T0353512

Certifiable Software Applications 1

Certifiable Software Applications 1

Main Processes

Jean-Louis Boulanger

ELSEVIER

First published 2016 in Great Britain and the United States by ISTE Press Ltd and Elsevier Ltd

ISTE Press Ltd
27-37 St George's Road
London SW19 4EU
UK

www.iste.co.uk

Elsevier Ltd
The Boulevard, Langford Lane
Kidlington, Oxford, OX5 1GB
UK

www.elsevier.com

Notices

For information on all our publications visit our website at http://store.elsevier.com/

British Library Cataloguing-in-Publication Data
A CIP record for this book is available from the British Library
Library of Congress Cataloging in Publication Data
A catalog record for this book is available from the Library of Congress
ISBN 978-1-78548-117-8

Printed and bound in the UK and US

Contents

Introduction

This introduction is shared across the different volumes of this series on the development of *certifiable* software applications.

Developing a software application is a difficult process that requires teamwork. The complexity of software applications is ever increasing and the amount has grown from a few tens of thousands to a few million. In order to be able to manage this complexity, development teams are of significant importance. The involvement of development teams in a software application, the internationalization of companies for a better distribution of work teams (multisite companies, use of outsourcing, etc.) – all these factors combined make it difficult to manage the complexity of a software application.

The complexity of developing a software application is further intensified by the race to obsolescence. The obsolescence of the hardware components entails the implementation of specific strategies (saving equipment, repository of tool sources, etc.) and mastering reproducibility and maintainability of the software application.

Another challenge is the requirement to demonstrate the safety of a software application. The demonstration of safety relies on the development of specific techniques (diversity, redundancy, fault tolerance, etc.) and/or controlling defects in the software application.

Even though the relationships related to systems and hardware architectures are introduced in these volumes, only the software aspect shall be discussed in detail [BOU 09].

This book series is a concrete presentation of the development of a critical software application. This approach is based on quality assurance as defined in ISO 9001 [ISO 08] and various industry standards such as DO 178 (aeronautics), IEC 61508 (programmable system), CENELEC 50128 (railway), ISO 26262 (automotive) and IEC 880 (nuclear). It must be noted that this book series is only a complement to other existing books such as the one written by Ian Sommerville [SOM 07].

Reader's guide

Volume 1 is dedicated to the establishment of quality assurance and safety assurance. The concept of a software application and the relationship with the system approach are addressed here. This chapter, therefore, discusses the fundamentals including the management of requirements.

Volume 2 describes the support processes, such as qualification tools, configuration management, verification and validation. Volume 2 is essential to understand what is necessary to develop a certifiable software application.

Volume 3 describes all the activities to be performed in the downward phase of the V cycle to produce a version of the software application. Activities such as specification, the establishment of an architecture and design of a software application are discussed here. This volume concludes with the presentation of production code of software application.

Volume 4 discusses the ascending phase of the V cycle along with a description of various stages of testing (unit tests, modular tests, component testing, integration tests and testing of the entire software) and various other associated tests. All these activities lead to the production of a version of the software application.

Acknowledgments

This book is a compilation of all my work carried out with the manufacturers to implement systems that are safe and secure for people.

1

System, Equipment and Software

1.1. Introduction

It is impossible to speak of software without referring to the system; in fact software does not exist without at least one execution platform that involves equipment and this equipment is integrated into a system. Contrary to popular belief, software is seldom reusable, generic or independent.

Very often, only one of the listed properties of the software is related to its independence with regard to the rest of the system; therefore, it may seem easy to modify just this one property; however, this is a gross miscalculation, as a software version is validated for a particular version of equipment and thus any change requires revalidation and analysis of impacts with respect to the equipment and the complete system.

The first chapter aims to put the software in the context of user equipment or systems and thus to reiterate the relationships and constraints that must be taken into account to develop a piece of software.

1.2. Impact on dependability

Automation of a number of command systems (railways, aerospace, automotive, etc.) and/or process controls (production, etc.) and replacement of poorly-integrated digital or analog systems (based on relay, for example) with high integration systems have led to a considerable expansion in the field of system dependability while taking into consideration the characteristics and specificities of computer systems.

Dependability [LAP 92, LIS 96, VII 88] involves four characteristics – reliability, availability, maintainability and safety (these concepts are discussed in Chapter 3).

The system safety includes applications which necessitate proper continuous operation, either due to the human lives involved (transport, nuclear, etc.) or due to the high investments at stake in the event of a calculation failure (space, chemical production process, etc.), or even due to the cost of inconvenience that could be caused due to failures (banking process, reliability of transport, etc.). It must be noted that in recent years, there is also a consideration of the impact on the environment.

Though system safety is an important subject which is always at the forefront, the other three subjects (RAM: Reliability, Availability and Maintainability) are just as important and may require great efforts. Let's take the example of maintenance; it is necessary to provision for maintenance from the time of designing (for example, consider dismantling capacity), and continue maintaining the system until its deactivation. Deactivation (Figure 1.1) does not mean the removal of the system, but decommissioning followed by a complete decommissioning of all the system parts.

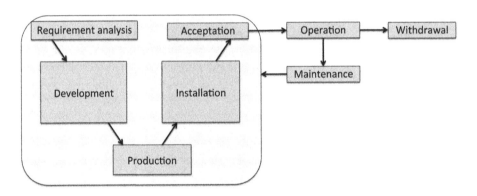

Figure 1.1. *Lifecycle of a system*

In the context of Figure 1.1, the maintenance phase concerns all the elements of the system. The software is a unique component as it is quite easy to modify and produce a new version, and it is presumed that its maintenance must be easy as well.

Software maintenance requires skills (trained personnel), means (machines, operating systems, tools, etc.), procedures and complete documentation of software and sources.

From the early stages of study (Figure 1.1 – requirement analysis) of such systems, the problems related to validation have always been a main concern of the designer: proper designing of mechanisms enable to respond to failures, to verify the design (simulations, tests, proofs, etc.) and to estimate, in a convincing manner, the relevant magnitudes measuring dependability performances.

1.3. Command and control system

Figure 1.2 shows an example of a rail system. The Operation Control Centre (OCC – top left picture[1]) allows control over the entire line and sends commands to the trains as well as to the signaling management system (bottom left picture represents a manual operation control center).

Figure 1.2. *The system in its environment[2]*

---

1 The top left photograph shows an old generation OCC (in this case, a drone), but the new OCCs are designed based on the traditional PCs and have developed from using physical technology (Optical Control Panel) to display lines using video projector.
2 Pictures by Jean-Louis Boulanger.

The operation control center[3] sends commands to the field through a set of relays (bottom middle picture shows an example of a room containing the relays associated with the signaling). In response to the commands, the field equipment adopts the required behavior (bottom right photo shows the operating signals).

Figure 1.2 introduces the complexity associated with the concrete system and it demonstrates that a complex system is not based on software, but on equipment that contains one or more pieces of software. Each of these programs is associated with safety objectives that can be different.

The software involved in supervision activities does not have as much impact on the *safety* of people as the software related to the automated control of trains. Therefore, in the context of systems requiring certification (aviation, railways, nuclear, programmable electronic based system, etc.), a safety level [BOU 11b] is associated to each software. This safety level is associated with a scale ranging from non-critical to high criticality. The concept of safety levels and the scales are discussed in Chapter 7.

Figure 1.3 helps to identify that the system to be developed is related to an environment that reacts to commands. It is, therefore, necessary to acquire a vision of the process status to control and dispose control means to send commands to the environment.

Environment

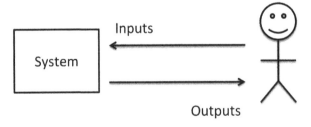

Figure 1.3. *System in its environment*

---

3 The picture shows a manual operating control center, but the operating control centers have been computerized for over several years, and are referred to as PMI ([BOU 11a] Chapter 8), PIPC and PAING ([BOU 09] Chapters 4 and 5).

The environment may consist of a physical element (motor, pump, etc.), but as a rule, there is an interaction with humans (operators, users, maintenance operators, etc.).

During the requirement analysis phase, it is essential to clearly identify all actors (operator, maintenance worker, client, etc.) and all the elements that interact with the system. The requirement analysis phase is essential and remains the source of many lapses and misunderstandings [BOU 06]. The requirement analysis must be viewed in relation to requirements engineering [BOU 14, HUL 05, POH 10]; Chapter 6 describes the management of requirements.

Figure 1.4 shows an example of modeling a control system of a railway crossing. This system enables one to control the intersection of at least one road and a railway track. The system interacts with different actors that include an OCC, road users (truck, car, etc.), railway users (train, high-speed train, freight train, maintenance train, etc.) and operators in charge of the operation and/or maintenance.

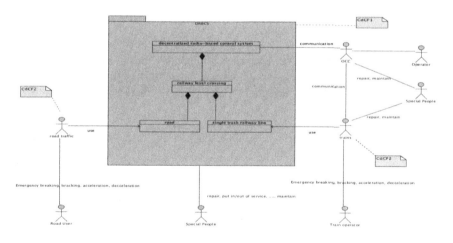

Figure 1.4. *Example of system model in its environment*

A class diagram [OMG 11, ROQ 06] has been used to model the fact that *Decentralized Radio Based Control System* consists of a crossing which in itself is constituted by a railway track and a road. For more information on this, and for a more detailed presentation of the model developed and the methodology used, see [BOU 07].

The important point in Figure 1.4 is the identification of the actors who interact with the management system which include road users, trains, OCC and, especially, maintenance workers or others (identified in the model as "special people").

The identification of all actors at the system level is very important, otherwise it may lead to omission of actions – such as maintenance activities – but also failure to recognize disturbances or malfunctions; the classic[4] example of the efficiency of a WiFi network may be related to the density of networks annexed to the system.

Figure 1.5 shows a traction-control equipment. A bogie consists of two axles. Some bogies are motorized and others are not. For the bogies with motors, the traction chain contains a TCU (Traction Control Unit) that is controlled via the train networks by the TCMS (Train Control Management System) and brake managements. The TCMS is the interface between the driver and the train. The train handler manages the acceleration and deceleration of the train. The figure shows an HV power supply from the catenary and LV power supply from the bogie. Figure 1.5 shows a complexity of interfaces (HV, LV, network, digital inputs and outputs, etc.).

We have discussed the importance of human factor in identifying the requirements, however, in Chapter 2, we shall not process the treatment of the human factor which, though essential, is not directly related to critical software applications.

1.4. System

First of all, we must remember that a software application is part of a system. The system can be divided into elements of different sizes that, in turn, consist of other elements.

At the lowest level is the software: one of the characteristics of the software is the lack of hardware architecture, i.e. there is no software.

---

4 Use of open networks such as WiFi involves a number of difficulties such as densification of networks (due to the rise in the number of private networks) and/or disturbances due to ancillary equipment. It must be noted that for a very long time the issue of open networks was not addressed in terms of operational dependability as it involved aspects such as confidentiality, intrusion, etc. which are covered under the term *safety*.

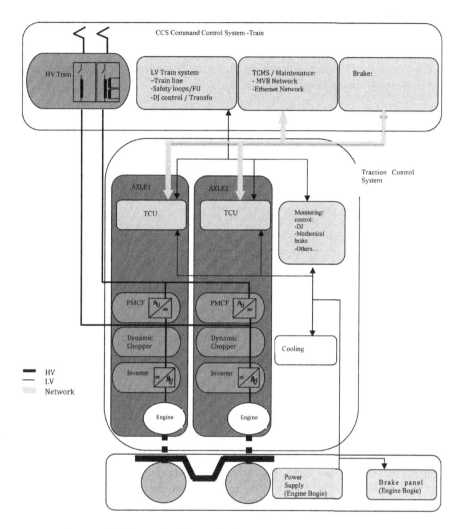

Figure 1.5. *Example of complex interaction between equipment*

We must remember that the validation (see Volume 2 of this series [BOU 16]) of software requires having hardware architecture and the validation results are applicable only for this hardware architecture. Thus, we identify the software in its operating environment (physical environment, hardware environment, operating procedures, set of integrated software and hardware, etc.). It is for this reason that the initial definitions of "software" refer to the concept of a system and a software-based system.

DEFINITION 1.1 (System).– *A system is a set of interacting elements organized to achieve one or more pre-stated results.*

The "organized" aspect of definition 1.1 may be understood at an organization level as indicated in the context of Figure 1.6.

DEFINITION 1.2 (Subsystem).– *A subsystem is a part of the system that performs a particular function.*

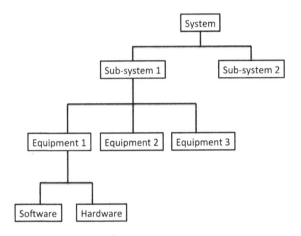

Figure 1.6. *From system to software*

Figure 1.6 provides a hierarchical view of the system. A system performs several functions. A system may be broken down into several subsystems, each performing functions that are subfunctions of the system's functions. At system level, the view must be complemented by a view of the interactions between the functions as shown in Figure 1.6.

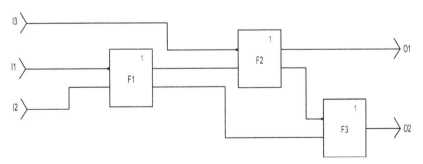

Figure 1.7. *Example of component decomposition*

A subsystem, therefore, supports several functions that can be broken down into various pieces of equipment. An equipment is not a functional element in itself; it must be complemented by other equipment in order to perform a system function.

DEFINITION 1.3 (Software-based system).– *Some elements of the system may be for entirety or part of the software.*

Figure 1.8 shows that a system is a structured set (computer systems, processes and context of use), which must create an organized whole unit. In the rest of this section, we shall focus on software applications that are part of the *computer/automatic system.*

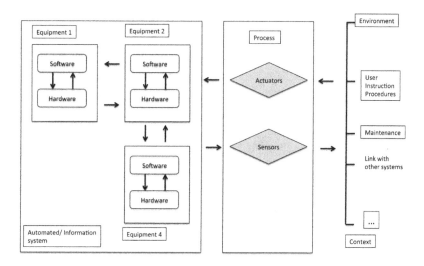

Figure 1.8. *System and interaction*

Figure 1.8 enables us to visualize that a programmable electronic-based system requires the definition of a context of use. This context of use includes the environment, operation (human, procedure, instruction, training, etc.), maintenance, links with other systems, and relationship with the authorities, etc.

Conversely, the context of use and developments may have a strong impact on the system and software that constitutes it. On the other hand, all the anomalies or unexpected behavior in the software will reveal unexpected behavior at the system level, which in turn will impact the context of use.

Figure 1.9 indicates the relationship between an equipment (computer) and the rest of its environment. Exchanges with actuators may require specific equipment (analog/digital converter, etc.). The figure shows a simplified case limited to one connection with other equipment, but in the context of network-based systems, it is quite common that a device is connected to more than three different networks.

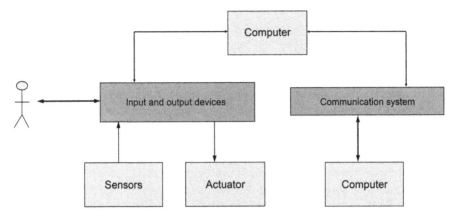

Figure 1.9. *System and interaction*

In view of the discussions related to Figures 1.8 and 1.9, the impacts of changes and/or developments are important factors. In fact, any system is a complex set of elements. Any change of an element must be validated locally, and it is necessary to ensure that the entire unit – i.e. the system – is still functional as planned, as a small change in the equipment can have a large impact on the entire system.

Under this section, it is shown that a system based on programmable electronic equipment is a complex subject, which must be well analyzed and disintegrated.

1.5. Development process

It is clear from the above discussion that a system is an organized unit and that the basic element termed as "part" participating in a function is called equipment – in the automotive industry it is called an ECU (Electronic Control Unit).

Equipment is further divided into three types of elements:

– hardware (hardware card, power supply, etc.);

– software;

– maintenance elements (cabinet, wiring, connector, etc.).

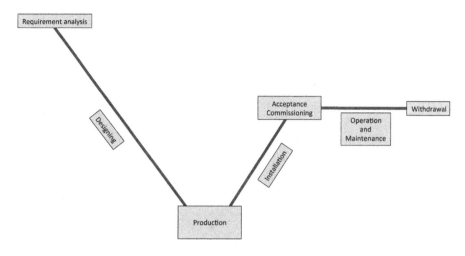

Figure 1.10. *Overall development cycle*

As shown in Figure 1.10, there are several phases in the life of a system:

– requirement analysis: understanding the limitations, constraints and requirements of the environment;

– design: decomposition, development of various components and plant validation;

– manufacturing: for mechanical, electrical, electronic components etc., a manufacturing phase is required;

– installation: on-site installation must follow certain rules to ensure that the installed system functions properly and site validation is set up;

– acceptance and commissioning: commissioning of the system can be regulated and a process can be followed which requires acceptance of the system supported by a test campaign;

– operation and maintenance: operation of the system requires a process, operating procedures and training of the personnel; but it can only be done by considering the failures. It is, therefore, necessary to define a preventive and corrective maintenance process. Maintenance of system and its components must be considered from the design phase;

– decommissioning: while preparing for the end of life of the system, retirement of the system must be planned.

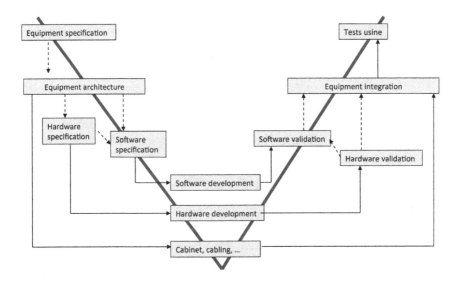

Figure 1.11. *Overall development cycle*

The design phase shown in Figure 1.10 must enable the breaking down of the system/subsystem into the equipment constituting it. On this basis, Figure 1.11 shows the developing process of the equipment that includes development of three components.

Therefore, software development requires knowledge of the equipment and hardware (specification, validation result) involved. And the knowledge of hardware (specification, interface, characteristics, concept of safety, etc.) is important as the development of software independent of hardware is an issue that shall be discussed again in the following chapters.

For quality purposes, the development process proposed in Figure 1.11 must be complemented with activities related to Quality Assurance (QA) and Configuration Management (CM).

QA (see Chapter 9) and CM (see Volume 2 of the series [BOU 16]) must cover the entire cycle of or a variation on the equipment, hardware and software. It is therefore necessary to set up a Software Quality Assurance (SQA) and Software Configuration Management (SQM).

1.6. Safety: from system to software

The safety management [VIL 88, LIS 96] of a system involves identification of risks and hazards and allocation of safety objectives (THR[5], DAL[6], SIL[7], ASIL) to various elements of the system. In order to perform safety analysis of a system, we must know the architecture (Figure 1.5) and must implement safety studies (see Chapter 4) such as preliminary analyses of risks, fault trees, FMEA, etc.

Figure 1.11 is an introduction to the development process of an equipment that does not take into account the Safety Assurance (SA) activities.

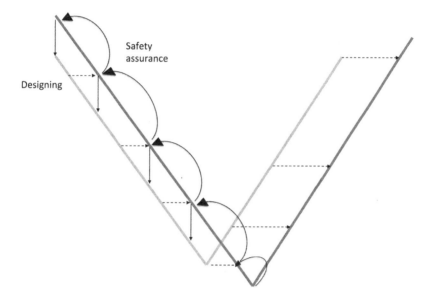

Figure 1.12. *Development and safety assurance*

Safety assurance is a process that is carried out simultaneously with the design activities. Figure 1.12 shows the impact of the safety assurance on the development process. Safety assurance begins before the implementation (necessity to identify the potential risks and safety requirements to be met) and ends after the process (necessity to formalize the safety demonstration based on the results).

---

5 THR for Tolerable Hazard Rate is the acceptable failure rate for a function, system and/or a subsystem.
6 DAL for Design Assurance Level is the desired confidence level used in aeronautics.
7 SIL for Safety Integrity Level is the requested/expected safety integrity level. It is used for E/E/EP systems and in railways. ASIL (Automotive SIL) is used for automotive domain.

Safety assurance follows the development process, but during the descending phase, this process can lead to loops – analysis of a step can identify new risks. Safety assurance and its implementation are introduced in Chapter 4 for "system" aspects and in Chapter 5 for "software" aspects.

Figure 1.13 (extracted from Boulanger [BOU 11b]) introduces the principle of allocation of safety objectives (THR, SIL) of a subsystem with equipment as developed for the railways (see standards CENELEC EN 50126 [CEN 00] and CENELEC EN 50129 [CEN 03]).

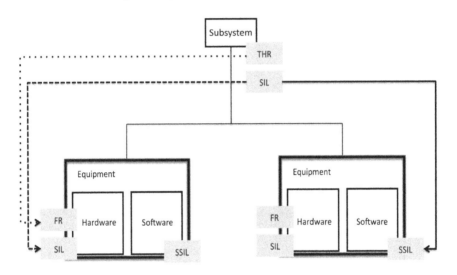

Figure 1.13. *Allocation of sub-system to equipment and their components[8]*

There is a division of THR allocated to each subsystem in FR (Failure Rate) allocated to hardware equipment constituting the subsystem depending on the architecture (hypothesis of independence) and division of SIL level allocated to each subsystem in SIL levels (SSIL) allocated to hardware equipment (software):

– the SIL level of the hardware is identical to the SIL level of the subsystem;

– the SSIL (Software SIL) level of the software is identical to the SIL level of the subsystem.

---

8 Figure 1.11 shows the allocation process as applied in railways; however, depending on the sector, a similar approach exists and justifies the level of confidence expected in the software.

It must be noted that a subsystem is assumed to be divided into two parts: "hardware" and "software".

The transition from subsystem SIL to equipment SIL is regulated; however, it is possible to take into account the architecture of the equipment to refine these SIL and SSIL.

If we implement a homogeneous architecture (identical hardware, identical OS[9], identical memory, etc.) [BOU 09, BOU 11a], it improves the consideration of random errors, but not of design and common errors (processor errors, etc.). Therefore, the SIL level required for the hardware must be the same as that of the subsystem.

If identical software is to be loaded thrice over this architecture, the software must have high level of SSIL. However, if the diversification of software applications can be differentiated and justified, then the implementation of three different pieces of software can justify a lower level of SSIL on these software.

The implementation of a heterogeneous architecture [BOU 09, BOU 11a] (three different processors, diversified memory units, etc.) can help to overcome the design problems and defects of the basic components while limiting common modes. It is then possible to indicate that each processing unit can be assigned to a lower SIL objective. For implementation of a single software application, the level of SSIL is always the highest.

The arguments presented above as examples show that it is possible, depending on the architecture and expert judgment, to refine the allocation of SIL and SSIL.

NOTE.– This allocation remains an expert judgment, therefore, it must be justified, and it is not a SIL algorithmic.

In conclusion, we must remember that safety is a combination and the impact of the software must be analyzed on the entire system during the design but especially during development, as a small software change can have a significant impact on the behavior of the entire unit.

Control over operational dependability is discussed further in Chapter 3 and the management of certifiable applications in Chapter 7.

---

9 OS is Operating System.

1.7. Software application

1.7.1. *What is software?*

In this chapter, the *software* element (in Chapter 2, the concept of software is introduced more formally) is described as an aggregate of calculating/processing an element that is executed on a hardware architecture so that the resultant entity can provide services associated with an equipment (see Figure 1.6).

Note that in this context, a software application is a part of software that performs a specific process/calculation.

1.7.2. *Generic, specific or dedicated*

Software can be a general (several uses or users) or dedicated application:

– a dedicated software application is for a single user or a very specific type of use. It is difficult to reuse it as is;

– a general software application is for a family of users and/or uses (operating system, compiler, recognized function such as ABS in automobiles, a generic application specialized for one type of use, etc.).

1.7.3. *Various types of software*

As part of development of an operationally safe and critical application, various types of software applications can be created:

– Application (or operational) software: they are normally embedded within a device. They are part of the final system and are delivered to the client as part of a project and/or product. Note that the external use test benches falls into this category.

There are two sub-types to this type of software:

- configurable applications: a data set allows specialization of software for a type of use;

- non-configurable applications.

– Development tool: it is a software application internal to a company and is not delivered to the client; it is intended to help in development (editor, IDE, code generator, compiler, charger, etc.) at large including testing (test environment, internal test bench, etc.).

– "Offline" tools: this last category of software helps in preparing elements, such as data, to be integrated in the final software application. They are part of the final application but are not implemented on the equipment. They may or may not be delivered to clients.

1.7.4. *Various types of uses*

A software application can be a demonstrator, a model or a finished product.

A demonstrator is a software application used by a client to refine the expression of their requirement to measure the level of potentially-rendered services. These software applications are not intended for operational use.

A model is an internal non-delivered research software used to verify a theory, an algorithm, or the feasibility of a technique (e.g. simulation) without the objective of generating results or completeness.

The finished product is a piece of software that has followed a development process, has been demonstrated to comply with the objectives and is intended to be delivered to a client.

1.8. Conclusion

In this chapter the complexity of the underlying systems based on programmable electronics was discussed. Here, we indicated the existence of a hierarchy flowing from system to software via subsystems equipment and electronic hardware. We have also learnt what a software application is and how it is positioned within a system.

It is an accepted fact that software is ubiquitous in our systems. Whether in critical systems or the systems of everyday life, software enables us to control (in principle) the variability of equipment through management of configurations and new versions. It is, therefore, a flexible component of systems where the flexibility is related to its ability to adapt to changes almost instantaneously unlike the fixed parts such as the electronic, mechanical or pneumatic components.

This flexibility makes it indispensable, though it has several difficulties. The first difficulty is in knowing that an equipment consists of software; this may be surprising but recent experiments show that even purely mechanical (or pneumatic, etc.) equipment may contain a bit of software in order to manage a setting which helps in configuring the product for various uses. The second difficulty lies in the ability to manage the configuration of a system and the consistency of various pieces of software, and this point is related to the third difficulty which is the ability to maintain the system over time and thus develop a new version of the software, knowing that the life of a certain system can be very long (5, 10, 40 or 50 years).

1.9. Glossary

ABS: Anti-Lock Braking System

ASIL: Automotive SIL

CENELEC: *Comité Européen de Normalisation Electrotechnique*
                  (European Committee for Electro-technical Standardization)

CM: Configuration Management

DAL: Design Assurance Level

DRBCS: Decentralized Radio-Based Control System

ECU: Electronic Control Unit

FDM: *Fiabilité, Dipsonibilité et Maintenabilité* (Reliability, Availability
                  and Maintainability)

FDMS :   *Fiabilité, Disponibilité, Maintenabilité et Sécurité* (Reliability,
                  Availability, Maintainability and Safety)

FMEA: Failure Mode and Effect Analysis

FR: Failure Rate

HV: High Voltage

IDE: Integrated Development Environment

LV: Low Voltage

OCC: Operation Control Center

OS: Operating System

PAING: *Poste Aiguillage Informatisé – Nouvelle Génération*
                  (Computerized Signaling Station – New Generation)

PC: Personal Computer

PCC: *Poste de Contrôle Centralisé* (Central Control Station)

PIPC: *Poste Informatique Petite Capacité* (Small capacity
                computer station)

PMI: *Poste de Manœuvre Informatisé* (Computerized work station)

QA: Quality Assurance

SA: Safety Assurance

SCM: Software Configuration Management

SdF: *Sûreté de Fonctionnement* (Operating safety)

SIL: Safety Integrity Level

SQA: Software Quality Assurance

SSIL: Software SIL

TCMS: Train Control and Management System

TCO: *Tableau de Control Optique* (Optical Control Table)

TCU: Traction Control Unit

THR: Tolerable Hazard Rate

ToR: *Tout ou Rien* (All or None)

2

Software Application

2.1. Introduction

In recent years, all systems (mechanical, electrical, automatic, electronic, physical, etc.), irrespective of their domain (energy, transport, production, banking, etc.), have seen the emergence of software. Introduction of software has been carried out in various forms, ranging from a simple addition of functionality to complete replacement of the initial system by a software-based system.

This approach is based on an idea that a "software-based system is more easily modifiable than the original systems". This reassuring statement must be demonstrated. In effect, production of a software application appears to be as simple as "writing a code, compiling it and deploying it" but the reality is more complex. A software defect is the first and foremost problem but there is also obsolescence of tools and related software (operating system, drivers, etc.) which cannot be ignored.

In the rest of this book, we shall discuss only the software aspects that lead us to the problem of defining what software is. Therefore, in this chapter we will introduce software applications and associated properties.

2.2. Software versus software applications

Section 1.7 identifies several types of software and the first property is that software can be generalized or dedicated. We have also identified software as part of a system and as a part that has a direct impact on the system behavior.

Figure 2.1 shows a basic representation of software. Software is thus a part of the system (or device). The system is then divided into three parts: the environment, hardware and software.

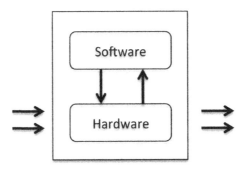

Figure 2.1. *Software in a system*

A simplified representation of Figure 2.1 shows software (in terms of executable) as an autonomous element, however, this is not quite true. Figure 2.2 introduce the software environment that uses tools and procedures and the download of software on the target through a maintenance tool and a process for use.

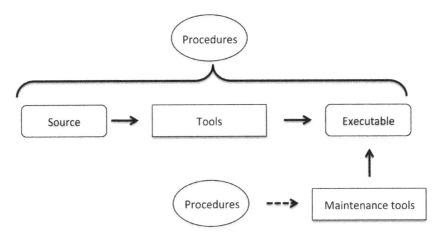

Figure 2.2. *Partial framework of software*

But to produce the executable, we need the source codes that are produced by tools and are associated with documentation. This source code may be managed in configuration. Figure 2.3 is more or less a complete system which still lacks a subset called software.

Figure 2.3 shows that software is a set that contains source codes, tools, processes, procedures, etc., from which the definition of 2.1, which was taken from [AFN 87][1], indicates that the awareness of software complexity is not something new.

DEFINITION 2.1 (Application software).– *All programs, processes and rules, and documentation relating to the functioning of an entire information-processing unit.*

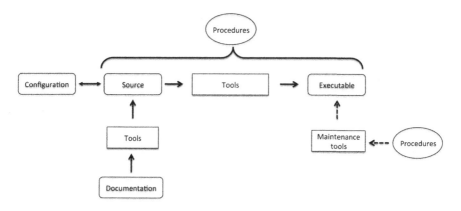

Figure 2.3. *A software application*

Contrary to what has been identified in section 1.6, definition 2.1 does not distinguish between the means (methods, processes, tools, etc.) to develop the software application, the products resulting from the development (documents, results of analyses, designs, sources, test scenarios, test results, specific tools, etc.) and the software application itself.

Figure 2.4 shows an example of a process equipped to perform a software application (editing, testing, compilation, version management, etc.).

---

1 Standard IEC 90003:2004 [IEC 04] uses the same definition but describes *software product.*

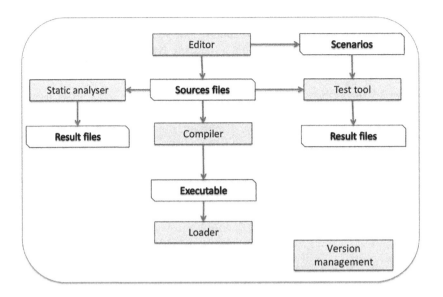

Figure 2.4. *Production process of software application*

Finally, definition 2.1 is associated with the concept of software application; where the concept of software is in turn associated with the executable concept.

2.3. Software application in its context

2.3.1. *General framework*

As shown in Figure 2.5, software generally uses an abstraction of the hardware architecture and its operating system through a lower layer called "basic software". The basic software is usually written in low-level languages such as assembly language and/or C language [KER 88]. It encapsulates the services of the operating system and the utilities, but it also allows more or less direct access to hardware resources.

If the software application is associated with a high level of safety, then the lower layers (basic software, utility and operating system) are also associated with safety objectives. The safety objective of lower layers is dependent on the hardware architecture (mono processor, 2oo2, nOOm[2], etc.) and safety concepts implemented.

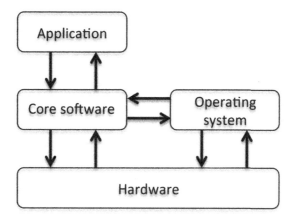

Figure 2.5. *Software in its environment*

In [BOU 09a, BOU 11], we have introduced actual examples of safe operating architectures. In this series, we shall assume that the safety analyses are performed and that for all software applications (lower layer included), a safety level is allocated.

2.3.2. *Reusability, maintainability and continuous service*

The architecture of software is an important point that must be looked into from a very early stage. Various topics such as reusability (implementation of elements previously developed on new projects), maintainability (possibility of developing over time) and business continuity (despite the changes and obsolescence) are addressed repeatedly.

Reusability is a key factor when trying to manage the cost of development. The code elements (service, unit, component, library, etc.) must have limited connection with the reference product and the external components (software, drivers, supplies, library, etc.). Figure 2.6 shows the dependencies that exist between a software

---

2 nOOm is n out of m. A redundant architecture n out of m performs m calculations and considers the result to be correct if n results are identical, see [BOU 09] – Chapter 1.

element and its environment (operating system, library, support hardware and interaction software).

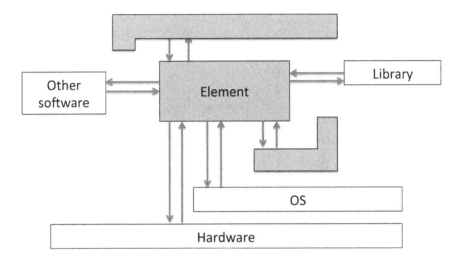

Figure 2.6. *Adherence*

DEFINITION 2.2 (Adherence of a software element).– *Adherence of a software element is defined by the list of software elements and/or the environment of the software element that are necessary for execution of this element.*

Once the concept of adherence is defined (definition 2.2), it is possible to connect it with the concept of reusability. The stronger the adherence, the more difficult it is to reuse the element without adaptation. Reusability is a commonly misunderstood concept, where some developers consider a reusable component as a software component offering many features – so a wide spectrum of possible applications is implemented but is never really used – whereas a reusable component offers minimum functionalities that are properly developed and completely documented and tested. Therefore, a reusable component is editable.

Software maintainability is related to the ability to develop a software application over a certain period (from a few days to decades). It is related to the establishment of a development and management process of changes. It is necessary to manage complexity. Maintainability will be discussed in more detail in the following chapters.

Continuity of service of a software application is generally not dealt with; however, it becomes a challenge for the safety of critical systems (transport, energy, services, etc.).

It must be possible to ensure that the software application is functional over a certain period of time, despite:

– changes in the software application: correction of defects and addition of features;

– obsolescence of hardware support: processors, memory, hard drives, USB keys, etc.;

– obsolescence of media software: operating systems[3], libraries, drivers, etc.;

– etc.

Furthermore, the standard applications are difficult to reuse and maintain as they are heavily dependent on hardware and software. Hence, several projects propose developing a software application independent of these materials. These architectures are called *modular architectures*.

2.3.3. *Modular architecture*

Figure 2.5 shows a basic architecture, but this principle has been generalized for a specific domain such as the aerospace and automotive industries through the IMA[4] (Integrated Modular Avionics (see [SPI 01] – section 33.2 and [EVE 06]) and AUTOSAR[5] (Automotive Open System Architecture (see [BOU 11] – Chapter 3 and [AUT 14]).

Both architectures are designed to introduce a clear separation between the performance software and hardware. This separation is achieved by implementing a

---

3 For example, when stopping the release of Windows XP, users were forced to move to Windows 7 and then, in the same year, were told that Windows 7 would no longer be maintained and that they needed to move to Windows 8 or even Windows 10.
4 In order to manage the delays and costs, aeronautics has established IMA. Compliance with a standard, reuse, and interchangeability are the three central concepts of IMA. Based on standardized and replaceable components, an IMA equipment can receive specific elements (cards, peripherals and software). For software, the development principles help to ensure the execution of external applications on a device.
5 For more information, visit http://www.autosar.org.

middleware that allows encapsulating and abstracting the hardware and thus, the software need to know the details of the hardware to achieve these behaviors.

Figure 2.7 shows a general view of the AUTOSAR architecture. The elements of the platform are abstract across software layers (services, drivers, abstraction, TENs). The real-time Run Time Environment (RTE) manages the execution of software application(s).

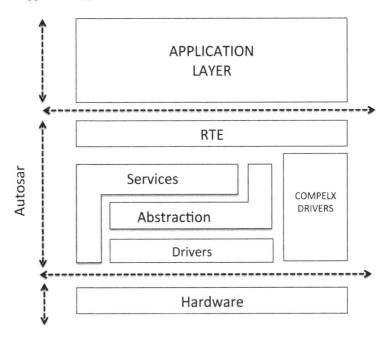

Figure 2.7. *AUTOSAR*

The introduction of an abstraction layer of the platform aims to introduce a wide degree of independence between the software application and execution platform.

This involves the following properties:

– standardization: AUTOSAR as well as software components can be standardized to abstract the hardware elements;

– transferability: as part of a new vehicle, it is possible to rearrange the assignment of software applications;

– adaptability: a software application can be extended to another vehicle or another platform;

– and so on.

Another property that is of interest is the ability to get the hardware support developed by various providers, which involves management costs, obsolescence and defects.

2.4. Generic software and parameterized software

Control/command systems currently developed are increasingly bigger; they introduce the concept of communication and are large consumers of data.

In software applications, it is possible to handle two types of data: constant data and variable data (global, local, function parameters, returns of functions, etc.). The variables acquired from the environment are called "variant" (see Figure 2.8) and they allow characterizing the state of the environment of the software application at any given time T (see definition 2.3).

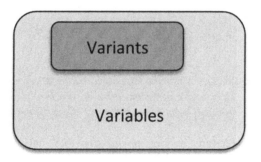

Figure 2.8. *Variables and variants*

DEFINITION 2.3 (Variant).– *A variant is a software variable which represents a data of the environment. This variable is acquired by the software application and can change its value for each cycle.*

The number of objects of a family is a constant for a software version but it might be necessary to evolve over time following an extension of the system. To do this, we should be able to develop a constant and produce a new version of the software application without having to redo all the verifications (proofreading, testing, etc.). This constant is called the parameter of the software application and is viewed as static (constant) during execution.

The parameters of a software application are static data (constants, see Figure 2.9) that can be of two types:

– fixed data called invariant, characterizing the environment (topology, trajectory, etc.), the system (object number, limit, etc.) and the characteristics (weight, length, speed, etc.);

– data evolving with the system state (wear, expansion, etc.).

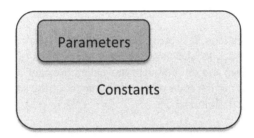

Figure 2.9. *Constants and parameters*

DEFINITION 2.4 (Parameter).– *A parameter is a constant data for a given instance of software application. This data can be modified to produce another version of the application or can be changed before execution to reflect the system status.*

A configurable software application is divisible into two parts, generic application and configuration. The instance of the generic application for a given use is called *specific application.*

DEFINITION 2.5 (Specific application).– *A specific application is a generic application to which a parameter has been associated. This specific application is only usable for a single installation.*

It must be noted that the concept of specific application covers the software and hardware aspects. Because the hardware is a fixed characteristic (an entry in the development of a piece of software – see Figure 2.10 – and a piece of software is validated for a platform), it is, therefore, possible to define the generic application (see definition 2.6).

DEFINITION 2.6 (Generic application).– *A generic application is composed of an execution platform (called a generic product), a software application and a configuration process. This software application is defined in terms of a set of configuration data that must be instantiated based on the end use (depending on the site, depending on the services to be activated, depending on the technical characteristics, etc.).*

Definition 2.6 identifies that the specific application is composed of three parts, and among these the configuration process is a delicate subject that will be discussed in Volume 2 [BOU 16a].

The concept of a generic application covers the concept of non-configured software, as there is neither instantiation nor any specific application.

As shown in Figure 2.10, the generic application is then the composition of a piece of generic software and an execution platform. The execution platform is a generic product and covers the hardware and software aspects (operating system, basic software, middleware layer for managing communications, etc.).

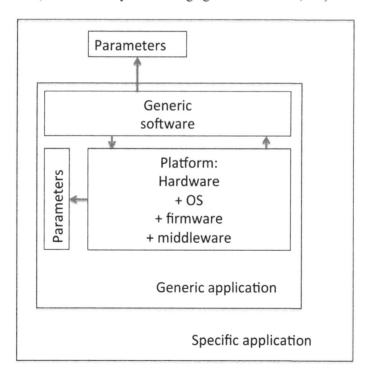

Figure 2.10. *Specific application versus generic application*

DEFINITION 2.7 (Generic product).– *A generic product is composed of a set of hardware and software elements. Its objective is to enable the execution of a software application. A generic product can be used for developing various systems.*

As indicated in definition 2.7, a generic product aims to run different types of software applications; the generic aspect does not allow for any specialization. The product concept is related to the fact that the set can be certified, independent of the area of use, for example, in case of programmable controllers.

Invariant data is known at system generation and defines the system configuration. It is, therefore, possible to define a system generically and to implant it in on another site through configuration.

For example, in the description of a metro line, it is possible to derive a set of data that are common to the entire system equipment. These data depend on the topology of the line, the characteristics of the trains and the technological choices (response time, CPU computation time, etc.). In the world of railways, they are called "topological invariants" [GEO 90].

A metro line (see the fictitious example in Figure 2.11) consists of tracks for train movements. These tracks consist of track circuits. Each track circuit is a track portion that is used to detect the presence of trains on that area. Track circuits are generally connected to two other track circuits, but in case they are connected to three other track circuits, they must be associated with a root, which is a device for selecting the path.

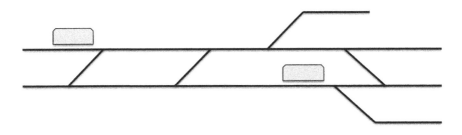

Figure 2.11. *Example of topology*

2.5. Module and component

It is important that we see a software application as a set of elements that interact to process a set of information. At this point, we speak of elements, as we have moved on from the concept of monolithic software toward the concept of a structured software seen as a set of elements.

DEFINITION 2.8 (Module).– *A module is a part of the software, known to be indivisible during development. It achieves a sufficiently explicit processing for it can be a direct transcription in a programming language.*

It is interesting to note that the standards (CENELEC 50128, IEC 61508, DO 178, etc.) in their versions of the late 90s, introduced the module concept whereas their updated versions in 2011 refer to the components.

A module is characterized by the following features:

– low complexity;

– limitation on the number of entry and exit points;

– limited number of parameters; and

– ability to be tested.

In light of these characteristics, a module can be a procedure, a function, a file, a package, a class, and, in the worst case, a piece of code. It, thus, appears that the module concept was vague enough that we could cover different languages and the level of granularity required by a project. Therefore, it is quite easy to match an ADA package, a file C and/or C++ class to a module.

As can be seen in Figure 2.12, a module may be dependent on another module (in C, STDIO.H module may be used by many other modules), which may make it difficult for it to be reused. In fact, in case of reuse of a module, it is not compiled (depending on another module) and some modules may be dependent on the compilers (modules associated with an implementation) and/or hardware platform. Figure 2.13 shows a module tree. Each module is managed by configuration. Module 4 reuse in another project requires recovering the associated sub-tree and if module 7 is a module attached to the compiler, it will be necessary to repeat the tests.

Another difficulty involves identification of entry points in the module, i.e. *which features are available?* and *what do they do?* because all the services of a module are accessible at the same level as in the source code.

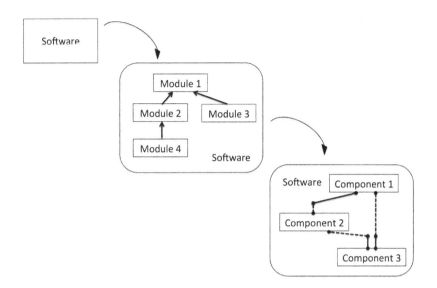

Figure 2.12. *Development of the software structure*

For each module, we shall implement a strategy of modular tests. The objective of this testing strategy is to show that the module services properly perform the processing. Some services can be internal (called by another without having specified functionality), partial (global service divided into several parts, and a single part addresses only one requirement), or not significant (a processing factorization performed without a specified feature) and it will be difficult to prove their proper functioning where, in fact, even the tests would be meaningless.

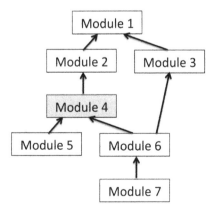

Figure 2.13. *Module tree*

In light of the difficulties associated with the module concept, the concept of the component was introduced (see Figure 2.12) with the idea that the component is an autonomous entity (compilable) with clearly identified interfaces.

There are two reasons for the popularity of this new paradigm: its use allows to develop applications faster and, above all, to reduce development costs. In fact, building an application consists of configuring the software components in the image of electronic components. More specifically, it refers to:

– designing and developing systems from prefabricated, preconceived and pretested components;

– reusing these components in other applications;

– facilitating their maintenance and development;

– supporting their adaptability and configurability to produce new functions and features.

Among these technologies, without being exhaustive, we can mention: CORBA [BAK 97], EJB [RAM 01], .NET [LOW 03], etc.

A commonly accepted definition of a component is that of C. Szyperski [SZY 98]:

"A software component is a unit of composition with contractually specified interfaces and explicit context dependencies only. A software component can be deployed and is subject to composition by third parties."

There are other definitions such as the ones given by B. Meyer [MEY 99] or J. Harris [HAR 99].

However, the analyses of these definitions deduce a set of properties, thus stating a component as:

– *auto-descriptive*: it has mechanisms that allow it to know and to dynamically change its characteristics;

– *composable*: it can connect with other components;

– *configurable*: it must be configurable via its configurable properties in a particular execution context;

– *reusable*: depending on the execution context, an adaptation step is most likely required;

– *autonomous*: it can be deployed, i.e. implemented within an architecture and executed independent of other components.

A component can be composed of other components. Such a component is called a composite component. The components included in a composite component are sometimes called internal components or subcomponents. So dualistically, the term father component can also be used.

With the main ideas of components introduced, we can say that from components rises the concepts of connectors, interface and composition.

Pragmatically, it is possible to define a component based on interfaces, defining the requirement and autonomy.

DEFINITION 2.9 (Component).– *A component is a software element performing a set of well-identified services, following a set of clearly identified requirements, having well-defined interfaces and is managed in configuration as a separate entity.*

Definition 2.9 refers to the concept of requirement. At this point of the discussion, it is necessary to recall that a requirement characterizes a need [BOU 14]. Chapter 10 is dedicated to the requirement management.

In light of definition 2.9, a component can be a software application, a bookstore, a commercial component (COTS), etc. The essential point of this definition is the autonomous aspect of the component. This ensures reusability and maintenance of the software application. In fact, if a component becomes obsolete (development of the operating system, hardware obsolescence, etc.), it is possible to replace the software component by another depending on the conditions of interfaces and requirements.

A component is independent and contains all the elements to ensure its proper functioning. Therefore, in the context of Figure 2.14, if we reuse the component 2 in a new project, it will be necessary to verify the use hypothesis of component 2 and then carry out the software /software integration.

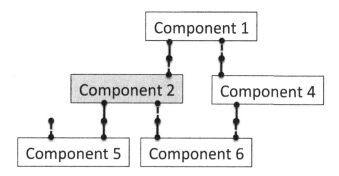

Figure 2.14. *Component architecture*

In another situation within the framework of Figure 2.14, if there is a change of hardware platform and component 6 is dedicated to the management of interfaces with the platform, it will be necessary to redo the software/software integration tests between components 2 and 6 but not retest the behavior of component 2.

In case of modification, the component management enables to limit the regression activities to the edge of components. Another advantage of the management of components lies in the granularity of tests – as in test components. It is necessary to test the services offered by the component that are completely specified.

2.6. Reused component and COTS

Following the definition of the concept of components, we can conclude that there are three types of components:

– new components: as part of a project, components are developed to meet the requirements of the project;

– reused components: as part of a project, it is possible to reuse components that have been developed in another project. For these components, the following are necessary:

- definition of component interfaces,

- specification of the component services,

- confirmation of the validity of the component (test, analysis, feedback, etc.),

- identification of use hypothesis of the component (representation of numbers, memory size, processor time, etc.);

– COTS (commercial off-the-shelf): some components are called COTS as they are provided by a third party (graphics library, communication protocol, library compiler, etc.). They are generally provided in the form of a library (see source code) but with little or no documentation and there is little information on their testing.

DEFINITION 2.10 (COTS).– *Software product available for purchase and use without the need to conduct development activities.*

In light of the rapidly changing and shortening lead times of development, it is necessary to reuse, as much as possible, the components of one project on another. However, reuse is also required for operating systems, or it is not possible to redevelop a complete new version and/or after a long period of operation (over 10 years) the need to add new functionality is addressed by interfacing existing software with new features, therefore, the component approach is required.

2.7. Product line

Developing a software application is one thing, but achieving a maintainable software application that is easily changeable and adaptable is another. Therefore, it may be worthwhile to develop not a product but a product line.

DEFINITION 2.11 (Variant).– *A variant of a software application is a version of it on which well-identified modifications were applied.*

Managing a product line that is industrially produced will lead to the establishment of a variant. This is particularly true for a product that has been developed with respect to the laws of a country and must be implemented for another country.

Figure 2.15 shows the ideal case (from development perspective and not from an economic point of view). Based on Product A characterized by a V1 version, behavior, interfaces, known defects, etc., we can continue the development of the product and create a variant that will follow its development. In the first case, the lack of interaction between the two projects will have an impact on costs (both versions developed on the same basis) and may have an impact on safety; faults detected on a project need not be shared with another project.

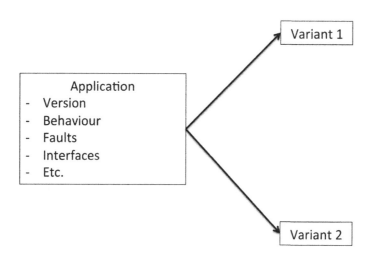

Figure 2.15. *Implementation of a variant*

DEFINITION 2.12 (Product line).– *A product line is a process for developing a product on the basis of a generic product and specializing it in order to take into account the specificities of a project while allowing to keep it consistent with other products already developed and to be developed.*

As discussed in section 2.4, the product can be separated into two elements: generic application and specific application. As a general rule, specific application consists of a configuration for selecting the executable services and defines certain data (number of objects, topology, characteristics of systems, etc.). But it is also possible to see the specific application as a way to define specific functions.

The definition of a generic application [BOU 99, BOU 00] remains a delicate point. Should all possible behaviors be included or should only the basic attributes be stated under generic application?

If generic application contains all potential behaviors, we shall have a final software application that will contain a lot of dead code. Generally speaking, this code is dead code by configuration (it is potentially testable at the generic application level). The existence of dead code is prohibited or must be minimized through safety critical application (as it has an impact on the lives of individuals or the company's assets). To prove the safety of dead code, the entire generic application must be verified and validated. Most of the time, it is not possible to completely check a generic application containing all potential behaviors.

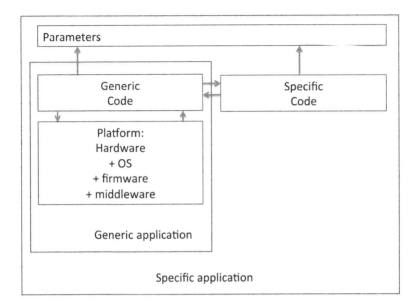

Figure 2.16. *Specific application*

If the specific application only contains the minimum, the important behaviors will be included in specific applications and the workload to be performed specifically for a project becomes more. It takes more when starting a new project using the nearest specific project.

The best solution is to take a median position (see Figure 2.16) and define an attainable generic application, and according to the specific applications make additions to the generic application.

Irrespective of the choices made, creating parallel development for developing variants must identify the process of reporting faults from one variant to another. A fault considered dangerous for a variant could be harmless for another variant; therefore, it is necessary to perform the analysis.

2.8. Conclusion

In this chapter we have defined what a software application is. We have identified two types of software applications – instantiable *generic applications* for a given use and *specific applications*.

We discussed the need to develop software application independent of the hardware platform (decreased adherence to the means of execution) that leads to the definition of new architecture (IMA, AUTOSAR, etc.) and the establishment an abstraction of the hardware platform.

In addition, it is necessary to limit the modifications in case of obsolescence and it is necessary to reuse a code to the maximum extent from one application to another. Hence, the concept of *component* was introduced to replace the concept of *module*.

In the next chapter we shall discuss safety assurance and its implementation for a software application.

2.9. Glossary

2oo2:   2-out-of-2 architecture

AUTOSAR[6]:   Automotive Open System Architecture

COTS: Commercial Off-The-Shelf

IEC[7]:   International Electrotechnical Commission

IMA: Integrated Modular Avionics

ISO[8]:   International Organization for Standardization

noOm: n-out-of-n architecture

OS: Operating System

RER: *Réseau Express Régional* (Suburban express train)

RTE: RunTime Environment

SACEM: *Système d'Aide à la Conduite, à l'Exploitation et à la Maintenance* (System to help production, use and maintenance)

---

6 http://www.autosar.org.
7 http://www.iec.ch.
8 http://www.iso.org.

Principle of Dependability

3.1. Introduction

Development of a software application is currently an activity accessible to everyone. The provision of development environment (Case Tool and/or IDE), offering modeling, verification and automatic code generation, has greatly simplified the development of a software application.

But the main feature of software is the presence of errors (BUG[1]). These errors can be automatically executed.

The presence of these errors is due to the *artisanal* nature of the development of a software application. The use of development environment gives the impression of industrializing the production of a software application but it is actually not. In fact, the tools of the development environment are developed conventionally and the use of development environment tends to overshadow the intrinsic complexity of the software through an almost clear graphical representation.

The presence of errors is a fact we have to deal with. With respect to errors, they must be accepted, managed and/or corrected.

After the introduction of the concept of error, fault and failure, and their application to software applications, we shall discuss the techniques that help to protect a software application and their implementation in this chapter.

---

1 The term *bug* was introduced by Grace Hopper, who is the founder of the first computer compiler and COBOL [SAM 78]. She could have named the programming errors after an insect that probably had caused failure on one of the machines used by her.

3.2. Dependability

3.2.1. *Basic concepts*

We will start first and foremost with dependability.

DEFINITION 3.1 (Dependability).– *Dependability is defined as the quality of service delivered by a system, as in the users of the service can trust in the system delivering it.*

In this book, we shall use definition 3.1 but it must be noted that there are many technical approaches to dependability, for example, for the standard IEC 1069 [IEC 91a], dependability is the measure to show that the said system exclusively and correctly executes (the) task(s) that has/have been assigned to it.

For more information on the dependability and its implementation, see [VIL 88, LIS 96, GEF 98] and for software-based systems, see [GEF 02, BOU 15].

Dependability – denoted (RAMS[2]) – is characterized by a set of attributes:

– *reliability*: property of a system to operate continuously, without error. Unlike availability, reliability is defined in terms of time interval and not in terms of a moment in time;

– *availability*: property of a given system to be used as it is. It often refers to the probability that a system is working properly and is available to perform its functions;

– *maintainability*: refers to the ease with which a failing system can be repaired and can be developed;

– *safety*: refers to the situation when a system fails temporarily, without any catastrophic event.

Other new attributes that are gaining importance are *security*[3] and RAMSS[4].

As indicated in Laprie [LAP 92], dependability of a complex system may be threatened by three types of events: failures, errors and faults.

---

2 *Reliability, Availability, Maintainability and Safety.*
3 Security is related to prevention of access and/or handling of unauthorized information, etc.
4 RAMS and Security.

System components are subject to failures and these failures may place the system in situations of potential accidents.

3.2.2. *Dependability constraints*

As stated in the standard IEC 61508 [IEC 08a], failure (sometimes called breakdown) is a disruption of the ability of a functional unit to perform a required function. As the performance of a required function necessarily excludes certain behaviors and as certain functions can be specified in terms of behavior to be avoided, occurrence of a behavior to be avoided is also considered a failure.

DEFINITION 3.2 (Failure).– *Failure (sometimes called breakdown[5]) is a disruption of the ability of a functional unit to perform a required function. As the performance of a required function necessarily excludes certain behaviors and as certain functions can be specified in terms of behavior to be avoided, occurrence of a behavior to be avoided is also considered a failure.*

From Definition 3.2, the need to define the concepts of normal behavior (safe) and abnormal behavior (unsafe) with a clear boundary between the two can be deduced.

Figure 3.1 shows that a system can be in different states. The important thing is to ensure that the system cannot reach a state of incorrect and dangerous functioning. We must, therefore, identify quickly a typology of systems states.

Figure 3.1 represents external states (correct, incorrect) of a system and the possible transitions between these states. The system states can be classified into three families:

– correct states: there is no dangerous situation;

– safe incorrect states: a failure is detected and the system is in a safe condition;

– incorrect states: it is an uncontrolled hazardous situation: there could be potential accidents.

---

5 The term *breakdown*, although widely used in different standards, should be avoided as it may be associated as much with the concept of failure (the car has broken down and does not start) as with concept of error and/or fault (the mechanic is looking into the breakdown to fix the car).

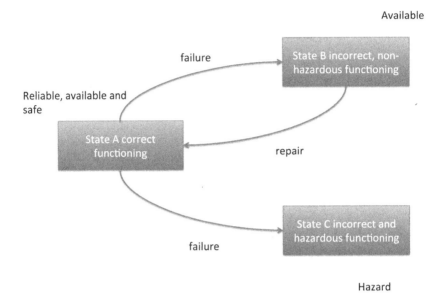

Figure 3.1. *Evolution of the overall state of a system*

From the external conditions (Figure 3.1), it is necessary to identify the internal states of the system (Figure 3.2) and to ensure that all external conditions are taken into account. There are, thus, different families of system state: normal behavior, degraded (loss of functionality) and faulty functioning (behavior is out of specification). The challenge is to ensure that all failures will bring the system to the proper state.

Generally, when the system reaches a fall-back state, there may be a complete or partial shutdown of services. Fall-back states may allow the system to return to the correct state following a repair action.

Failures can be random or systematic. Random failure occurs in an unpredictable manner and is found to be the result of a set of degradations affecting the hardware aspects of the system. In general, random failure can be quantified due to its nature (wear, aging etc.).

Systematic failure is deterministically linked to a cause. The cause of the failure can only be removed through recovery of development process (design, manufacturing, documentation) or recovery of procedures. Given the nature, systematic failure is not quantifiable.

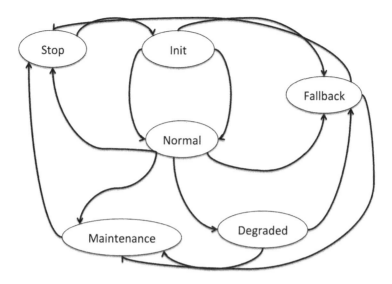

Figure 3.2. *Evolution of the internal state of a system*

Failure is an externally observable manifestation of a fault (the standard IEC 61508 [IEC 08a] refers to it as *anomaly*).

DEFINITION 3.3 (Error).– *Error is an internal consequence of a fault during the implementation of the product (a variable or a state of the erroneous program).*

Despite all the precautions taken during the development of a component, it may be subject to defects related to design, verification of defects, defective usage, defects in maintaining the system in operational condition, etc.

From defects, it is possible to derive the concept of fault. A fault is the cause of error (e.g. burned circuit, electromagnetic interference, design fault, etc.). It should be noted that the failure of an internal element will cause a fault to occur (e.g. short circuit, etc.). Fault (see definition 3.4), which is the most commonly accepted term, therefore, refers to the introduction of a defect in the component.

DEFINITION 3.4 (Fault).– *A fault is any non-compliance introduced in the product (e.g. an incorrect code).*

As observed, it must be noted that the confidence in the system dependability may be compromised due to the occurrence of obstructions such as faults, errors and failures.

Figure 3.3 shows the fundamental chain that connects all the obstructions. The occurrence of a failure can lead to a fault which in turn may provoke error(s); this (these) new error(s) may lead to emergence of a new failure.

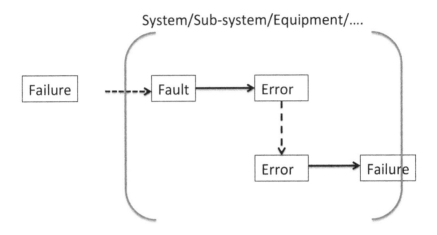

Figure 3.3. *Fundamental chain*

The connection between the constraints must be viewed with respect to the entire system as shown in the example in Figure 3.4. A failure at the component level following a fault (short circuit) on a transistor will result in a fault at the card level (a locked storage area 1, for example). This fault, when activated, causes failure of the card (wrong value reflected while reading the card) which in turn leads to a fault in the equipment and if the wrong value is used to produce an output at the equipment level there will be a failure of the equipment.

The fundamental chain (Figure 3.3) can be generated in a single system (Figure 3.4), and create interlocking of components (subsystems, equipment, software, hardware), or from system to system (Figure 3.5); failure generating an error on the following system.

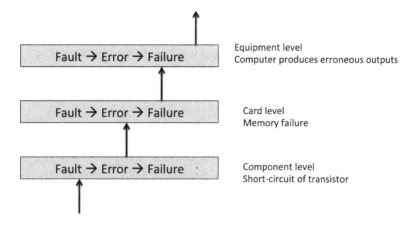

Figure 3.4. *Propagation in a system*

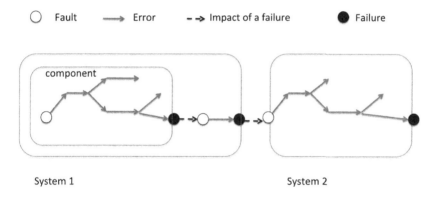

Figure 3.5. *Fundamental chain from system to system*

With the entire vocabulary of dependability having been defined clearly, we shall now present only the concepts that are useful for our discussion; [LAP 92] contains all the definitions necessary for the understanding of this field.

3.2.3. *Methods*

There are four techniques to manage faults and to create a dependable system:

– *fault prevention*: it is the "ability to prevent the occurrence or introduction of faults";

– *faults elimination*: this is the "ability to reduce the presence (number and severity) of faults";

– *faults tolerance*: this is the "ability of a system to perform its services even in the presence of faults";

– *fault predicting*: it is the "ability to estimate the presence, creation and consequences of faults".

There are several ways to combine the fault management techniques; Figure 3.6 shows two approaches. In the first approach, avoidance and elimination of faults are selected to build a system with very little fault or no fault (which is quite difficult). Whereas acceptance of faults is based on the prediction and fault tolerance where faults are accepted and managed.

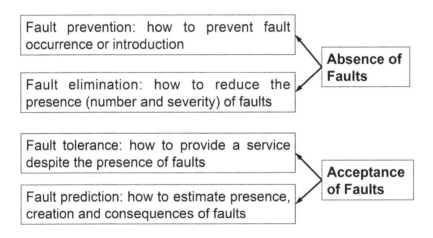

Figure 3.6. *Absence of faults versus acceptance of faults*

Figure 3.7 shows all the components of dependability falling within three categories: attributes, constraints and methods.

3.2.4. *Example of a constraint*

Figure 3.8 shows an example of application of failures. As previously indicated, a failure is detected when there is a behavioral difference of the system with respect to what has been specified. This failure occurs at the limits of the system through a set of errors that are internal to the system and have consequences on the production of outputs.

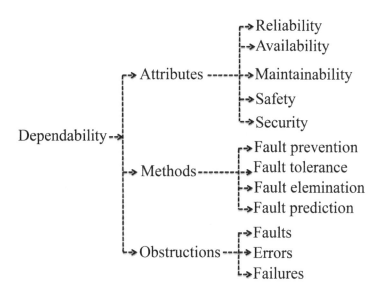

Figure 3.7. *Dependability*

In this case, the source of errors is a fault in the embedded executable. These defects can be of two kinds: either they are errors introduced by the programmer (BUG) or they are defects introduced by the tools (executable generation, downloading facilities, etc.) or by hardware failures: memory failure, short circuits on a component, external disturbance (e.g. EMC[6]), etc.

It must be noted that faults can be introduced during the design process (fault in the software, system sizing, etc.), during production (generating the executable, manufacturing equipment, etc.), during installation, use and/or during maintenance.

The diagram in Figure 3.8 can thus be adapted for different situations. Figure 3.9 shows the impact of human error.

In the previous section, we noted that there were two types of failures: random failures and systematic failures. Random failures are due to the production process, aging, wear, deterioration, external events, etc. Systematic failures are reproducible; in fact they are caused due to design flaws.

---

6 EMC stands for Electromagnetic Compatibility.

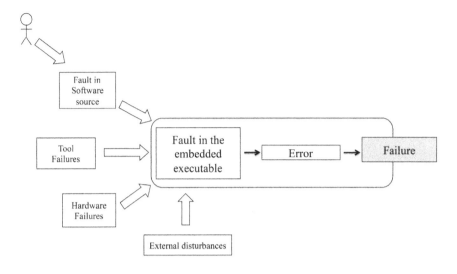

Figure 3.8. *Example of propagation*

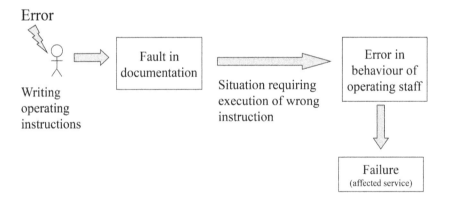

Figure 3.9. *Impact of a human error*

Note that a random failure can be due to a design flaw (underestimation of the effect of temperature on the processor). As we will see below, there are several techniques (diversity, redundancy, etc.) to detect and/or control random failures. Systematic failures are more difficult to manage because their management relies on quality (pre-established and systematic practice) and verification and validation activities.

3.2.5. *Classification of faults*

Faults can be classified as follows:

– permanent faults: they persist indefinitely (or at least until repair) after their occurrence (short circuit, default software, etc.);

– intermittent faults: they occur sporadically. This is a temporary situation that occurs sporadically such as loss of a relay contact;

– transient faults: they occur in isolation such as electromagnetic interference.

As shown in Figure 3.10, a version of LAAS [ARL 06], it is possible to construct a classification of errors based on various criteria:

– phenomenological causes, natural or human-induced;

– intentional: intentional without malice, intentionally with malice, accidental;

– creation or occurrence phase of fault: during development or operation;

– boundary of the system: internal or external;

– persistence: permanent or temporary.

As for situation:

– in case 1, there may be a manufacturing defect, etc.;

– in case 2, there may be a component failure, etc.;

– in case 3, there may be an interference, etc.;

– in case 4, it could be bugs, etc.;

– in case 5, there may be an operator error, etc.;

– in case 6, it could be a "backdoor", etc.;

– in case 7, it could be viruses, worms, etc.;

– in case 8, it could be of hacking, etc.

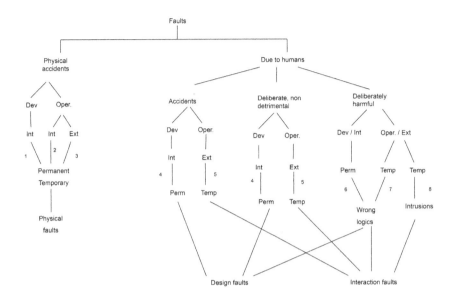

Figure 3.10. *Classification of faults*

In terms of RAMS management, the fault cases with physical causes, accidental and/or deliberate non-harmful human causes are taken into account by safety studies. But the faults with deliberate harmful human causes are not addressed. For faults in cases 6 (backdoor, etc.), 7 (viruses, worms, etc.) and 8 (hacking, etc.), it may be necessary to implement other practices [BOU 14b, CAM 14, KOB 14].

3.2.6. *Adaptation to software applications*

In a software application, there are *failures* as soon as the behavior of the software application does not conform to its specification. This means that failure of a software application is detectable through the output analysis of the application.

Since a software application does not wear out (no degradation) but can only age[7], the application failure is *systematic*. A failure is related to one or more *errors*. Errors are internal to the software application and are a consequence of the

---

7 The behavior of a software application evolves with time and changes in support technologies (processor, memory, hard disk, etc.), hence, a software application *ages*.

propagation of other errors or activation of a *fault*. A fault is located in a specific part of the software application. Activation of the fault will generate an error that can result in a failure or error propagation.

Figure 3.11 shows an example of error propagation in a software application. The first step is related to presence of fault in the software. The second step shows that after a certain running time the fault was activated that led to the propagation of errors in the software. The third step shows that an error has reached the limits of software and failure is visible. The failure may be an erroneous value, erratic behavior of the software (free-stop, etc.), etc.

Note that the fault is the result of a failure and that failure can be a human error (typing "+" instead of "–"), a hardware failure (a memory bit blocked at 1) or environment failure (bit changes related to the program memory or data following an EMC field and /or a particle).

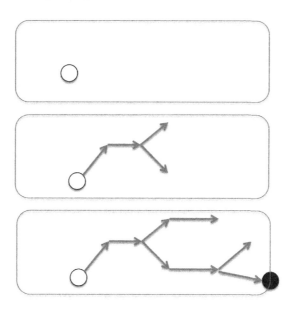

Figure 3.11. *Error propagation*

Figure 3.12 allows replacement of a software application in its environment. Its environment consists of libraries, basic software, utilities, an operating system (referred to as OS) and a hardware architecture. Each element of the environment that may be faulty (CPU defects, memory defects in an OS or basic software, etc.) can introduce faults in the software application.

In the context of software applications, it should be noted that environment failures (see Figure 3.8) take into account the failures from support tools to the development of software applications (compiler, download tool, testing tools, code generators, etc.) and the tools used for loading the application on the target device.

The following are the types of failures introducing faults in a software application:

– *design failures*: designer introduces a fault in the software;

– *failures in the support tools*: failure of a tool introduces a fault in the executable on the target computer (failure of code generator, compiler, the linker, loader, etc.);

– *failures in other software elements* (OS, libraries, utilities, etc.): these failures can disrupt the software application either directly (bad value, bad formatting, etc.) or indirectly (modification of the program in memory, poor management of disruptions, blockages in a hardware component, etc.);

– *hardware failures*: changes in memory information, improper execution of the software application, etc.

– and so on.

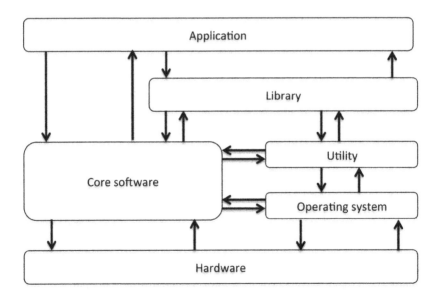

Figure 3.12. *Software in its environment*

Figure 3.13 shows the various failures that can introduce a fault in the software application. Development of a software application is related to the cases 1, 2, 3 and 4. Case 5 is processed at the software level (establishment of the identity of the executable) and the platform. The platform must handle cases 6, 7 and 8. For the faults related to compatibility (which can occur in cases 5, 6, 8), it is necessary to establish a process for deploying a software version.

Table 3.1 – which is a partial list of failures affecting software – explains the failures identified in Figure 3.13. Note that the last column shows the characterization of the element involved in failure.

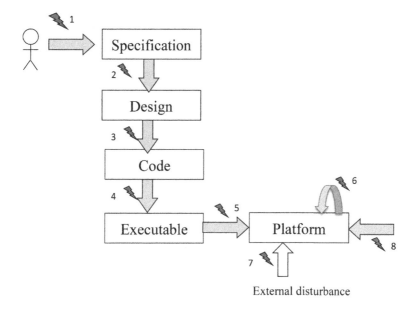

Figure 3.13. *Software in its environment*

3.3. Description of software errors

Now that we have presented the various concepts associated with operational safety and especially failures that could impact the software application, we shall introduce different types of errors in this section. This refers to the errors that may occur within a running program.

	Various causes	Consequence	Vector
1	A fault may be introduced during specification	This fault could be present in the executable and is not detected	Human
2	During the design process, the designer introduces a fault in the documentation (architecture, design, etc.)	This fault could be present in the executable and is detected	Human
3	During the production of code (manual) the programmer introduces a fault		Human
	While generating a code, the tool introduces at least one fault		Device
4	Failure in the production chain of the executable (code generation, compiler, linker, etc.)		Device
	Incorrect input file of the executable production chain		Human
			Device
5	Failure of the loading tools on software application platform. The executable is different from the one provided as input		Device
	Incorrect version of the downloaded executable (human error)		Human
6	Platform failure, executable in memory is modified		Platform
	Platform failure, data in memory is modified		Platform
	Platform is not compatible with this version of the software		Human
	Environment conditions (temperature, humidity, etc.) are not respected		Human
			Environment
7	External disturbance (ECM, particles) modify the program in memory		Environment
	External disturbance (ECM, particles) modify the data used by the software application		Environment
8	The interface elements do not provide the correct data (incompatibility, etc.)		Environment
			Human
	Data acquired are used incorrectly (incorrect cycle, etc.)		Platform
	Incorrect connection of interfaces		Human

Table 3.1. *Failure affecting the software*

Error classes	Error types
– Incorrect evaluation of an equation – Obtaining incorrect result from an operation – Incorrect use of operands	⇒ Result error
– Error in sequencing operations – Incorrect connection – Erroneous loop processing	⇒ Algorithm error
– Error in synchronization primitive – Incorrect synchronization parameter – Unplanned synchronization	⇒ Synchronization error
– Errors in data definition – Errors in data initialization – Errors in data handling – Unauthorized modification of data	⇒ Error in processed data
– Error in procedure call (error in input data during call, no procedure call) – Procedure output error (error in output data during feedback) – Parameter transmission error between procedures (parameter addressing error)	⇒ Interfacing error between procedures
– Error in defining transmitted data – Error in data transmissions – Erroneous frequency of transfers	⇒ Data transfer error with the environment

Table 3.2. *Error classes*

3.4. Safety critical software

Existence of faults leading to system failures is thus a point to be considered while developing a software application. As we identified under section 3.2.3, there are four techniques for achieving a *dependable* system:

– *faults prevention*;

– *faults elimination*;

– *faults tolerance*;

– *faults predicting*.

In the following sections we shall analyze these techniques and study their applications in developing a software application.

3.4.1. *Prevention of faults*

Prevention of faults is based on the rigor in the development process. The rigor of development process requires the establishment of quality assurance. Quality assurance is, therefore, applicable when developing a software application.

It is first recommendation in all standards (aeronautics, railways, nuclear, general, etc.) is the implementation of software quality asssurance.

ISO 9001:2008 [ISO 08] remains the applicable standard (explicitly cited in various standards), but it is quite acceptable to have a certified process such as CMMI[8] (Capability Maturity Model for Integration) or SPICE (Software Process Improvement and Capability dEtermination or [ISO 04a]). In railways, IRIS[9] [UNI 09] has been defined to include, under a single certification, the compliance with ISO 9001: 2008 and CENELEC (50126 [CEN 00], 50128 [CEN 11a] and 50129 [CEN 03]) referential.

---

8 CMMi is a maturity model dedicated to software industry which combines all good practices to be implemented in development projects. For more information, visit the site of *Software Engineering Institute*: www.sei.cmu.edu/cmmi.

9 IRIS is *International Railway Industry Standard*. For more information, visit www.iris-rail.org.

Managing quality of a software application is discussed in detail in Chapter 9.

Interestingly, it has been shown that one of the main sources of defects is in improper acquisition and description of the requirement. Therefore, formalization of requirements is also widely recommended by various standards and it is accompanied by the use of semi-formal and formal methods.

3.4.2. Elimination of faults

Elimination of faults involves detection of errors and correction of their effects. Detection of a fault can be linked to the performance of a test revealing a failure. But generalization of the detection of faults involves establishing *quality control* and *verification* and *validation* activities.

Quality control must be associated with the existence of quality assurance. It must be ensured that the measures that have been defined are effectively implemented. Quality control is associated with controlling the quality of a software application. It is discussed in detail in Chapter 9.

The verification and validation activities help to ensure that the product was properly developed (no fault is introduced) and corresponds to the identified requirements. Verification and validation are discussed in detail in Volume 2 [BOU 16a].

Correction of the effect of a fault requires formalization of the anomaly, analysis, correction and verification of correction and non-regression of the product. Formalization of the anomaly and management of the correction are discussed in Chapter 9, which deals with the quality management, and in Volume 2 [BOU 16a] dealing with the maintenance of a software application.

3.4.3. Tolerance to faults

Tolerance to faults aims at inhibiting the defects of the software application. For this purpose, we must implement a fault tolerant programming that tries to recover the situation when an error is detected.

The error detection implies acceptance of the presence of fault and identification of errors can be detected and corrected. Correcting or inhibiting an error involves:

– knowing a safe state (hold state);

– knowing that a correction action is set in place for each detectable error;

– knowing previous correct states and existence of alternatives to circumvent the error.

Establishing fault tolerance for software applications is one possibility that has been widely used and led to several techniques such as:

– error handling;

– error recovery;

– defensive programming;

– double execution;

– data redundancy;

– and so on.

These techniques are discussed in detail in Chapter 6.

3.4.4. *Prediction of faults*

Development of a software application is, and remains, a creative human activity. Predicting faults of a software application is linked to the analysis of a person's behavior. While it is possible to provide a typology of defects and a comprehensive list of faults that a developer could introduce in a software application, it is not possible to quantify the number of defects.

There are a number of tasks that are related to *reliability* of the software. These tasks propose methods for quantifying the reliability of software that are based on the awareness of identified defects and controlling changes in the software application.

This type of quantification is based on an improvement of the process and does not take into account several factors:

– human factor, it is difficult to guarantee the quality of work that is likely to be "artisanal";

– discontinuity of the process improvement:

  - time between two versions may be longer or shorter,

- it is not possible to ensure that it is the same set of people who would develop the following version;

– lack of information about anomalies of the product in service;

– and so on.

The various standards applicable for developing a software application with dependability objectives offer no guarantee with regard to the reliability of software applications. A dependable software without any faults must also be reliable.

3.4.5. *Review*

To conclude this section, we can say that the safety of a software application can be ensured by establishing quality assurance that takes into account all the stages of verification and validation associated with quality control and through establishment of safety techniques.

Safety techniques and their impact on the software application are discussed in the next chapter.

While designing a software-based equipment with dependability objectives, the following three types of failure must be taken into account:

– random failures of hardware components;

– systematic design failures of both hardware and software;

– specification "errors" at the system level; these errors can have serious consequences on operation and maintenance of systems.

3.5. Conclusion

In this chapter, we described the constraints (fault, error and failure) faced in terms of dependability management of a software application. We discussed the safety techniques of a software application and we have shown that the main characteristic of all of these techniques was to make the code more complex and thus, make safety demonstration harder (test, analysis, etc.) and especially render *maintainability* of the software application more difficult.

Maintainability of a software application is the most important attribute after safety. In fact, depending on the sector in which it is used, a software application has more or less a long life (15 years for the automotive sector, 40 to 50 years for the railway and aviation sectors, 50 years for the nuclear sector, etc.); the ability to maintain a software application related to safety is, therefore, essential.

In Chapter 4 we shall analyze the various safety management techniques in a software application.

3.6. Glossary

CENELEC[10]:   *Comité Européen de Normalisation Electrotechnique* (European Committee for Electrotechnical Standardization)

CMMi[11]:   Capability Maturity Model for integration

E/E/PES: Electric/Electronic/Programmable Electronic Systems

EMC: Electromagnetic Compatibility

IDE: Integrated Development Environment

IEC[12]:   International Electrotechnical Commission

IRIS[13]:   International Railway Industry Standard

ISO[14]:   International Organization for Standardization

OS: Operating System

RAMS: Reliability, Availability, Maintainability, Safety

RAMSS: Reliability, Availability, Maintainability, Safety, Security

SPICE: Software Process Improvement and Capability dEtermination

---

10 http://www.cenelec.eu.
11 http://www.sei.cmu.edu/cmmi.
12 http://www.iec.ch.
13 http://www.iris-rail.org.
14 http://www.iso.org.

Safety Management of a Software Application

4.1. Introduction

In Chapter 3, we identified that the dependability (see Definition 3.1) of a system must be managed through the entire lifecycle from requirement analysis to the decommissioning of the system (see Figure 4.1).

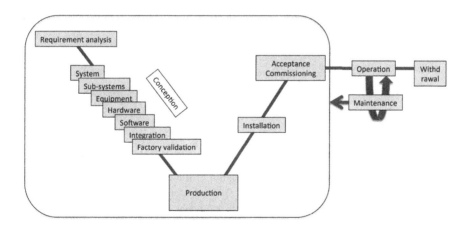

Figure 4.1. *From requirement analysis to decommissioning of the system*

One of the important changes that has occurred in recent years is the establishment of safety demonstrations that take into account all phases from requirement analysis to decommissioning of the system. In fact, the safety of a system may be compromised by manufacturing (use of non-compliant elements, etc.), installation, operation and maintenance. Considering decommissioning of all or part of the system very early in safety activities ensures compliance with environmental requirements and managing the safety of the site.

Managing the dependability of a system requires establishment of an independent production team (development, verification and validation) which is in charge of carrying out RAMS[1] activities. Generally speaking, RAMS's activities are divided into two parts: RAM and Safety. Safety refers to identifying risks and hazards and demonstrates that the system complies with the safety objectives.

4.2. General approach

The demonstration of the safety of a system involves the following steps:

– identifying undesirable events (hazards);

– identifying risks;

– defining safety activities;

– drafting out "safety" requirements;

– developing a "safe" design;

– implementing a "safe" solution;

– ensuring safety of the process;

– verifying or ensuring that the tests cover the safety requirements;

– confirming that the safety objectives are met.

As indicated in Chapter 1 (see Figure 1.11), the software must be seen as part of a whole, i.e. as an equipment, and before identifying the limits of a software application, it is necessary to identify the limits of the equipment. From the limits of the equipment and on the basis of a set of rules of architectures and safety concepts (nOOm architecture, diversity, etc.), it is possible to identify the limit of the "hardware" and "software".

To this process, it is possible to add the safety analyses that are to be carried out at every level, which is shown in Figure 4.2.

---

1 RAMS: Reliability, Availability, Maintainability and Safety.

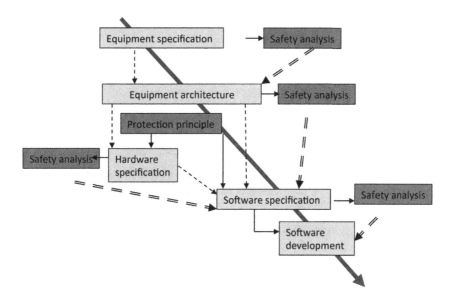

Figure 4.2. *Relationship between specifications and safety studies*

Based on Figure 4.2, we see that at the beginning of the development of a software application, a number of studies must be carried out to identify functional requirements, safety requirements and assumptions and constraints of use of the software application.

The hypotheses of use of a software application is important to frame the scope of its use and therefore, the scope of the demonstration of the safety of the software application.

4.3. Danger, undesirable events, accidents, risks

The purpose of this section is to present the language that can be used in analyses related to safety management.

4.3.1. *Definitions*

During the operation of a dependable critical system, we try to avoid any accident. An accident (see Definition 4.1) is a situation that can be associated with different types of damages (individual, collective).

DEFINITION 4.1 (Accident).– *An accident is an event or series of unexpected events leading to death, injury, loss of a system or service, or environmental damage.*

By their nature, accidents, in order to be avoided, must be taken into account while developing the system. In land transport, as indicated in [BAR 90], accidents can be classified into different families:

– system accidents: system users are passive and suffer damages that are attributable to staff failures (maintenance, intervention, operation, etc.), internal system failures or abnormal environmental conditions;

– user accidents: this accident category refers to events that are attributed to one or more users (discomfort, panic, suicide, etc.) and have little to do with the system;

– system-user accidents: unlike system accidents, here the user is active and interacts with the system. Behind the accident, there is misuse of the system (e.g. non-conformance of the audio signal of doors closing in a metro).

An accident may be characterized by some severe consequences, such as:

– a certain number of deaths and/or injuries to persons;

– destruction of company property (loss of an aircraft, loss of an airport, etc.);

– impact on the environment;

– impact on land (contamination of an area, etc.);

– impact on the company's image.

The definition of accident raises the concept of an event which can be refined by introducing the concept of an undesirable event (see definition 4.2).

DEFINITION 4.2 (Undesirable event).– *An undesirable event is an event that should not happen or has a low probability of occurrence.*

Damages can be classified into two families: collective damages and individual damages.

A user accident is likely to cause individual damage, while the other two categories of accidents can cause individual or collective damages. The level of severity[2] of these damages can be defined as: insignificant (minor), marginal (significant), critical and catastrophic.

---

2 We have selected the railway sector [CEN 00], but we have indicated within parentheses whenever there is another term used in other sectors.

The accident situation is the final outcome; there is an intermediate situation which is a potential accident. The concept of potential accident refers to a known situation that can lead to an accident.

In the list of potential accidents are situations specific to the selected domain, such as derailment, collision and more general situations such as passenger fall, running over an individual, jamming of an individual, electrocution, fire, explosion, flood, etc.

DEFINITION 4.3 (Potential accident).– *A potential accident is an event or series of events and contingencies that could lead to an accident following the occurrence of an additional event not controlled by the system.*

The concept of potential accidents is similar to the concept of "near miss" used in fields such as aeronautics and characterizes an unspecified state of the system in which there is no physical integrity of persons nor destruction of equipment, but which could have led to the damage of the physical integrity of persons and/or destruction of equipment.

Table 4.1 shows an example of a potential accident list for the railways [HAD 98]. The potential accident situation is related to the concept of hazard (see Definition 4.4).

DEFINITION 4.4 (Hazard).– *A hazard is a condition that could lead to a potential accident.*

A hazard (see definition 4.4) is therefore a dangerous situation whose consequences can harm humans (injury or death of persons), company (production loss, financial loss, loss of image, etc.) and environment (degradation of environment and fauna, pollution, etc.). The source of the hazard can be uncertain or voluntary (deterministic), therefore, referring to the terms danger or threat. The term threat is generally used in the context of safety operations (planning safety, facility safety, etc.) and/or security.

Hazards can be classified into three families:

– hazards caused by the system or equipment;

– hazards caused by man (failure of operating personnel, failure of maintenance personnel, passenger intervention, etc.);

– hazards associated with abnormal environmental circumstances (earthquake, wind, fog, heat, humidity, etc.).

Potential accident	
Falling of passenger	Passenger falling out from the train onto the platform Passenger falling in the train at the station Passenger falling from the platform onto the track
Injury to passage	Passenger unable to leave the train Passenger is caught between the doors of the train and the platform Passenger is on the track and hit by a train
Derailing	Derailment due to over speeding Derailment due to in correctly positioned needle
Collision	Collision with another train Collision with an obstacle
Injury to staff	Staff on the track hit by a train
Asphyxiation/ poisoning	–
Burns	–
Electrocution	–
Fire	Fire in the train Fire outside the train

Table 4.1. *Example of a list of potential accidents in railways*

Identification of hazardous situations for a given system involves conducting systematic reviews in two complementary phases:

– an empirical phase based on the feedback (existing list, accident analysis, etc.);

– a creative and/or predictive phase which may be based on brainstorming, forecasting studies, etc.

The concept of hazards (a hazardous situation) is directly related to the concept of failure.

Figure 4.3 shows the path that goes from the dreaded event to an accident. It must be noted that a potential accident cannot occur in the presence of a favorable operating environment. In fact, if there is a crossing of a red light on a separate track with little traffic, the risk is lower on a main track. Similarly, transition from a dreaded event to a hazardous situation is related to a technical context.

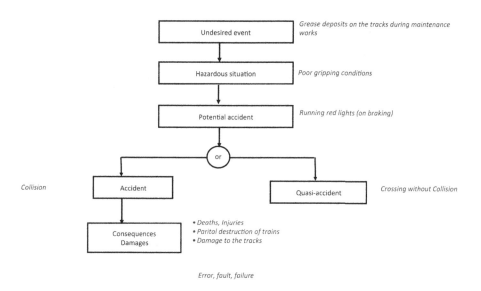

Figure 4.3. *Chain of events leading to accident*

Figure 4.4 shows the complete diagram of the sequence of events from cause to potential accidents (for details refer to [BLA 08] as example).

The concept of cause has been introduced to connect the various types of failures that the system can be subjected to, such as failure of one or more functions (a function can be transversal to several internal equipment) failures of one or more equipment, human errors and external factors (EMC, etc.).

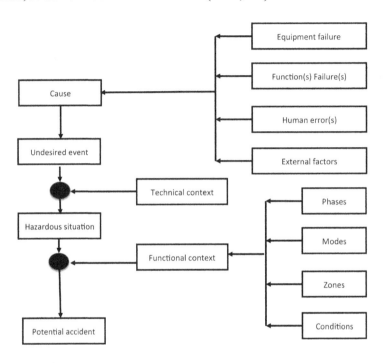

Figure 4.4. *Chain of events leading to a potential accident*

Figure 4.5 shows how a potential accident, a combinatory process, is set in motion. It is then the responsibility of the analyst to select the representative scenarios (Cause – Undesirable Event – Hazardous Situation – Potential Accident).

4.4. System safety

4.4.1. *Definition*

In rail transportation, two safety principles are used [BIE 98]: intrinsic safety (see Definition 4.5) and probabilistic safety (see Definition 4.6).

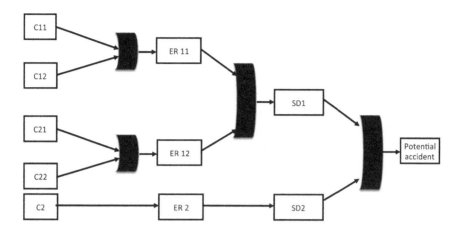

Figure 4.5. *Combination of events leading
to potential accident*

DEFINITION 4.5 (Intrinsic safety).– *A system is intrinsically safe if it is ensured that any failure of one or more components will move the system to a more restrictive state than it is at the time of the failure.*

An equipment which falls under the principle of the intrinsic safety is defined, using a pre-established set of assumptions, by carrying out desired functions in a given environment such as the occurrence of one or more failures of its constituents, drives the system in a known state not reflected by a more permissive situation or involving more dangerous consequences than those that would have existed without failure.

Intrinsic safety is thus related to the concept of safety state or fall-back state. The fall-back state is a specific state that ensures system safety. It must be noted that for rail transportation, complete stop is generally the most restrictive state (except in tunnels), which is not the case with aeronautics.

Intrinsic safety is based on the physical properties of the components, it is necessary to know the behavior of the components in the event of one or more faults, which leads us to use only those components whose complexity is manageable.

DEFINITION 4.6 (Probabilistic safety).– *Probabilistic safety involves demonstrating that the likelihood of a dangerous situation is below a predefined threshold.*

Probabilistic safety is, therefore, to accept that zero risk does not exist (all scenarios leading to dangerous consequences have not been removed); it will be described hereafter. The combination of probabilistic safety and intrinsic safety defines tested safety.

Equipment is said to be controlled for safety if it is able to detect a fault that would lead to a state in which severity of consequences that would be unacceptable and can command a safe configuration. In such a chain, the final link must be intrinsically safe.

DEFINITION 4.7 (Controlled safety).– *A device is said to be controlled for safety against certain failures when the catastrophic consequences due to these failures are inhibited by other independent equipment that detects and controls a restrictive condition.*

The concept of controlled safety is related to the ability to detect a failure (see Definition 4.8).

DEFINITION 4.8 (Detected failure).– *A failure is said to be detected if, when the failure occurs, the system switches to a safe state.*

Two distinct types of threats are identified: accidents and malice with regard to *safety* and *security*.

DEFINITION 4.9 (Computer safety).– *Computer safety is defined by the set of measures implemented to minimize the vulnerability of a computer system against accidental or intentional threats.*

Safety involves protection of computer systems against accidents caused by the environment or system faults. This is emphasized in the computer systems that control real-time processes and have human lives at stake (automatic transport, nuclear power station, etc.). Real-time systems are subject to very strong temporal requirements.

DEFINITION 4.10 (Physical safety).– *Relates to prevention of disasters (safety).*

Protection of computer systems against malicious actions (intrusion, vandalism, etc.) induces security. In general, we find ourselves working with systems performing sensitive processes or containing sensitive data (bank account management, etc.).

With the introduction of new technologies in computer-based systems, this is not entirely true. In the context of transportation (automotive, railways [BOU 14a], aeronautics, etc.), technologies such as WiFi, GSM, GSM-R[3] or powerline are implemented and measures with regard to security must be set in place.

DEFINITION 4.11 (Security).– *This refers to prevention of attacks (intrusion, loss of confidentiality, etc.).*

The basic principle is not to put the security objective on the communication medium; it is not safe and it is necessary to secure the system considering this hypothesis.

It is generally referred to as "grey channel" (see Figure 4.6). The applications to communicate through the "grey channel" must have a mechanism for encoding/ decoding the information exchanged. This mechanism should allow assumptions of security objectives.

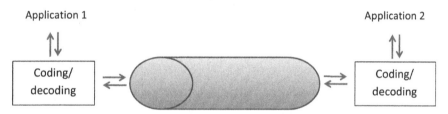

Figure 4.6. *Combination of events leading to potential accident*

4.4.2. *Safety management*

Dependability [LIS 95, VIL 88] of a system is implemented through a number of activities based on studies. These studies must be a prerequisite for designing of a required safe system.

Figure 4.7 shows the dependability implementation cycle for a computer system. The first step is to carefully assess the requirement; the studies related to operational safety must enable understanding, identification of risks and considering the consequences, and then defining dependability objectives (RAM and/or S) for the system.

Studies related to dependability follow the lifecycle phases (specification, design, implementation and evolution).

---

3 GSM-R is a specific application dedicated to railways.

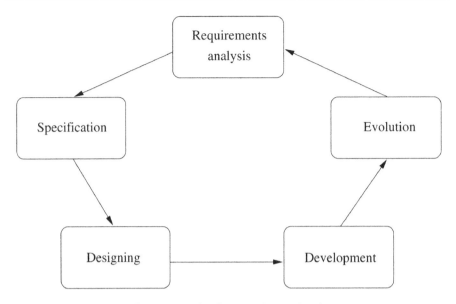

Figure 4.7. *Implementation cycle of functional safety*

The specification phase is an important step as it identifies the system requirements. These requirements are of two types: non-safety-related requirements (functional requirements, non-functional requirements such as performance, etc.) and safety-related requirements (see Figure 4.8).

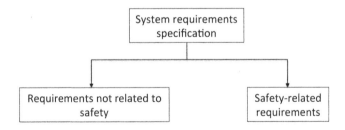

Figure 4.8. *Specification of system requirements*

As shown in Figure 4.9, it is possible to draw a connection between risks, consequences and associated failures.

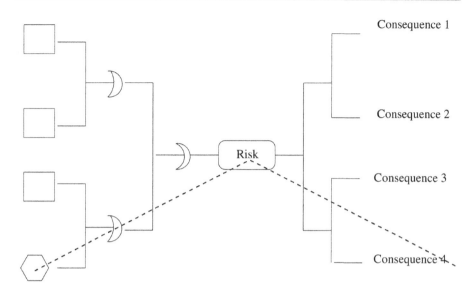

Figure 4.9. *Relationship between failure,*
risk and consequences

DEFINITION 4.12 (Risk).– *Risk is a combination of:*

– probability of occurrence of an event or combination of events leading to a hazardous situation, or frequency of such events;

– consequences of this hazardous situation.

According to definition 4.12 and in accordance with [IEC 08b], risk is, therefore, a combination of the likelihood of injury and its severity. Severity is characterized by the damage and the consequences of the accident (see Figure 4.10).

For every hazardous situation, we must define a probability of occurrence or frequency; for this, a set of categories are defined (see Table 4.1, which is extracted from the CENELEC 50126 standard [CEN 00]), where each category is associated with a frequency range.

In Table 4.2, the term *often* indicates that the hazardous situation has occurred and will occur again.

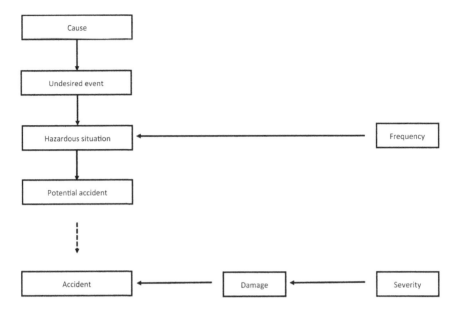

Figure 4.10. *Frequency and severity*

Category	Description
Frequent	Likely to occur frequently. Hazardous situation is continually present.
Probable	May occur on several occasions. Hazardous situation can be expected to occur often.
Occasional	May occur from time to time. Hazardous situation can be expected to occur.
Rare	Likely to occur at some point in the system lifecycle. It is reasonable to expect that the dangerous situation occurs.
Improbable	Unlikely to occur but possible. Presumably the dangerous situation may occur on one-off basis.
Unlikely	Extremely improbable. Presumably the dangerous situation will not occur.

Table 4.2. *Frequency of a hazardous situation*

DEFINITION 4.13 (Hazardous situation).– *A hazardous situation is one in which a person is exposed to dangerous event(s). The hazard is a potential source of danger in the short and/or long term.*

Definition 4.13 introduces a relationship between risk and potential accident. A hazardous situation is one of the links to an accident scenario. It corresponds to an unstable state but reversible of the system.

Level	Consequences for people or environment	Consequences for the service
Catastrophic	Several dead and/or seriously injured and/or major environmental damage	
Critical	One dead and/or seriously injured and/or serious threat to environment	Loss of an important system
Marginal	Minor injuries and/or serious threats to the environment	Severe damage to one or more systems
Insignificant	One person slightly injured	Minor damage to a system

Table 4.3. *Severity of dangerous situations*

For every hazardous situation, we must analyze the consequences on the system, people and the environment. Quantification of consequences can be performed by defining the severity level. Table 4.3 is taken from the CENELEC 50126 standard and relates to consequences.

Depending on the type of system, consequences can be classified under two families:

– first, there may be an impact on property, environment and/or individuals (transport, energy, etc.);

– second, there may be impact on services with loss of all or part of the system (spatial, telecommunication, etc.).

Given the diversity of risks and the impact they can have on the system, it is best to define categories and to associate actions to these categories. Table 4.4 is an example of categorization. As part of the undesirable category, there is a relation with the supervisory authority. In the railway sector, the supervisory authority is the operating company.

Risk category	Action to be taken for each category
Unacceptable	Must be eliminated
Undesirable	Acceptable only when it is impossible to reduce risk and with the authorization of the operating company or, where applicable, of the supervisory authority
Acceptable	Acceptable with appropriate monitoring and approval of the rail operating company
Negligible	Acceptable with approval of the rail operating company

Table 4.4. *Qualitative category of risks*

In order to assess the risk from the above definitions, the standards recommend establishment of a severity-occurrence matrix. For example, let's take the matrix (Table 4.5) from CENELEC 50126.

Frequency of a dangerous event	Risk level (risk category)			
Frequent	Undesirable	Unacceptable	Unacceptable	Unacceptable
Probable	Acceptable	Undesirable	Unacceptable	Unacceptable
Occasional	Acceptable	Undesirable	Undesirable	Unacceptable
Rare	Negligible	Acceptable	Undesirable	Undesirable
Improbable	Negligible	Negligible	Acceptable	Acceptable
Unlikely	Negligible	Negligible	Negligible	Negligible
	Insignificant	Marginal	Critical	Catastrophic
	Level of severity of consequences of a hazardous situation			

Table 4.5. *Qualitative category of risks*

NOTE.– In Tables 4.2, 4.3, 4.4 and 4.5, the content is taken directly from the standard CENELEC 50126. The formulation of the elements reflects the general nature of the application considered. Every implementation must begin with definition of these terms and related categories.

Acceptable risk is the value of a risk resulting from an explicit decision objectively established. This acceptability threshold is denoted by THR (Tolerable Hazard Rate). THR is expressed as the probability of occurrence of a failure expressed as 10^{-x} per hour. When identifying dangerous situations, it is necessary to associate them with THR that are part of the specification.

For a particular system, it is the responsibility of the operating company to provide the maximum acceptable occurrence rate(s) of hazards (THR). The safety management process for the railway sector is defined in CENELEC 50126 [CEN 00] and is given in Figures 4.1 and 4.7.

Risk management with a capacity exceeding the threshold of acceptability involves:

– reducing the likelihood of occurrence through preventive counter-measures that aim to reduce the vulnerability of elements of the system that are most exposed to this dangerous situation;

– reducing the severity of consequences by setting protection in place.

From an initial description of the system and a list of hazardous situations, a risk analysis can be performed to identify the measures that have only acceptable risks. These measures should be considered while developing the system.

Concerning the risks, it is possible to eliminate the hazard, as it is the most effective way to reduce risk. However, the elimination of hazards is often not possible. In these cases, we need to reduce risks to an acceptable level.

In order to reduce risks, we need to reduce the frequency of hazard and/or reduce the hazard severity (consequences). Reducing the frequency and/or severity of the hazard is commonly referred to as "risk management".

Figure 4.11 shows a mapping of the risk management process which is an iterative loop consisting of three phases: identify, evaluate and act.

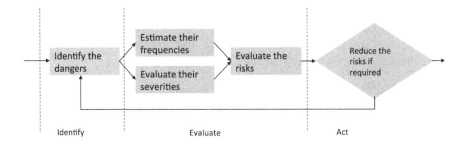

Figure 4.11. *Risk management process*

The objectives of risk management are:

– Step 1: identify the hazards associated with the system:

- systematically identify and prioritize all reasonably foreseeable hazards associated with the system in its application environment.

- identify sequences of events leading to hazards.

– Step 2: evaluate the hazards:

- estimate the frequency of occurrence of each hazard.

- evaluate the probable severity of the consequences of each hazard.

- evaluate the risk to the system due to each hazard.

– Step 3: establish a process to manage the risk:

- create a register of hazardous situations[4] (RHS).

Based on the list of safety requirements and rate of occurrence (THR, etc.), it is possible to define a safety integrity level.

4.4.3. *Safety integrity*

In the various fields (aeronautics, nuclear, space, railways, etc.), similar concept of safety levels are observed. But the concept of safety integrity has been introduced for the first time in IEC 61508 [IEC 08b].

---

4 This also refers to a *Hazard Log* (HL).

The concept of safety integrity was then divided into different sub-standards. For the railway sector, the concept of safety level is given in CENELEC 50126, 50128 and 50129.

The concept of safety integrity (see Figure 4.12) consists of two components:

– random failures management;

– systematic failures management.

The main difference between random failures and systematic failures lies in the fact that the systematic failures cannot be quantified using probabilistic calculations.

Random failures are hardware related – they appear randomly in time and due to aging and wear of the materials. By their nature, software applications are not subject to random failures.

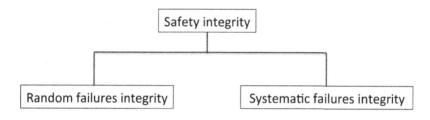

Figure 4.12. *Safety integrity*

Systematic failures can be due to problems in hardware and/or software. They can also occur due to human error during the various life phases of the system (specification and/or design problem, manufacturing problem, a problem during installation, problem introduced during maintenance, etc.).

As for systematic failures, it is necessary to implement various methods or techniques that allow us to obtain a sufficient level of confidence in the achieved safety integrity level.

Figure 4.8 shows a cut-out of the requirements specification in two families – safety-related requirements and non-safety-related requirements. Considering the above statements, it is possible to refine this division as shown in Figure 4.13. This figure introduces a new partitioning of the safety requirements into safety functional requirements and safety integrity requirements.

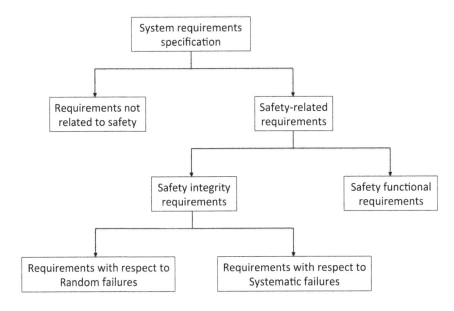

Figure 4.13. *Specification of system requirements*

Safety functional requirements include the safety requirements related to functioning of the safety functions of the system.

The concept of safety integrity involves the ability of a system to fulfill its safety functions under specified conditions within a defined operating environment and during a given period. Safety integrity (section 4.7 of CENELEC 50126 [CEN 00]) is related to the probability of not achieving the required safety function.

Unlike the standard IEC 61508 [IEC 08b], CENELEC 50126 (which applies to the entire rail system) does not define the correlation between the safety integrity and probabilities of failure. However, it must be defined for a given application. The safety functions are assigned to safety systems or to external devices for risk reduction.

4.4.4. SIL management

The standards applicable to aerospace and nuclear domains are not prescriptive, they require implementation of activities but it is always possible to select others.

On the contrary, the standards IEC 61508 [IEC 08b], CENELEC EN 50126, EN 50128 and EN 50129 describe the requirements necessary to achieve each level of safety integrity. These requirements are more stringent for the highest levels of safety integrity to ensure lowest probability of hazard failure.

As shown in Figure 4.14, safety integrity is managed by two practical groups. With regard to integrity versus random failures, we must manage the quantitative objectives (Failure Rate – FR) and qualitative objectives. For integrity versus systematic failures, we must manage the objectives of quality management, safety and safety of hardware elements.

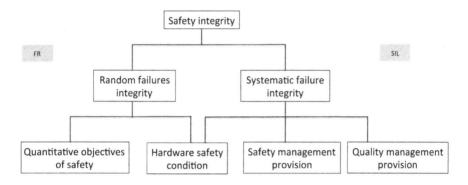

Figure 4.14. *Safety integrity management*

We shall review safety integrity management against systematic failures:

– the provisions for safety management of hardware elements are based on safety analysis methods (preliminary risk analysis [GUE 08], FMEA [IEC 91b], HAZOP, Area Analysis, FTA [IEC 06a], etc.), design methods[5] (redundancy, diversification, etc.), management of degraded modes and defining strategies and managing technical documentation;

– the provisions of quality management are based on quality management (implementation of ISO 9001:2008 or equivalent), managing staff qualifications and establishing autonomy;

– the provisions of safety management are based on a comprehensive management of safety (defining a strategy applying to the hardware and software elements of the system), safety demonstration, safety management software

---

5 For more information, see Chapter 1 of [BOU 09].

applications (implementation of SEEA[6], controlled development methods and "safe" programming technique) and management of technical documentation related to various activities (activities must be auditable).

4.4.5. *Safety integrity level*

As mentioned before, the safety objective of an application is referred to as "safety integrity level". The definition and classification of safety is unique for each sector (aeronautics, railways, automobile, auto, nuclear, etc.).

The generic standard IEC 61508 [IEC 08b] describes the sub-standards covering various areas as shown in Figure 4.15.

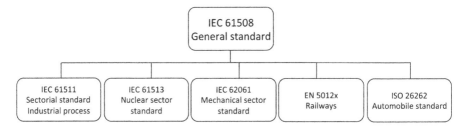

Figure 4.15. *CEI/IEC 61508 and definitions[7]*

The various standards introduce the concept of "safety integrity level". The "safety integrity level" may be associated with a system, subsystem, equipment, system function, software application and/or a software function. It may be interesting to present and compare the various "safety integrity levels".

The standards IEC 61508, IEC 61511 and CENELEC 5012x introduce the concept of SIL (Safety Integrity Level), which can have four discrete values (1 to 4) to specify the requirements for safety integrity.

---

6 SEEA (Software Error and Effects Analysis) is the only safety study carried out on a part or an entire software application. This safety analysis is introduced in Chapter 5.

7 Figure 4.12 shows a link between IEC 61508 and IEC 61513 standards, but this link is not correct. In fact, the nuclear standards existed even before the standard IEC 61508 and the link is only a naming link.

For the standard IEC 61508 [IEC 08b], the four levels of SIL for a safety function are characterized by the impact of failures:

– SIL 4: catastrophic impact (the highest level);

– SIL 3: impact on the community;

– SIL 2: major protection for installation and production or risk of injury to employees;

– SIL 1: minor protection for installation and production (lowest).

The standard for aeronautics sector [ARP 96a] defines the concept of DAL (Design Assurance Level) for an aircraft's safety objective which has the following levels:

– Level A: Catastrophic problem – safety of the flight or landing is compromised – crash of the airplane;

– Level B: Major problem causing serious damage or death of several occupants;

– Level C: Serious problem resulting in dysfunction of vital equipment of the unit;

– Level D: Problem that could disturb flight safety;

– Level E: Problem with no effect on flight safety.

For automotive industry (see ISO 26262 [ISO 11]), this is referred to as *Automotive* SIL (ASIL).

Table 4.6 provides a comparison of safety levels identified in the various standards. This comparison is only an indication. In fact, the principles of identification of risk and safety levels from one area to another are very specific [BLA 12, BAU 10, MAC 12].

It must be noted that Table 4.6 refers to the safety integrity levels for the system or its subparts (equipment, subsystem). Table 4.6 raises the question: *what is the compatibility of the safety integrity levels?* As a partial response to this question, it can be recalled that in the aeronautics sector, for risk analyses we take into consideration the entire aircraft whereas for railway sector we refer to the parts of the system (equipment, subsystems).

	No impact	Impact on the system		Impact on the system and persons		Impact on persons
50126/50129	Non SIL	SIL1	SIL2	SIL3		SIL4
IEC 61508	–	SIL1	SIL2	SIL3		SIL4
ISO 26262	–	ASIL A	ASILB	ASIL C	ASIL D	–
Aeronautic	DAL E	DAL D	DAL C	DAL B		DAL A
Nuclear[8]	–	C	B	A		A
Spatial	–	Critical		Critical		Catastrophic

Table 4.6. *Comparison of safety levels*

Another perspective regarding the identification of the safety integrity level: IEC 61508 [IEC 08b] proposes formulas that take into account different loads (low or high), whereas railways standards are based on initial knowledge of associated risks and probabilities of associated failures that are provided by the authorities. The last point about compatibility levels of safety refers to the allocation principles; ISO 26262 standard provides arithmetic rules recursively whereas aeronautics standards provide rules that are applicable only once and the railways standards offer no rules.

In the end, it may seem impossible to compare the levels in order to facilitate acceptance from one level to another. The railway sector introduces the concept of *cross-acceptance*, which is a recognition process of a certificate or demonstration of the existing safety. Part 1 of the application guide of the standard CENELEC EN 50129 [CEN 07] describes the principles of cross-acceptance.

It must be noted that the safety integrity level (ASIL, DAL, SIL, etc.) should be determined by experts and must be assigned to an item which fulfills one or more functions in an isolated manner.

---

8 For the nuclear sector, the applicable standards are IEC 61513 for system aspects and IEC 61880 [IEC 06b] for the software.

4.4.6. *Overall safety cycle*

4.4.6.1. *Recall*

Figure 4.1 shows that safety must be ensured from the requirement acquisition phase until the decommissioning phase of the system. Figure 4.2 precisely shows that safety studies (system, subsystem, equipment, hardware and software) must be implemented at every level.

System dependability offers tools such as FMEA [IEC 91b], FMECA and/or the fault trees that are generally used at the system level and/or on the hardware architecture to identify the impact of failures on the analyzed elements [VIL 88].

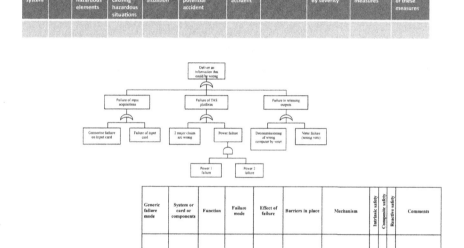

Figure 4.16. *Example of safety assessment*

Systematic research of failures and analyzing their effects on the system can be carried out through activities (see Figure 4.16), such as Preliminary Risk Analysis (PRA) [GUE 08], Failure Modes Effects Analysis (FMEA) [IEC 91b], Fault Trees Analysis (FTA) [IEC 06a], etc.

4.4.6.2. *Iterative process*

The process of defining SILs from hazards to the lower level elements (hardware and software) is a process that requires a loop, as shown in Figure 4.17. This loop ensures that all predefined objectives have been met.

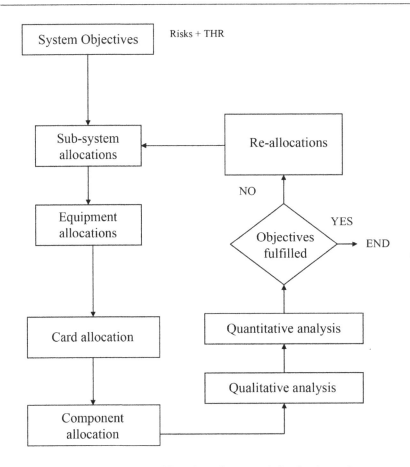

Figure 4.17. *Allocation of system to basic elements*

4.4.6.3. *Identification of safety requirements*

Figure 4.13 introduces safety-related requirements; however, the establishment of the link between risk analysis and safety requirements is not stated. Risk management identifies barriers that help in avoiding potential accidents and/or decrease the severity of the consequences of an accident.

Figure 4.18 shows the barriers following the events leading to an accident. As a general rule, the barriers refer to the equipment and system functions and/or the implementation of specific operating procedures.

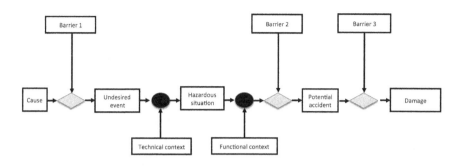

Figure 4.18. *Introduction of barriers*

Safety studies help in defining safety requirements that are supported by barriers. Figure 4.19 shows a certain number of elements (shaded boxes) which may be the safety requirement supports.

It must be noted that the process starts with the identification of risks and enables identification of the safety-related system functions to develop them from system to equipment in order to identify devices that support the safety functions. In the end, each piece of equipment is associated with a collection of requirements that is a function of risk.

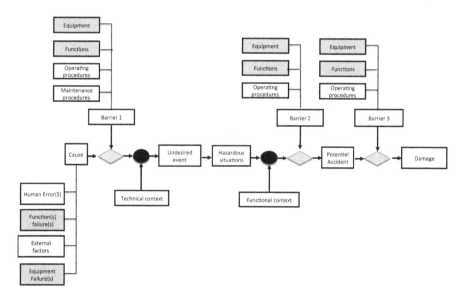

Figure 4.19. *Positioning of safety requirements*

Further, it must be noted that one of the major points for this type of analysis is the logging of selections and justifications.

SIL can then be defined as the confidence level in line with safety requirements allocated to a function and/or equipment.

4.4.6.4. *Preliminary Hazard Analysis*

Preliminary Hazard Analysis (PHA) [GUE 08] is a method for identifying and evaluating risks, their causes, their consequences and the severity of these consequences.

The fundamental role of PHA is to identify, assess and prioritize risks. The objective of risk analysis is to deduce the means and corrective actions to eliminate or at least control hazardous situations and highlighted potential accidents.

The APR process involves:

– identifying, as exhaustively as possible, the Undesirable Events (UE) resulting from the failure of system functions;

– prioritizing UE based on criteria taking into account the severity of the events;

– proposing risk reduction actions calling for measures of prevention or protection of the system;

– re-determining the level of severity of each UE, taking into account the measures implemented.

System:									Page:		
									Date:		
Function	Initiator event (Failure Mode of the function)	Consequence on the system and description of scenario	Undesired Event U.E No		Severity	Frequency	Risk Management Action	Final severity	Final frequency

Figure 4.20. *Example of PHA*

PHA is particularly useful in the early stages of the lifecycle of new systems for which we cannot rely on the feedback.

4.4.6.5. *Analysis of failure modes and their effects*

The Failure Modes and Effects Analysis (FMEA) [IEC 91b] is a systematic risk analysis of causes and effects of failures that may affect the components of a system. FMEA (C) is the extension of the FMEA to analyze the criticality.

This analysis aims to determine the importance of each failure mode with respect to its influence on the normal behavior of the system; it assesses the impact of failures on the reliability and safety of the system.

The objective is to identify existing barriers in order to limit the impact of failures. In the absence of such protection methods, additional mechanisms such as detection/recovery are proposed to tolerate the faults. Alternatively, workaround methods based on the use of operating procedures may also be proposed.

FMEA (C) is devised from a functional representation of the system or structural level (decomposition of the system into hardware/software components).

Failure modes selected for each function are:

– loss of function (in a sustainable manner);

– no function;

– degraded or incorrect function (in a sustainable manner);

– unintended function (in a sustainable manner);

– no breakdown of the function.

4.4.6.6. *Common mode*

The validity of the safety studies may depend on the independence of functions as both the functions are independent if:

– all failures on a function do not affect the correct functioning of the other function without being detected;

– all realistic or specified external influences do not affect the correct functioning of both the functions without being detected.

4.5. Safety Assurance Plan

A Safety Assurance Plan (SAP) must be in place to identify:

– product limits and hypotheses taken into consideration;

– project organization and demonstrate the independence of the safety team with respect to the design team;

– risk management;

– the means (tools, database, feedback, etc.);

– the safety assurance management process of the project and the methods implemented;

– etc.

Appendix 1 proposes a general template for SAP; however, it can be adapted for each sector and each project.

4.6. Safety case

4.6.1. *Structure of the safety case*

Safety studies are performed to demonstrate that a system meets the safety requirements. As we have explained throughout this chapter, it is possible to identify the risks that could affect the safety of a system based on the hazardous situation. A safety level is thus associated with all or part of our system safety level to identify the objectives, means and/or practices to be implemented.

The main difficulty of risk management is the demonstration of the system safety. Safety case[9] (SC) is used in support of this demonstration. Safety case demonstrates that the objectives are achieved, and the means and practices are implemented.

The safety case (see Figure 4.21) is divided into four points:

– a demonstration of quality management, independence of teams and competence of those involved in safety management;

– demonstration of technical safety. This demonstration is based on the principles of safety, independence of elements, etc.;

9 The term safety case (SC) is used very often.

– demonstration of the lack of impact of a simple mistake and controlled behavior in case of double fault. For this, it is usually necessary to demonstrate the absence of common mode;

– demonstration that certified or reused products are used correctly.

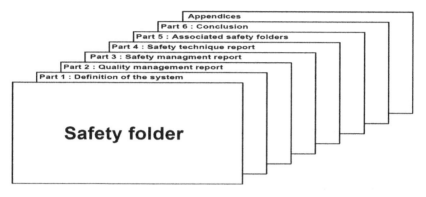

Figure 4.21. *Safety case*

A safety case (see Figure 4.20) may be based on another safety case (a component in use that has already been evaluated and/or certified).

The generic standard IEC 61508 [IEC 08b], applicable to electronics-based and programmable electronic systems (E/E/EP), covers this point and proposes a general approach and for the railway sector, the standard CENELEC EN 50129 [CEN 03] sets the format for safety case.

4.6.2. *Exported constraints*

Based on the results of the safety demonstration presented in the safety case (Figure 4.20), it is possible to export to the future users the use of constraints called exported constraints or *Safety Related Application Constraints* (SRAC).

The exported constraints may include:

– design hypotheses;

– use constraints identified through safety studies;

– unresolved anomalies;

– etc.

The exported constraints can be assumed through:

– operating procedures;

– maintenance procedures.

4.6.3. *Product*

As shown in Figure 4.22, a product (system, subsystem, equipment or platform) is characterized by a function (V1), interfaces and constraints (C1). C1 constraints consist of design hypothesis, constraints (limits, partial behavior, etc.) and use restrictions.

The design of a product P2 on the basis of a product P1 requires verification:

– that the functional V1 of P1 conforms to the requirements identified in the functional V2 of P2;

– that the functional P1 not used in the product P2 cannot jeopardize the safety of P2;

– that the interfaces of P1 comply with the interfaces identified in P2;

– that HCR (Hypothesis, Constraints and Restrictions) of P1 are assumable by P2 (check that the execution hypotheses of P1 are acceptable and that the exported constraints are acceptable and assumed by P2, etc.).

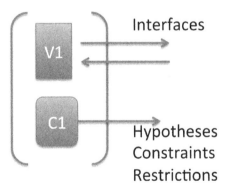

Figure 4.22. *Product*

Cross-acceptance is a phase of verifying that the normative context, hypotheses and exported constraints of an evaluation report and/or certification are consistent with the intended use of the project. The application guide in Part 1 of the standard CENELEC 50129 [CEN 07] describes the principles of *cross-acceptance*.

4.7. Reliability, availability and maintainability

4.7.1. *Requirement*

Until now, we have focused on the safety aspect of the system as safety remains the main aspect of dependability that is required to be analyzed for critical systems. There are few or no requirements of reliability or availability arising from the normative and legislative framework; however, that is not the case for maintainability.

The lack of normative or legislative constraints does not mean that there are no constraints. It is no longer uncommon to see specifications identifying 99.99% reliability and penalties in case of non-compliance with the availability and reliability objectives.

For critical systems (DAL A, SIL3-4, ASIL D), safety implementation principles are most often against system availability, as by design [BOU 09, BOU 11] they stop in the face of failure ("fail stop") for safe behavior on failure ("fail safe"). For example, in the railway sector, safety status is "train stop" and has a strong impact on overall system availability. This feature, specific to applications (including land transport and energy) with a resting state identified as safety, is achievable by relatively simple and fast methods and is not shared in other sectors including air transport where the functions involved in safety must remain available no matter what.

As for software, faults are limited to design faults (which may also be varied and involve components to the related software itself, e.g. documentation). The need for prevention and elimination of faults through various methods prescribed for higher safety levels (DAL A, SIL3-4, ASIL D) has the additional effect of also improving the reliability level of software through better control of their complexity and quality.

For maintainability (see Figure 4.1), the normative and legislative environment (European and international) shows the need to be able to maintain the system for long periods (15, 30, 40 or 50 years) with the same level of safety.

The ability to manage maintenance requires formalization of processes, training and sustainability of the implemented tools.

The establishment maintainability involves obsolescence management (inventory management, identification of sensitive components, implementation of multiple sources, etc.) and sustainability skills (regular training of persons, knowledge transfer, planning starts, etc.).

4.7.2. Problems specific to using off-the-shelf components

In the railway sector, the COTS aspect is currently very pronounced for ancillary equipment (such as video surveillance, passenger announcements, etc.) and for subsystems such as media communications networks. For equipment enabling to establish these communication networks (routers, switches, network cards, hubs, etc.), irrespective of whether or not it contains configurable embedded software, it is currently difficult to demonstrate its reliability and availability, if there is no reference to an already existing installation, through feedback, with all the difficulties included (different contexts of use, etc.).

Safety demonstrations of sub-critical systems are sometimes based on reliability and availability requirements of support subsystems, including communication networks for functions distributed on air/ground (communications operator/driver for manual or gear train driving systems/ground equipment for automated systems). That is why in the recent past (see SAET METEOR – commissioned in 1998) railway sector networks used network equipment developed specifically for the application, and therefore, it was possible to demonstrate the level of safety excluding any standard off-the-shelf equipment.

The railway sector (see European interoperability specifications [COU 96]), the automotive sector (see standard AUTOSAR, [BOU 11 – Chapter 3]) and the aviation sector (see IMA A380 [BEL 02]) are now raising a legitimate concern of economic efficiency, toward the use of standard components based on COTS. The success of this development will then pass through reliability management and availability of COTS, whose suppliers will necessarily evolve (if they want to conquer this new market) to take into account the requirements of these new customers whose objective is to achieve safety features from COTS.

It is therefore likely (and desirable) that in the near future an off-the-shelf component may have as part of its documentation, dependability demonstration elements (failure modes to be considered in system design using the component and perhaps the associated rate of occurrence, etc.) which the industrial users/contractors of critical COTS-based systems can integrate into their safety records.

4.7.3. *FDM plan*

FDM activities are defined in a FDM plan which includes:

– the organization in place;

– the FDM objectives;

– for each stage of the lifecycle of the system, the inputs, activities, outputs and tools implemented must be identified.

4.8. Critical systems

The so-called critical systems are those which in case of failure may jeopardize the life of an individual or individuals. For this class of systems, we must conduct studies that will aim to demonstrate the absence of failures that are against safety. But all systems are not critical and there are scales that define criticality levels that are associated with targets.

4.9. Conclusion

In this chapter we introduced the vocabulary of dependability and associated processes. We deliberately focused on the aspects of systems and subsystems. In the following chapter we shall discuss about the implementation of dependability in software.

The concept of safety integrity has been identified because, although it is common to all areas, its definition and identification depend on specific business processes making difficult the reuse of a product from one sector to another.

Safety management of a critical system requires us to define a process based primarily on test activities that are complemented by reviews, safety analyses, etc.

With regard to the aspect of reliability for critical systems, it results from quality control. In contrast to non-critical systems, which are often COTS or contain COTS, there is currently some difficulty in defining actual reliability when it is a primary piece of information.

4.10. Appendix 1 – Safety Assurance Plan

The *Safety Assurance Plan* (SAP) of a project must contain the elements[10] that are described in the following section.

---

10 This SAP presentation is an example to explain various elements that must be identified in SAP.

The following subjects shall be addressed:

– Section 1: presentation of the project and scope of safety assurance;

– Section 2: identification of standards and mandatory regulations. The purpose of this section is to identify the set of standards and regulations to be respected while managing safety assurance. It is necessary to clearly identify the titles, references and versions of these documents;

– Section 3: provision of a glossary and definitions of important terms for project and safety assurance studies;

– Section 4: presentation of safety assurance context.

In this section, we shall identify the initial events to be taken into account, frequency quantification principles, severity and risks.

– Section 5: description of activities. For each stage of the product lifecycle (system, subsystem, equipment) under analysis, it is necessary to identify the activities to be performed, the documents in inputs and outputs, resources and tools.

This section could be divided into several subsections to manage several levels (system, subsystem, equipment) and hardware and software aspects.

– Section 6: description of management processes and acceptance of preexisting products, COTS and certified products;

– Section 7: description of the construction of safety demonstrations;

– Appendix A: provision of type of plans to carry out studies identified in section 5.

– Appendix B: presentation of implementation methods: tools, database, etc.

4.11. Glossary

ARP: Aerospace Recommended Practice

ASIL: Automotive SIL

AUTOSAR: AUTomotive Open System ARchitecture

CCR: Critical Code Reading

CENELEC[11]:   *Comité Européen de Normalisation Electrotechnique*
                 (European Committee for Electrotechnical Standardization)

---

11 Visit the site www.cenelec.eu.

COTS: Component Off The Shelf

DAL: Design Assurance Level

E/E/PE: Electric/Electronic/Programmable Electronic system

EMC: Electromagnetic Compatibility

FMEA: Failure Modes and Effects Analysis

FMECA: Failure Mode, Effects and Criticality Analysis

FR: Failure Rate

FTA: Fault Tree Analysis

HAZOP: HAZard and OPerability

HCR: Hypothesis, Constraints and Restrictions

HL: Hazard-Log

IEC[12]:   International Electrotechnical Commission

ISO[13]:   International Organization for Standardization

nOOm: n Out Of m

PRA: Preliminary Risk Analysis

PSS: Product assurance and Safety Standards

RAM: Reliability, Availability and Maintainability

RAMS: Reliability, Availability, Maintainability, Safety

RHS: Register of Hazardous Situations

SAP: Safety Assurance Plan

SC: Safety Case

SEEA: Software Errors and Effects Analysis

SIL: Safety Integrity Level

SRAC: Safety Related Application Constraints

THR: Tolerable Hazard Rate

UE: Undesirable Event

---

12 Visit the site: http://www.iec.ch.
13 Visit the site: http://www.iso.org.

Safety of a Software Application

5.1. Introduction

In the previous chapters we discussed dependability (see definition 3.1) and its implementation in the framework of a system, subsystem or device (see Figure 1.6).

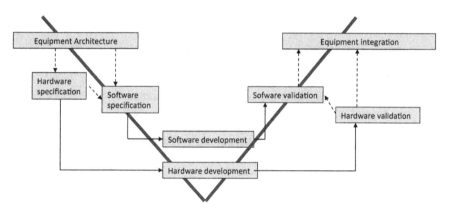

Figure 5.1. *Development of a software application in the overall process*

Development of a software application[1] must be seen in the overall development of a system as shown in Figure 5.1.

---

1 This refers to realizing software application and not just developing a software application.

Development of a software application involves development activities, but also verification, validation, manufacturing, installation, maintenance and decommissioning of the software application (see Figure 5.2).

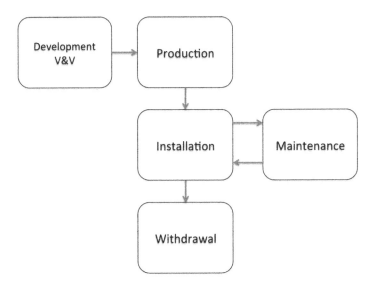

Figure 5.2. *Different steps in the development of a piece of software*

The verification and validation activities are important and are more or less developed depending on the level of safety required.

Manufacturing (also called *production*) of the final software application and installation (also known as deployment) are crucial and require implementation of specific processes. Executable generation (production) must ensure that the executable available is the right one (use of proper source files, use of correct generation chain, non-corruption of the executable during transfers, etc.) and it must be possible to reproduce identically if necessary (formalization of the generation process, generation of environmental formalization, etc.). The deployment of software is a known situation (see updates by Windows or applets) but requires proper formalization and management. In fact, it is not acceptable that, after the deployment of software, the system stops being functional (loss of service).

Maintenance is a delicate issue in software; in fact, software in itself is fault (bug)-ridden and correcting a fault or adding a behavior is an action that will either introduce or develop a new fault, even if we are able to correct it. The difficulty of the maintenance activity of a software application is that two different teams work on a modification considered minor in too short a time.

The decommissioning of a software application is mentioned but it is not a cumbersome process such as the decommissioning of a complex system or a nuclear power plant or a railway installation.

5.2. General approach

Dependability must cover the entire lifecycle of a system (from designing to its decommissioning, see Figure 1.1) but must also take into consideration the various components of a system (see Figure 1.6) and software as part of equipment.

5.2.1. Software reliability

5.2.1.1. Issues

Reliability of a system (see section 3.2.1) is an important element that can be measured and which must be controlled over time. In the context of industrial projects, the objective of reliability is becoming more restrictive; it is not uncommon to see targets higher than 99%.

When the software application is introduced in a fault tree (at system level), the associated probability takes either a value of 0 (no failure as it is developed with a qualitative objective) or a value of 1 (always failing).

Software application is an element that is dependent on an execution environment (runtime platform, real environment, network, etc.). As mentioned already, software application is of an intangible nature, and mistakes are limited to design faults (no wear or damage). In addition, the software uses the data (global variables, local variables, parameters, constants, etc.) which are stored, and software behavior is dependent on stored values. Measuring the reliability of a software application, above all, is to enlist (therefore, count) various different situations it may encounter, and this may seem to be an impossible task.

In addition, if we analyze the allocation process of safety objectives (see Chapter 4), we note that on the basis of risk analysis (severity and frequency) an objective is identified for systematic failures and random failures of the system and on the basis of the objective related to systematic failures. The safety objective of the software application is identified, and because of the risk analysis process, the objectives related to systematic failures of the software application are therefore qualitative objectives.

Furthermore, it is not reasonable to calculate the software reliability, as software is an intangible object that has faults and may have new ones. However, as the production of the software is based on a human process (regardless of automation, skills, etc.), the risk lies in modifications to correct known errors or adding new behaviors. In fact, each modification of software application may add more faults or reveal existing faults. This risk is related to the fact that the team executing the modification, though using an approach similar to the initial approach, may not follow the same mental thought pattern.

Thus each software application development requires the same skill level, same level of formalization, the same deadlines, etc. and unfortunately if the software needs to modified, it must be done, most of the time, in a very short span of time (the system service cannot be stopped for too long), with appropriate methods (we try to minimize activities to be carried out) and with different people (the original people involved are then working on another project or are no longer part of the company), etc.

As a software application is analyzed as part of an entire system, reliability is considered as a property of the whole. The same software in two different systems will have different behavior and a different impact on the overall reliability.

Hence, the term *software reliability* should not be used, as it is not possible to measure this characteristic for a software application.

5.2.1.2. Reliable software

Software reliability is a term to be avoided, though it is used widely and there are suggestions that the term *reliable software* could be used instead. Safety-critical software is called reliable software.

In fact, for developing safety-critical software, the need to prevent and eliminate in various sectors (railways, aerospace, nuclear, automotive, etc.), also has the effect of improving the reliability level through better control of their complexity and their quality.

For non-critical and less critical types of applications, the software implementation process is, however, less constrained (as in the choice of language and tools that the processes use especially for verification and validation), which induces quality of any software, resulting in lower reliability of software, which can therefore induce behavior contrary to availability.

To be more precise, in the context of non-critical or less critical systems, manufacturers can use a "component off the shelf" (COTS). Controlling the quality of COTS has a direct impact on the reliability and availability of systems used, and remains a topical issue, in a context of increasing the search for efficiency.

Managing COTS – and their impact on RAMS – is to extend to the pre-existing software applications. In order to control the costs, it is reasonable to reuse existing software applications that could be developed with or without referential and may not have the same level of quality requirement. However, this involves the same problem: how can we ensure that the recycled portion performs its intended function? Is it in the right context for the use of pre-existing software? Are we using the pre-existing software properly?

5.2.1.3. Conclusion

Ultimately, managing the reliability of software applications is to manage a development process for all the life phases of a software application. Finally, a safety-critical software application is a reliable software application.

5.2.2. Availability

On a similar reasoning as that used for reliability, availability is not a measurable property for a software application. The behavior of a software application is directly related to hardware support and the rest of the system.

However, it may be necessary at the software application level to set load objectives such as:

– maximum number of error messages and/or warnings that may be stored;

– number of reading/writing devices on storage media (xPROM, USB key, hard disk, etc.);

– maximum number of messages for various network interfaces.

5.2.3. Maintenance

The main problem in managing the maintenance of a software application is its lifespan. For the railway sector, the lifetime is 40–50 years, for aeronautics it is 40 years, for the nuclear sector it is 50 years, and for the automobile sector it is 15 years. Given these lifetimes, we must take steps to ensure the maintenance of service and the software application.

Finally, maintenance of a software application is a difficult activity, where following a modification, we must maintain a level of safety while controlling the cost of changes and minimizing the impact on a system in service. The ability to maintain a software application requires the effective management of software (sources, documents, etc.), tools and means of executions (machine to compile and/or for testing, etc.).

To ensure the maintainability of a software application, it may be necessary to identify the following properties:

– the maximum CPU load consumed by the application;

– memory size used by the application, data, maintenance information.

5.2.4. *Safety*

5.2.4.1. *Safety management*

The safety management system comes into picture when a system has an impact on:

– death and/or injury to persons;

– property of the company;

– environment.

Safety management is formalized in a Safety Assurance Plan (SAP) that describes the lifecycle management of safety, organization set in place (hierarchy, authority, independence) and methods to be applied.

For software, safety management is a unique process as the classical concepts (risk, danger, etc.) and conventional techniques (FTA [IEC 06a], FMEA [IEC 91], etc.) do not apply directly. Safety management refers to managing failures and the absence of fault. For this, at the software application level, the methods used are different, such as:

– review: document review, code review, etc.;

– analysis and follow-up of safety requirements;

– Software Errors and Effect Analysis (SEEA);

– residual fault analysis;

– managing complexities;

– quality assurance management of the application.

Under dependability, the methods, tools and activities to be performed on the software application as well as the skills of those in charge of these studies are specific, which is why it is more pertinent to implement a Software Safety Assurance Plan (SSAP). SSAP is described in section 5.7.

5.2.4.2. *Impact of the software*

As inputs for developing a software application, it is necessary:

– to have a safety objective;

– to set safety principles of the platform and have a concept of safety;

– to complete safety studies (FMEA, FTA, etc.) to identify safety requirements affecting the software.

These safety studies are described in the project Safety Insurance Plan (SAP). As part of the safety studies, it may be necessary to identify mitigations to control the risk and these are expressed in the form of requirements to be adhered to by the system. Some of these requirements may or may not be safety requirements.

Safety studies enable us to identify the safety levels of the various components (mechanical, electrical, hardware, software, etc.). Safety levels are given under section 4.4.5 and for the software sector, they are explained under section 5.3.

Safety studies also enable us to identify various families of requirements. In Figure 4.13 we have summarized the families of requirements as a requirement tree.

Safety requirements must ensure that during the situations identified as dangerous, the reactions of the software applications will not worsen the situation and make it more complex.

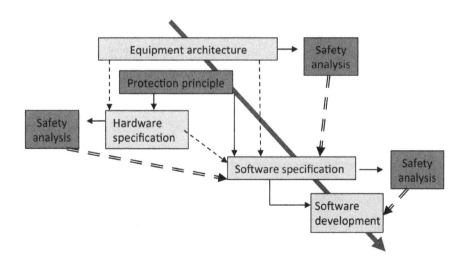

Figure 5.3. *Relationship between specifications and safety studies*

Based on this, it is possible to develop a software application and set up safety studies related to the software application (see section 5.4). Figure 5.3 shows dependability management with respect to software applications.

5.2.5. *Impact of the software*

A software application is a special element that has its own cycle of development and life but needs an environment to run. The verification activities (static analysis, test host, etc.) of a piece of software cannot guarantee its performance; therefore, it is necessary to implement software application tests in its environment (actual platform, OS, etc.) to prove their serviceability; this refers to the term validation of the software application.

As we have said before, system safety studies identify the safety integrity level of the equipment and on the basis of an analysis of the architecture of this equipment, it is possible to allocate a safety integrity level for each software application and every associated element: operating system, hardware card, etc. Section 4.4.5 describes the safety integrity levels.

In software applications, we sometimes refer to the concept of safe software application. Thus, software applications can be classified as safe or unsafe.

DEFINITION 5.1 (Safe Software Application).– *Software applications whose malfunction could lead to limiting the system's ability to ensure expected services in terms of reliability of information provided to the operator without compromising on system safety.*

DEFINITION 5.2 (Unsafe Software Application).– *Software applications whose malfunction could affect the safety of the system that supports it.*

5.3. Safety level

The overall safety objective is called "software safety level" and it depends on the type of architecture implemented and the overall objectives of the equipment. For each sector (aeronautics, railway, automobile, nuclear, etc.) there is a definition and classification of safety.

The standard IEC 61508 identifies the concept of SIL (Safety Integrity Level) which is used for both the system as well as the software.

The standard CENELEC EN 50128 in its 2001 version [CEN 01] introduced the concept of Software SIL (SSIL). This allowed the distinction between the system SIL that is dependent on probability and software SIL that is dependent on the system SIL. The 2011 version of the standard [CEN 11] refers to the integrity of the software but no longer uses the term SSIL. The railway sector continues to distinguish between SIL and SSIL.

The difference between SIL and software SIL is important because at the system level, systematic failures can be managed through architecture (implementation of redundancy, diversity and asymmetry) whereas at software level these have to be managed through quality-management (see Chapter 6), skills, resources, process, etc.

Note that the standard DO 178 (Versions B and C), which applies to the development of a software application, introduces the concept of *software level* that is derived from DAL (Design Assurance Level) [ARP 96c].

5.4. Safety demonstration activity of a software application

5.4.1. *Safety analysis*

5.4.1.1. *Introduction*

To conduct safety studies on a software application, there exist two approaches:

– the first approach is deductive, for each function and output, identifying potential errors that may appear. This study is similar to an FTA associated with the software;

– the second approach is inductive where the analysis is performed by functions. For each function, inputs are identified and for each input, potential errors are identified. Then the whole function is analyzed to deduce the impact on the outputs. This analysis is similar to FMEA but is applied to a software application.

In this approach, we locally analyze the effect of errors and identify the barriers to be implemented to avoid impact on the entire software and/or system.

5.4.1.2. *Fault tree, FMEA of a software application*

5.4.1.2.1. Fault tree

In software applications, Fault Tree Analysis (FTA) can be used in two ways:

– while developing a fault tree at system level, it is inevitable to arrive at the software application as a source of failure affecting the system (see Figure 5.4). This raises a problem: what failure rate must be associated with the software application? Practice is that we either use 1 meaning that the software application is still failing, or 0 which means that we have taken necessary measures to reinforce the software application so it has minimum defects. Depending on the probabilities used in the fault tree, we identify the safety integrity level associated with the software application;

– in software applications, failure is visible on its outputs. Also, based on knowledge of the software application architecture, it is possible to create a fault tree for each fault of the outputs of software application and thus analyze the contribution of each part of the software application.

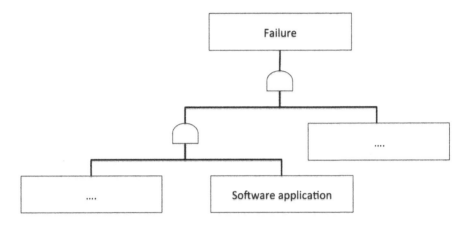

Figure 5.4. *Example of fault tree linked to a system*

Figure 5.5 shows an example of a fault tree related to software failure. Creating a fault tree for software is a long (depending on the number of outputs, number of functions, number of data, etc.) and complex (it is necessary to analyze all behaviors) activity.

When all the software fault trees are created, it is possible to identify the critical parts (data, functions, etc.), requiring special precautions.

Several issues must be taken into account while implementing this technique:

– there is no tool available, it is a manual analysis of the entire code and behaviors (even stored data) of the code;

– this analysis must be repeated in entirety during a change in the software application.

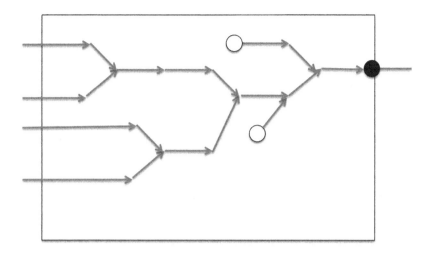

Figure 5.5. *Example of fault tree linked to a software failure*

In the 2001 version of CENELEC EN 50128 applicable to the railway sector, FTA appears in Table A.3 dedicated to the description of architecture. In the 2011 version of the standard, FTA was removed because it is very difficult to create for complex software and to maintain after each software change.

As mentioned previously, in general, the entire software application (one function calls another function, global variables are shared and used by various functions, the core libraries are interacting with all services, etc.) is involved in the production of a faulty output. Fault Tree Analysis applied to a software application is still used in the automotive sector [MIH 14].

5.4.1.2.2. FMEA

FMEA can be performed from a functional representation of a system or at structural level (Breaking down of the system hardware/software components).

For an electronic card, FMEA is an applicable technique to identify potential problems, though it is not feasible for a software application. The systematic side of fault identification and specific characteristics of software architectures (explicit and implicit flow, memory, size, number of connections, etc.) make FMEA an impractical approach on a software application.

Hence, there is a need for establishing a more local approach or component-by-component analysis of the fault impact; this study is called "software errors and effects analysis".

5.4.1.3. *Software Errors and Effect Analysis: SEEA*

5.4.1.3.1. Introduction

While developing the very first applications for metro such as SACEM [GUI 90, HEN 94], several questions were raised regarding the impact of software errors on the complete system. This elicited two types of responses:

– establishment of a safety architecture to detect random faults and/or of the process (compile, download, etc.) through implementation of safe coded processor;

– minimizing systematic errors of the software through formal implementation.

However, in the case of MAGGALY [MAI 93], which is an automatic metro using software, it has been proposed to carry out the FMEA study, but on the software application. This analysis derived from FMEA was called Software Errors Effects Analysis (SEEA); for more information see [THI 86].

This analysis allows for the characterization of the criticality of software through its constituents. The purpose of this method is to expose to designers the critical points identified, and to allow those responsible for validation to refine their approach.

SEEA must be carried out at the preliminary design stage so that the proposed software changes can be considered at the earliest.

5.4.1.3.2. Basic principles

The basic idea SEEA is to analyze the impact of an error on a software application or at least a part of the software application. This involves two approaches:

– the first approach is a deductive approach, for all input we identified the potential error and propagated it in the software. This study is similar to the FMEA. The number of cases to analyze can quickly become very big and difficult to manage;

– the second approach is inductive and we can analyze the software function by function. For each function, we identify the input and the impact of an error on the output. This analysis is similar to FMEA but applied on the software function. In this approach, we can analyze the error effects locally and identify the barrier to prevent the impact on the complete software and/or on the system.

SEEA can be performed on a specification (if it is based on a structured approach: function and data flow), architecture (for example, detect the impact of failures related to unsafe components on safety components), or a code to identify defensive programming elements to be implemented following potential errors on inputs and processing.

The standard CENELEC EN 50128 in its 2011 version classified the implementation of SEEA at the architecture level as highly recommended (HR). In the railway sector, SEEA is generally carried out on the software application code.

SEEA is divided into five stages:

1) Definition of the principles of SEEA: this first step should enable to restrict the scope of the study; the error classes to be taken into account, the severity levels, etc. must be identified. Table 5.1 identifies an example of error classes defined by type.

2) Define the scope: identify the list of components/modules/etc. for which SEEA must be carried out.

3) Identify the hypotheses related to SEEA: hypothesis about the propagation of errors (analyze function by function or search for the function causing the fault) and hypothesis about the positioning of barriers (close to failure or edge of the system).

4) Carry out SEEA: for components/modules/etc. identified as part of Phase 2, we carry out an analysis of the impact of failures identified in Phase 1 by taking into account the hypotheses of Phase 3. This analysis takes into account the following steps:

i) propagation error in the component until its output;

ii) error propagation on the outputs of the components analyzed to the outputs of the system in order to assess the risk of failure;

iii) analysis of the severity of the effect of software failures in the system (a table will be used to characterize the severity) and identifying safety requirements that would be impacted;

iv) identification of barriers to be implemented for each error affecting system safety;

v) definition of the level of criticality. This level of criticality depends on the severity and nature of the safety barrier to be implemented.

5) Verification of the possibility of setting up safety barriers and respecting the identified level of criticality.

The approach presented above is a general approach and we currently use a specific SEEA for each industry. As a general rule, SEEA is carried out to avoid the propagation of faults over the rest of the software application as it involves significant cost in study which could be as much as for creating a fault tree. Certain industries carry out SEEA to confirm the level of criticality of functions/modules/components constituting the software application.

Error classes	Impact of the error
Incorrect calculation Function returning an incorrect value	Incorrect output
Error in processing sequencing Connection error Incorrect loop management	Error in algorithm
Error in synchronization mechanisms Parameter error during synchronization Unrequested synchronization	Synchronization error
Error in data definition Error in data initialization Error in data manipulation Unauthorized modification of data	Error in data processing
Error in procedure calls (no call, incorrect parameter, etc.) Error on procedure return (error in return data) Error in passing parameters during procedure call (incorrect parameter, incorrect addressing, etc.)	Interface error between procedures
Error in data transmission Error in defining transmitted data Error in transfer frequency	Error in transferring data with the environment

Table 5.1. *Examples of error classes*

Finally, we must remember that as SEEA involves analyzing the code, it is interesting to use it along with the Critical Code Review (CCR).

5.4.1.3.3. Conclusion

SEEA is a very interesting approach for analyzing the architecture of a software application or its code. It helps to cover the following points:

– identification of gaps in the architecture and/or the code and the impact on the system;

– identification of barriers and protections to be implemented;

– justification of barriers and protections by introducing a link on failures and their impact on the system;

– identification of consequences of failure on other components and the software application;

– justification for the classification of failures;

– identification of additional verifications.

SEEA has been implemented in the context of software applications with varying degrees of success. Note that the standards CENELEC EN 50128, ISO 26262 and IEC 61508 recommend the implementation of SEEA.

The standard CENELEC EN 50128 recommends the implementation of SEEA to verify an architecture and the code.

5.4.2. *Code analysis*

The main purpose of a software application is the code, which is why it is essential to manipulate the code and verify that the code of the software application complies with specific properties.

5.4.2.1. *Critical Code Review: CCR*

CCR is an activity that involves reviewing the entire or part of the code of a software application. This reviewing process covers at least four objectives:

– verifying the conformance of a code with project documentation such as software design documents required to describe data handling, types, algorithms and traceability with requirements with which the component review must comply;

– verifying the proper implementation of barriers and protections that have been identified to be implemented;

– verifying that the programming rules are respected;

– verifying that the requirements identified to be related to safety are correctly implemented.

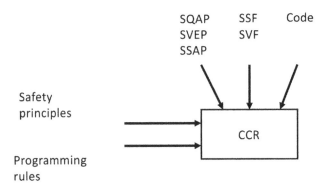

Figure 5.6. *Critical Code Review*

5.4.2.2. *Programming rules*

One of the difficulties related to programming is the fact that programming languages are not perfect and hence we must take a subset of a language and define specific protections in the form of programming rules.

Programming rules are composed of:

– rules for naming objects to increase readability;

– rules related to typing, standards recommending the use of a strong typing language and the choice of a language like C that requires addition of defensive programming to restrict the objects to functional type as defined in the specifications;

– rules prohibiting certain constructions (e.g. do not use pointers) or recommending specific forms to protect certain constructions (in case of use of pointer, verify before and after use);

– rules exported by reused elements and/or pre-existing components;

– rules exported by execution platform (SRAC – Safety Related Application Constraints) and/or by the operating system.

CCR is generally formalized as:

– a form (checklist) that requires identification of a component, its version, level of safety and document repository taken into consideration;

– a table listing the programming rules with an evaluation of whether the rule is applicable, or properly applied and in case of faults there will be a justification or a link to fault report.

5.4.3. *Compliance with safety requirements*

During the input of the software application development process, there must be a system specification as well as a list of safety requirements that the software application must take into account.

As shown in Figure 5.7, the software application design team implements traceability between input material and content of the documentation of software application.

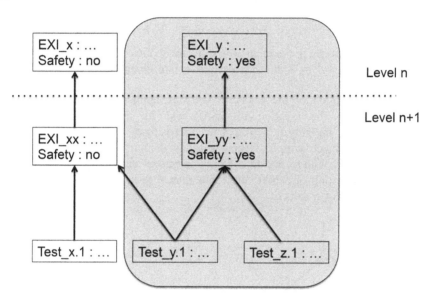

Figure 5.7. *Requirement analysis*

The safety team is responsible for ensuring proper consideration of the safety requirements until they are proven "agreed" and must, therefore, carry out verification. This verification must indicate that the safety requirements have been properly considered and traced and the associated tests are sufficient.

5.4.4. *Fault analysis*

During the various stages of developing a software application, faults such as document faults, tests with errors, traceability defects, etc. are detected.

It is, thus, necessary that the team in charge of demonstrating safety analysis fault evaluate the impact of each fault on product safety. For each fault, a level of criticality must be identified and managed by the safety team.

5.5. Conclusion

System safety involves managing the safety of various parts such as hardware and software applications. The software application is a particular product whose implementation must at least comply with the ISO 9001: 2008 and standards related to the field of application.

Thus, it is necessary to prove that the software application assumes the allocated safety objective as well as all the safety requirements allocated to the software.

This demonstration of the safety of software applications involves planning activities through the creation of SSAP and its application. Increasingly, manufacturers are applying the concept of "safety case" to software applications. The safety-case objective is to formalize safety demonstration that the software application assumes with respect to its safety objectives and requirements, as well as to allow for the setting of export constraints related to its use and restrictions that may result from known defects.

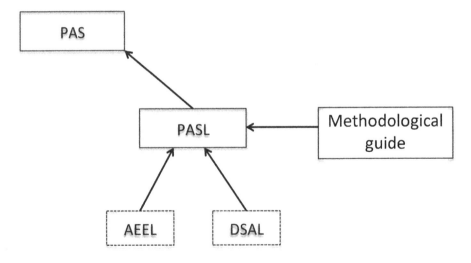

Figure 5.8. *Safety document*

Figure 5.8 shows the entire documentation for the software to be developed:

– a Software Safety Assurance Plan defining the organization, methodology and activities to be undertaken to demonstrate software safety;

– a methodological guide describing the methods and ensuring playback;

– code analysis through SEEA;

– safety case of the software application that contains the elements related to software safety demonstration.

5.6. SSAP template

SSAP must contain the following elements:

The subjects to be considered are:

– Section 1: identification of SSAP objective and field of application.

– Section 2: identification of standards and mandatory regulations.

The objective of this section is to identify the set of standards and regulations to be observed during the implementation of a software. It is necessary to clearly identify the standards, references and versions of these documents:

– Section 3: establishment of glossary with all the terms and acronyms used.

– Section 4: project organization (software part) with a positioning of the safety team.

Each role (manager, engineer, etc.) must be described through a job description identifying the responsibilities and skills. We must demonstrate the independence of the safety team with respect to the project team; the skills of the safety team members must be justified (it can rely on a local process in a project and HR management of the company).

– Section 5: identification of safety policies.

Description of safety principles that can be based on internal methodology guides, management, safety levels and activities to be performed depending on the safety level, etc.

– Section 6: safety approaches.

This section must identify all activities to be performed (elements inputs, activities, persons involved, output elements) to manage the safety of software applications. In general, the V-cycle of software development is used with specific activities for safety teams.

Activities are of the following types:

- review;

- SEEA;

- analysis of safety requirement traceability;

- analysis of traceability between requirements and test cases;

- residual fault analysis; etc.

– Section 7: demonstration of safety.

This section must describe how safety demonstration process must be carried out and formalized. In general, a Software Application Safety Case (SASC) which contains the results of the different activities identified in Section 6 is created and it must conclude whether or not the software application achieved its safety objectives and under what conditions.

– Section 8: traceability with standards and regulations.

The objective of this section is to demonstrate that regulations and standards are to be respected by the project.

– Section 9: type of plan of different documents related to safety studies.

5.7. Glossary

ARP:	Aerospace Recommended Practice
ASIL:	Automotive SIL
CCR:	Critical Code Review
CENELEC[2]:	*Comité Européen de Normalisation Electrotechnique* (European Committee for Electrotechnical Standardization)
COTS:	Component Off-The-Shelf
DAL:	Design Assurance Level
DS:	*Dossier de Sécurité*
E/E/PE:	Electric/Electronic/Programmable Electronic system

---

2 http://www.cenelec.eu.

EMC:	Electromagnetic Compatibility
FMEA:	Failure Modes and Effects Analysis
FMECA:	Failure Mode, Effects and Criticality Analysis
FTA:	Fault Tree Analysis
HL:	Hazard-Log
IEC[3]:	International Electrotechnical Commission
ISO[4]:	International Organization for Standardization
nOOm:	n Out Of m
PRA:	Preliminary Risk Analysis
RAM:	Reliability, Availability and Maintainability
RAMS:	Reliability, Availability, Maintainability and Safety
SAP:	Safety Assurance Plan
SASC:	Software Application Safety Case
SC:	Safety Case
SEEA:	Software Error Effect Analysis
SIL:	Safety Integrity Level
SRAC:	Safety Related Application Constraints
SSAP:	Software Safety Assurance Plan
SSIL:	Software Safety Integrity Level
THR:	Tolerable Hazard Rate

---

3 http://www.iec.ch.
4 http://www.iso.org.

6

Technique to Manage Software Safety

6.1. Introduction

In Chapters 3 and 4 we discussed the general principles of dependability and the management of Safety Assurance (SA). In Chapter 5, we discussed the management of SA for a software application. In this chapter, we shall present the safety principles for a software application.

The techniques implemented are similar (or at least are based on the same principles) to those used for hardware (redundancy, diversity, etc.), but include software aspects.

First, we shall present the software safety techniques (software redundancy, data redundancy, defensive programming, error detection, forward recovery, backward recovery, etc.) and then we will show how they complicate the development of a software application.

Based on this, we can introduce the concept of Quality Assurance (QA) and the relationship with safety integrity level (confidence level to be attained). In several areas, a specific standard (DO 178, CENELEC 50128 and IEC 60880) or a part of the standard pertaining to the sector (ISO 26262 – part 6, IEC 61508 – part 3, etc.) is dedicated to the implementation of software applications, taking into account the safety integrity level (SIL) to be attained.

6.2. Techniques for software safety

6.2.1. *Introduction*

There are a number of techniques to manage the incorrect states of a software application. These techniques are used to manage a software application state (to verify whether the software application is in the correct state) and offer some technical assistance to return it to correct state.

These techniques must be viewed as a set of programming rules to be applied systematically. However, it is also possible to see them as being part of a safety concept. The safety concept is related to the overall architecture of an equipment; it covers the hardware, software and the overall behavior of the equipment. It becomes a set of rules to apply systematically and some of these are standardized for one domain.

Several techniques are available to manage the software safety, some of which are:

– error management (section 6.2.2);

– recovery from errors (section 6.2.3);

– defensive programming (section 6.2.4);

– double execution of the software application (section 6.2.5);

– data redundancy (section 6.2.6).

The objective of this section is to present the various techniques and identify their strengths and weaknesses.

6.2.2. *Error management*

6.2.2.1. *Principles*

The implementation of a specification involves the problematic situation: "how to indicate the presence of an error or exceptional conditions while running a service (function, procedure, piece of code, etc.)?".

Under normal conditions, the result of an operation is of a certain kind (for implementation of a certain type), whereas under exceptional circumstances, this result cannot take any one of the specific values because of the error condition. The indication of an error can normally not be in the field of return type; therefore, there is type incompatibility.

There are several approaches to solve this problem. The first solution involves extending the type and, thus, defining a special constant as "undefined" and, in the case of faults, returning the "undefined" result. The second solution is to introduce an error identification parameter and the operation returns an *n-uplet* with one of the components that indicates whether the operation was successful or not. Although the first solution is the most convenient one, it is only applicable at the specification level because at implementation level, it is not always possible to find the equivalent in terms of programming language. Therefore, the second solution is used in implementation.

The identification of an error must be associated with processing. If the execution of an operation does not generate an error, the error indicator is set to "success". Otherwise it will have a "fail" value. The calling process must then test the error indicator to determine success or failure of the request. Thus, for each operation, we have an implementation as shown in Figure 6.1.

```
SEARCH
    ...
    operation(x, y, z, fail);
    IF fail
        THEN – process the fault
    ...
    ENDIF
    ...
    END
```

Figure 6.1. *Error management mechanism:*
operation with parameter

This implementation may be simplified by replacing the procedure by a function returning a status indicating the success or failure of the operation (see Figure 6.2).

```
SEARCH
    ...
    IF operation(x,y,z) = fail
    THEN – process the fault
    ...
    ENDIF
    ...
    END
```

Figure 6.2. *Error management mechanism: function return*

In many cases, the processing of a fault causes a break in the execution flow in progress and, therefore, uses a branch or a return to the caller by propagating the observed fault as shown in Figure 6.3.

```
START
    ...
    IF operation(x,y,z) = fail
        THEN return fail
    ...
    ENDIF
    ...
    END
```

Figure 6.3. *Propagation of fault*

Another approach to error management is the use of the exception mechanism (see Figure 6.4) offered by certain modern programming languages (ADA [ANS 83, ISO 12a], Eiffel, C ++, etc.).

```
START
        ...
        operation(x,y,z)
        ...
    EXCEPTION
            FAIL: Fault processing
    END
```

Figure 6.4. *Implementation of an exception*

As shown in Figure 6.4, exception management enables a clear coding but delocalizes error processing and increases the complexity. This complexity is induced through generalizing exceptions; thus, it becomes more difficult to create a link between an exception and a service or a service call that generated the exception.

Figure 6.4 shows the correct case that must be implemented, but in view of the complexity of exceptions (too many exceptions, incorrect understanding which has generated the exception, etc.). Figure 6.5 shows that the implementation is the most often opted for. The failure of a service generates a failure of calling service and generally this situation continues until the failure of the main application.

```
START
        ...
        operation(x,y,z)
        ...
EXCEPTION
        Fail: Remove Fail exception
END
```

Figure 6.5. *Fault generates a fault*

6.2.2.2. *Summary*

Error processing is one of the difficult aspects of design; the conventional methods of error management can be easily ignored by programmers (lapse in return codes, not processing error codes, systematic propagation of errors codes, non-recovery of exceptions, etc.).

In view of the addition of specific treatments (adding a parameter, condition, connection, etc.) for error management, the complete error processing by conventional methods greatly complicates the logic of a program.

The cyclomatic complexity ($V(g)$) is incremented by at least one for each error processing and it becomes very difficult to understand, maintain and test a software application integrating this type of technique.

6.2.3. *Error recovery*

6.2.3.1. *Presentation*

Error recovery is a technique that aims to put the system in a correct state after error detection. After error detection, there are two possibilities, either to return (recover through retrieval) to a correct state of the system in order to run an alternative software application or to execute a series of actions aimed at correcting the current state to achieve a correct state of the system (recovery through continuation).

Error recovery is therefore a technique that allows the error compensation. There are two recovery mechanisms:

– the recovery of errors through retrieval: the system state is saved periodically and allows a fallback in case of errors;

– error recovery through continuation: in case of error, we look for a new acceptable but generally degraded one. Continuation is only possible when we have a list of errors to process.

6.2.3.2. *Error recovery through retrieval*

Recovery (backward error recovery) involves restoring the system to its previous safe state. For this, you must perform regular backups of the system and must be able to load one of these backups. Upon detection of an erroneous situation, it is possible to reload a previous situation and resume execution. If the error is generated from the environment or a fugitive failure, the system is expected to resume proper operation. If there is a systematic failure (hardware or software), the system will return to the wrong state. Some systems have several alternatives in addition to the software application, and activate another replica of the application during the retrieval.

The main advantage lies in the fact that the erroneous state is deleted and this deletion is not based on the search for the place of infringement or its cause. The backward error recovery can therefore be used to cover unexpected faults, including design errors.

The recovery may be of *low grain* or *high grain*. Recovery by *high grain* is to replace the last correct overall condition and re-run the same software application completely. The recovery by *low grain* is for a finer recovery strategy, reinstallation of correct local state (limited to a function, for example), alternative execution, etc.

The *high grain* recovery has the advantage of only implementing a single recovery point and remains suitable for systems that are subjected exceptionally to hardware failures.

Figure 6.6 shows an example of a missile that has a target and must pass through an "eventful" (wind, temperature, electromagnetic fields, explosion, radiation, etc.) interception area. The system saves its state regularly and in case of accidental reboot, the previous status can be restored to continue the mission. For this type of system, it is not necessary to have an alternative, and high grain recovery is sufficient.

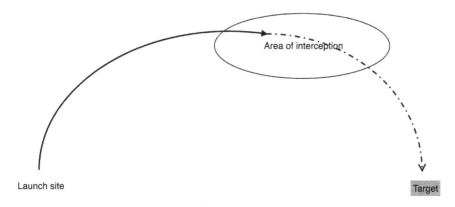

Figure 6.6. *Example of a system using continuation of execution through recovery*

But in the case of system-based error detection, an alternative concept is important to inhibit a fault. It is then necessary to have programming structure for taking into account the alternatives. The alternative concept allows taking into account a broader family of failures including software design failures.

```
ENSURE <test acceptance >
BY
          <primary module>
ELSE
          <alternative module>
ELSE
          < alternative module >
          ...
ELSE
          < alternative module >
ELSE
          error
END
```

Figure 6.7. *Possible syntax of recovery blocks*

Figure 6.7 shows an example of syntax for describing recovery blocks. The structure is based on the identification of an acceptance test and a series of alternatives where the alternatives are introduced in a specific order.

As shown in Figure 6.8, at the input of a block there is an automatic recovery point (backup for the current state) and at the output an acceptance test. The acceptance test (assertion) is used to test whether the system is in an acceptable state after the execution of a block.

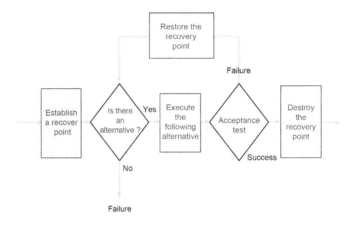

Figure 6.8. *Execution principle of recovery blocks*

The principle of execution (see Figure 6.8) is as follows:

– if the acceptance test fails, the program is restored to the recovery point at the beginning of the block and an alternative module is executed;

– if the alternative module also fails the acceptance test, the program is restored to the recovery point and another module is executed, and so on;

– if all modules fail then the block fails and the recovery must be triggered at a higher level.

```
ENSURE Rounding_err_has_acceptable_tolerance
BY
      Explicit Kutta Method
ELSE
      Implicit Kutta Method
ELSE
      error
END
```

Figure 6.9. *Example of recovery block*

In the first example shown in Figure 6.9, the *Explicit Kutta* method is fast but inaccurate when the equations are "stiff", so it is evaluated as the first alternative. The *Implicit Kutta* method is more expensive but can handle "stiff" equations. The proposed solution will process (see Figure 6.9) all the equations and potentially also tolerate design errors in the *Explicit Kutta* method if the acceptance test is sufficiently flexible.

As shown in the second example in Figure 6.10, the recovery blocks can be inter-connected or nested. If all alternatives in a nested recovery block fail the acceptance test, the recovery point is restored externally and an alternative module to this block will be executed.

The acceptance test provides an error detection mechanism to implement the software application redundancy. Design of acceptance tests is crucial to the effectiveness of the "recovery block". There is a compromise between providing comprehensive acceptance test and keeping the load associated with them to a minimum, so that a flawless execution is not affected. Note that the term used is *acceptance* and not *accuracy* as this allows a component to provide a degraded service.

```
ENSURE rounding_err_has_acceptable_tolerance
BY
    ENSURE sensible_value
    BY
        Explicit Kutta Method
    ELSE
        Predictor-Corrector K-step Method
    ELSE
        Error
    END
ELSE
    ENSURE sensible_value
    BY
        Implicit Kutta Method
    ELSE
        Variable Order K-Step Method
    ELSE
        error
    END
ELSE
    error
END
```

Figure 6.10. *Example of inter-connected/nested recovery blocks*

All error detecting techniques may be used to form an acceptance test. Figure 6.11 shows examples of acceptance test. However, they should be paid special attention as failing acceptance tests may result in the non-detection of residual errors.

Domain verification (assertion):
    0<= speed <= 500
Structural verification:
    The last element of the point list on "null" value:
Verification of control float:
    Update a flag
    Launch a processing
    Verification of the flag status
Time verification:
    Software watchdog
Information verification:
    CRC, parity bit, …
Reverse verification:
    Calculation of yy = square root (xx) and verification if yy*yy =xx

Figure 6.11. *Example of acceptance tests*

The example given in Figures 6.9 and 6.10 is a classic that has been repeated in several books and articles on software safety; however, the example is not representative of the problem that we are trying to address.

If we have several alternatives for a piece of code (function, procedure, program, etc.), this solution can be implemented with no particular difficulty, but there is an increase in the maintenance cost (multiple versions of code), an increase in development cost (several developments and diversity demonstrations) and an increase in the complexity and therefore increased test effort.

6.2.3.3. *Error recovery through continuation*

Recovery through continuation (forward error recovery) involves continuing to run the application from the erroneous state by making selective corrections to the system status. This includes making the controlled environment "safe" since it may have been damaged by the failure.

Continuation is, therefore, an activity specific to each system and depends on the accuracy of predictions about the location and cause of errors (i.e. identifying damages).

The modern programming languages (ADA [ANS 83, ISO 12a], Eiffel, C ++, etc.) provide a mechanism called exceptions management that enables us to control recovery through continuation.

Implementing error recovery through continuation is a difficult activity. This principle must be systematically used (recovery of all exceptions) and verified. The difficulty lies in testing the principle: how can we demonstrate the effectiveness of the mechanism?

It must be remembered that one of the causes of the accident of the Ariane 5 rocket was related to non-recovery of exceptions, which caused the decommissioning of two safety controllers and destruction of the rocket.

6.2.3.4. Summary

Recovery through restoration is generally used in practice (backup of data in banking system, etc.). It may be purely hardware- or software-based. Recovery through restoration must be accompanied by the existence of at least one other alternative which increases the complexity from 1 to 2 or more than 3 with acceptance test and backup mechanism and status restoration. Recovery through restoration is fairly simple to implement and requires maintenance alternatives.

Recovery through continuation requires having an error list and the ability to correct these errors. The addition of error detection point and execution control point will complicate the code and increase test combinations to be performed to validate the application. Recovery by continuation renders the maintenance of software application more difficult. Each change may introduce new potential errors and a new execution control point.

6.2.4. Defensive programming

6.2.4.1. Presentation

Defensive programming is an approach in which the programmer assumes that there may be undetected faults or inconsistencies in code. So, what is defensive programming?

In IEC 60880 [IEC 06], section B.3a, it is recommended that "plausibility checks must be carried out (defensive programming)". IEC 61508 [IEC 11], section C.2.5, explains defensive programming as the objective "to produce programs capable of detecting the order flow or abnormal data or abnormal data values being executed and react to those mistakes in a predetermined and acceptable manner" and the methods for this include: data control (type, field limits, plausibility check, etc.), plausibility checks for input data and intermediate variables, output data control through observation, monitoring software integrity and implementation methods.

6.2.4.2. *Principles*

Defensive programming, therefore, involves adding a system status verifying code after each modification and ensuring that the status change is consistent.

If any inconsistency is detected, one of the following strategies may be implemented:

– status change is cancelled;

– we return to correct state of the system;

– error diagnosis is done and the processing is stopped.

Two types of defensive programming are identified:

– weak defensive programming: execution is continued;

– strong defensive programming: software application stops.

Thus, defensive programming is the opposite of offensive programming. Offensive programming is based on the idea that it is the responsibility of those who use a service to verify the conditions of use of this service.

Defensive programming can be implemented through the following four techniques:

– establishing control on consistency/coherence of the system status (verification of inputs, verification of outputs, etc.);

– error management (section 6.2.2);

– error recovery through continuation (section 6.2.3.2);

– establishing assertion.

6.2.4.2.1. Controlling consistence/coherence of the state

System status control involves managing the initial state of the system. The first method involves implementing restrictive initialization of all variables (global and local). The choice of initialization values must be related to the concept of safe state.

Managing the consistency/coherence of the state of a software application involves input control; therefore, we must avoid spreading an erroneous input within the software application. On the contrary, the second approach involves systematic verification of input data (parameters of a function call, global variable, function call returns, etc.).

```
root function (in xx: integer, out yy : integer): boolean
begin
        if (xx < 0) then return False
        ...
        ...
        return True
end
```

Figure 6.12. *Example of defensive[1] programming*

"Root" processing, in Figure 6.12, applies the principles of defensive programming. If the *xx* parameter is negative, the anomaly is identified and the responsibility of decision for action on failure is *delegated* to the caller. This case is typical behavior of a library that cannot take a decision not knowing its execution environment.

```
IF (xx>0) THEN ... ENDIF
IF (xx>0) THEN ... ELSE No processing ENDIF
```

Figure 6.13. *Example of IF structure in defensive programming*

Figure 6.13 shows a structure example of IF defensive programming. The third approach is related to data control during processing. For this, for each programming structure, one must take into account all the used cases. For an IF statement (Figure 6.13), a THEN branch must be systematically included, and for a CASE instruction, DEFAULT case must be systematically included (see Figure 6.14).

```
CASE xx OF
1 : BEGIN ... END;
2 : BEGIN ... END;
ELSE ERROR
END
```

Figure 6.14. *Example of ACCORDING TO structure in defensive programming*

---

1 The language used in Figure 6.11 is PASCAL.

Figure 6.14 shows a CASE example of defensive programming structure. There are several advantages to the application of this rule. The first is in managing a random anomaly that could modify the data, but it also allows for the management of a systematic anomaly. In fact, in the development context, a person involved can change the Account Type to add a new value (see Figure 6.15). This modification may be related to a lapse in update of all the structures handling this type.

enum AccountType
{
Savings,
Checking,
MoneyMarket
}
	switch (accountType)
	{ case AccountType.Checking:
	  // do something ...
	case AccountType.Savings:
	  // do something ...
	case AccountType.MoneyMarket:
	  // do something ...
	default:
	  Debug.Fail("Invalidaccounttype.");
	}

Figure 6.15. *Example of CASE structure in defensive programming[2]*

Defensive programming can be implemented through assertion, as shown in Figure 6.16.

```
int f (int x)
{
assertion (x>0) ; //precondition
...
y = ...
...
assertion (y>0) ; //postcondition
return (y) ;
}
```

Figure 6.16. *Example of assertion in C*

6.2.4.2.2. Data plausibility

The values of the variables seem plausible, given the knowledge of the program. The plausibility is interesting because it does not allow the treatment to be repeated

---

2 Program in C#.

in order to check the validity of data, while trying to verify properties; it must be noted that the acceptance tests of Figure 6.11 are similar to plausibility tests.

The consistency of input data is based on the fact that there is a redundancy in all inputs:

– two different acquisitions, for example, by same string or by two different strings;

– a single acquisition of more information, for example speed measured on two tires threaded differently;

– information may be sent coded;

– two opposing inputs are available; etc.

For some systems, there are post conditions (see Figure 6.16) that verify consistency of the processing to be carried out. These post-conditions link the calculated outputs and inputs.

Some post-conditions address a specific aspect (e.g. measuring an angle) and are related to the physical phenomena (maximum acceleration), implementation choices (the last item in a list is always the *null* element, etc.).

For example, during measurement of the angle of a steering wheel of an automobile, the angle cannot change by more than 90° with respect to the cycle time.

6.2.4.2.3. Plausibility of execution

The techniques related to the plausibility of execution are related to the question: "does the program follow a foreseeable and expected execution flow?":

– analysis and signature verification (for code as well as for data);

– error detection.

The consistency of execution enables us to assess whether a software application follows the paths that have been previously validated. For this, we must be able to trace the execution of a software application. Execution of a software application is composed of a set of *traces*. Each trace is a series of checkpoints (execution path).

The graph in Figure 6.17 is a representation of a program with two consecutive IF instructions and a WHILE statement. An analysis of execution paths in operation can lead to the selection of two execution traces. The characterization of these traces is done by the introduction of checkpoints. These checkpoints can be local (more information is stored) or global (a single variable is used) indicators.

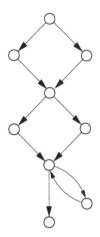

Figure 6.17. *Execution trace*

For example (see Figure 6.18), it is possible to have a variable set to 0, which when passing through a THEN branch is incremented by 1; which when passing through an ELSE branch is decreased by one and at the end of the execution must have value 2 or −2.

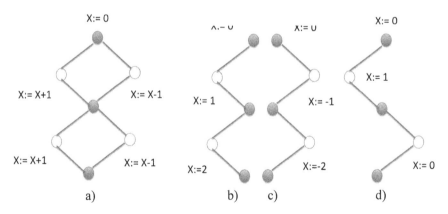

Figure 6.18. *Execution trace control*

In some systems with high levels of criticality, the checkpoints are numerous and allow fine or total control of execution.

The more numerous and/or complex the traces, the greater the number of checkpoints, and this has consequences on memory space (memory traces and current trace), execution time (additional processing) and on complexity of code (addition of non-related functional processing, complex code and associated analyses).

6.2.4.2.4. Assertion management

An assertion is a condition that must be true in order to continue running the program. Assertions can be used as pre-conditions and post-conditions.

A pre-condition (Figure 6.19) ensures that the execution of the software application will not continue if certain conditions are not met. Pre-conditions are placed at the beginning of the procedure (function and/ or method). This is the most common way to program defensively. The basic idea is: "a program cannot be run outside nominal conditions".

```
Public void print(String message)
{
assert message!= null: "Error: message is null";
System.out.println(message);
}
```

Figure 6.19. *Example of assertion in C*

Use of assertions as post-conditions (Figure 6.20) is much rare. The post-conditions help to ensure that the client contract terms are met. They are often placed at the output of the procedure (function and/or method). For example, making sure to a customer that the suggested method will never return an empty list.

```
Public List<String> filter(List<String> mails)
{
...
assert myList!= null:"Error:list null";
return myList;
}
```

Figure 6.20. *Example of assertion in C*

Assertions have an impact on execution time. This overload is induced by the fact that it is necessary to verify things that should never occur. It should be noted that some languages allow for inhibition of assertions, thereby removing all protections.

6.2.4.3. *Review*

Defensive programming is one of the techniques which is required in nearly all standards and is widely used. But there is sometimes confusion between defensive programming and fault management of software application. While identifying a situation where the software application does not respond properly, it is possible to establish a palliative code without actually understanding the fault.

Defensive programming consists of two problems:

– identifying problem situations (division by zero, root of a negative number, etc.) for all or part of software application;

– identifying corrective actions to be implemented by systematically avoiding to escalate the problem to calling services.

The first effect of defensive programming is the long execution time. But by nature, defensive programming complicates the code and thus renders tests and maintenance of the software application more difficult. As for the tests, defensive programming generates situations which are:

– either difficult to test: some defects are taken into account by several barriers and therefore, it is impossible to trigger internal barriers (protected by other barriers);

– or impossible to produce: sequence of failure is an example of a difficult test to be implemented.

6.2.5. *Double execution of a software application*

6.2.5.1. *Principles*

The execution redundancy involves running the same software application twice using the same processing unit (CPU, etc.). The results are usually compared by a device outside the processor; and any inconsistencies cause degradation of the calculation unit (behavior fail stop). This technique is often used in the programmable logic controllers (PLC – Programmable Logic Controller).

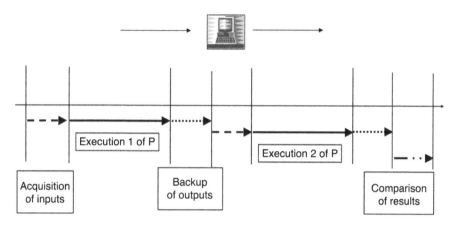

Figure 6.21. *Principle of execution redundancy*

Figure 6.21 shows the temporal diagram of execution redundancy. It can be noted that the triplet "acquisition, implementation, backup" appears twice and in the end there is a comparison of the saved results.

The use of execution redundancy may be implemented to detect memory failures. To do so, a unique program is loaded in two different memory areas (two areas for addressing two different memories, two different storage media, etc.). Memory failures (RAM, ROM, EPROM, EEPROM, etc.) as well as intermittent failures of the processing unit (CPU, ALU[3], FPU, etc.) can thus be detected.

Note that certain failures of shared hardware devices (comparison unit, processing unit) are not detected and, therefore, remain unaddressed. There exist two possibilities for error masking:

– the result of the comparison results can always be positive regardless of the inputs (failure of comparison method which is a common failure mode);

– subtle failures (for example, A–B is performed systematically instead of A+B) of the ALU of the processing unit can give the same wrong result for each execution (processing unit is a common failure mode).

---

3 Arithmetic Logic Unit.

```
int F(a,b)                          int F(b,a)
{                                   {
    int y = 0;                          int y = 0;
    y = 2*a+b+1                         y = -(-2*a-b-1)
    return y                            return y
}                                   }
```

Figure 6.22. *Code diversification*

One of the solutions involves introducing:

– autotests during execution;

– comparison of discordant data is generally avoided until the fold-up;

– comprehensive functional testing of the processing unit.

For an effective detection, the test coverage must be sufficient (application instructions coverage, etc.) and it must be executed at the right time (regular initialization, for each cycle, till the end of the mission, etc.). The main disadvantage of this solution is cost performance (related to the size of self-tests and their frequencies).

The second solution involves introducing code diversification. This diversification can be "light" and in this case, we speak of voluntary asymmetry of coding of two applications. It is possible to force use of two different instruction sets for programming the application; for example, one of the programs uses A+B and the second uses $-(- AB)$ as shown in Figure 6.22.

An asymmetry of data may be introduced by addressing objects differently (variables, constants, parameters, functions and procedures) in memory for each of the two programs.

xx	yy
a+b	$-(-a-b)$
A or B	NOT (NOT(A) and NOT(B))
....	

Table 6.1. *Example of diversification rules*

It should be noted that these voluntary asymmetries can be automatically inserted within the same program. For both types of asymmetry, we must pay attention to the compilation phase and check that the asymmetry is always present in the final executable phase.

In general, the redundancy is complete (the entire application is executed twice), but a partial redundancy may also be sufficient (Figure 6.23(b)).

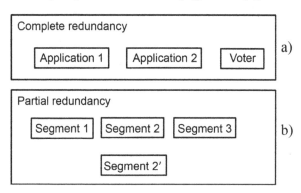

Figure 6.23. *Complete redundancy a) and partial redundancy b)*

The introduction of a calculation using floating variables within a safety function requires the establishment of a safety technique. The introduction of a partial redundancy of calculation of floating variables should be based on diversity; this diversity can be, for example, using different libraries. It should then be able to accept a certain error during comparison.

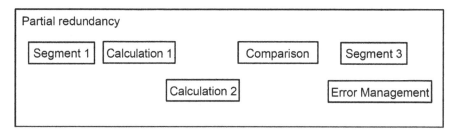

Figure 6.24. *Partial redundancy*

Software diversity can be accompanied by hardware diversity. Figure 6.24 introduces a partial redundancy that can be coupled with diversity, but it is possible to add hardware architecture to it (see Figure 6.25) offering FPU[4] of the main

---

4 FPU: Floating Point Unit.

processor and an annex unit for performing calculations. The diversification of the code is a little stronger as two sets of instructions are used. Here, the concept of error acceptance is very essential.

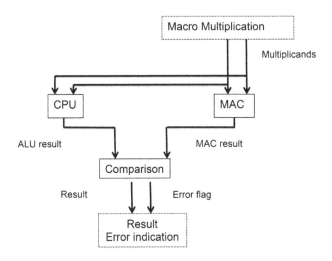

Figure 6.25. *Double execution and comparison process*

6.2.5.2. *Example 1*

The introduction of a partial asymmetry has the advantage of being fairly simple to implement, but its main defect is fairly low ability to detect failures. It is possible to generalize this solution through diversifying the application to be executed. There are various possibilities: having two development teams, having two different code generators, etc.

For example, Figure 6.26 shows how EBICAB 900 functions. There is a diversification of the application to be executed in application A and B. Application A is divided into F1, F2, F3, and Application B into F1', F2', F3'. Three development teams are then required; two independent teams are responsible for executing two applications, the third team is responsible for the specification (which is common) and synchronization. Since there is only one acquisition phase, the data are protected (CRC[5], etc.). The data manipulated by application A are diversified (stored differently in the memory, bit to bit mirror, etc.) with respect to application B.

---

5 CRC, or Cyclic Redundancy Check, is a powerful and a simple method to control data integrity.

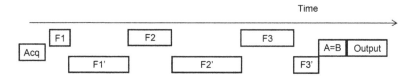

Figure 6.26. *EBBICAB temporal execution principle*

6.2.5.3. *Example 2*

As a second example, we will talk about a piece of campaign equipment that connects a central work station and the tags (elements used in giving commands). In this application, there is one software application formally developed using Method B [ABR 96] and a processing unit. Method B is a formal method which guarantees (through mathematical proofs) that the software is correct with respect to the ownership. This warranty is useful, but it does not cover the code generator, the executable generation chain (compiler, *linker*, etc.) and the loading equipment.

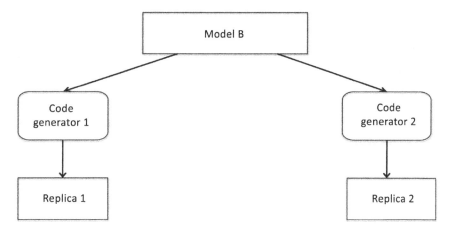

Figure 6.27. *Diversification*

As shown in Figure 6.27, in this application, there are two code generators and two channels for generating executables (two compilers). This allows for two different versions of the executable. It is thus possible to show that the addressing tables (variables, constants, functions, parameters, etc.) of the two executables are actually different. Hence, loading each version of the application is done in different memory spaces.

6.2.5.4. *Example 3*

In this example, we will focus on embedded information consoles on trains. In the console displaying the train speed information, the undesirable event is "Display of erroneous drive order or speed".

A possible choice for the safety (SIL2) of a display is to use reactive safety [CEN 03]. This technique requires that the time of detection and inactivation after the occurrence of a failure must not exceed the limits specified for a potentially dangerous transient output.

The definition of reactive safety, as defined in the CENELEC EN 50129 [CEN 03], is as follows:

> "This technique allows a safety feature to be achieved using a single entity, provided its safe operation is ensured by rapid detection and inactivation of any dangerous failure. Although an entity carries out the actual safety feature, detection/control/test feature should be regarded as a second entity which is independent to avoid any common mode failure."

The maximum tolerated duration for an erroneous permissive information must be less than or equal to the limit of perception of the human eye.

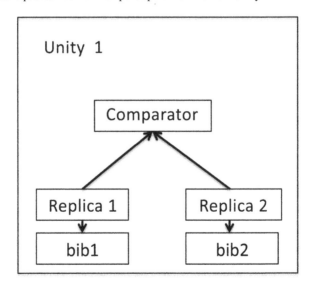

Figure 6.28. *Diversification of media libraries*

A console consists of a processing unit that houses two applications; the objective of each application is to construct an image to be displayed. As a general rule, an image is composed of critical information and non-critical information.

A comparison mechanism enables to verify that both applications have produced a similar image. The similar term indicates that the comparison is performed on "critical" parts. Depending on the available power, we can compare just the data necessary for the whole image. Comparator is a common failure mode that can be a voter in this type of architecture.

Comparison can be performed on the images produced or we can allow the display of one of the images and compare the display memory (VRAM) with the memory containing the second image; it is then possible to detect failures on memory screen.

The main difficulty of graphics applications is the construction of an image through a library which is a COTS. Graphic libraries can be very easily validated and contain a large number of faults.

In fact there is a single application of SIL2 level, but it is linked to two different libraries by providing graphic primitives based on different algorithms.

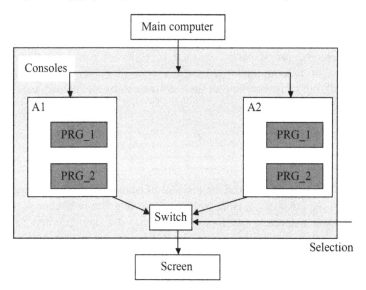

Figure 6.29. *Safe and available architecture*

Diversification of media libraries and execution redundancy can be combined with unit redundancy to associate high availability with safety, as shown in Figure 6.29.

As shown in Figure 6.29, the system consists of two identical consoles A1 and A2. One console is called "primary" and the other is called "secondary". In case of failure of the primary console, a "switch" allows to activate the secondary console.

6.2.5.5. *Example 4*

An independent safety component, sometimes called *safety bag*, is a component that intercepts the actions requested by a user or a system component and controls their validity following the safety rules established during development (this is a plausibility control form). The independent safety component has its own representation of system state which must be sufficiently precise and recent to allow application of all rules it supervises. This technique is introduced in Klein [KLE 91].

6.2.5.6. *Review*

The execution redundancy is a fairly simple technique whose main advantage is the use of a single processing unit. The major drawback is the execution time, implementation of double processing with vote and the fact that an auto test takes at least 2.5–3.5 times longer than a single processing. Hence, this type of solution is used for systems where the processing time is not critical.

The implementation of partial or total diversity of the code allows a good detection rate of random and systematic errors (depending on the degree of diversification), but increases the cost (two software to be maintained, etc.).

6.2.6. *Data redundancy*

6.2.6.1. *Introduction*

In section 6.2.3, we introduced the concept of error recovery and in section 6.2.4 the concept of dual execution. Both techniques can involve redundancy of software application. Data redundancy is focused solely on the data handled by software application.

Data redundancy requires identifying the data to be protected. It is either necessary to protect all data or only a subset of the data.

In the simplest form, data redundancy is to duplicate memory variables and comparing the contents. Once the data list is identified and managed the safety, simply make double assignment of the data. The duplication can be managed through a safety mechanism that makes it transparent to the programmer (dedicated call service, etc.). To do this, it is necessary to define the writing and reading services that will manipulate the two images. It should also identify checkpoints for consistency of the two images.

```
F (...):
START

...

WRITE (A, 10)

...

WRITE (B, READ (A)+READ(B))

...

END
```

Figure 6.30. *Example of program with data redundancy*

Figure 6.30 shows an example of function *F* that will write the value 10 in the variable *A* that in turn will write the value *A+B* in the variable *B*; for this purpose, we use read and write services. Figure 6.31 shows an example for implementation of read and write services that handles two replicas of a variable.

```
WRITE (x, v)
START
    V1(x) = v
    V2(x) = v
END

READ (x)
START
IF V1(x) = V2(x)
            THEN RETURN (V1(x))
            SINON ERREUR
END IF
END
```

Figure 6.31. *Implementation of write operation*

The two images may be the same or different. If the replicas are identical, an equality test must be used. Replicas can be complementary (mirrors), in which case, it must be verified if the sum of the two replicas is zero ($V1(x)+V2(x)=0$).

Diversification of replicas will allow us to take into account the random and systematic failure of the hardware used (processor, memory, etc.). In fact, an equal comparison to zero is easier to validate than an equality comparison between any two values.

To ensure the safety from memory failure on data, it is necessary to diversify the memory areas, the memory banks and even the type of memory.

6.2.6.2. *Generalization*

In Goloubeva ([GOL 06] – Chapter 2) a more systematic data redundancy mechanism is shown that can be applied through a general algorithm (or tool) to a piece of code and/or a software application.

There are three rules:

– any variable x is duplicated at $x0$ and $x1$;

– any writing operation is carried out $x0$ and $x1$;

– after each reading of the variable x, the two copies must be verified.

START
    A := B;
END
	START
	    A0 := B0;
	    A1 := B1;
	    IF (B0 != B1)
	        THEN ERROR();
	    ENDIF
	END

Figure 6.32. *Protection of a simple assignment*

Figures 6.32 and 6.33 show the result of implementing the algorithm presented in section 6.2.5.1 on two very simple programs that can be summarized in a single assignment.

START
    A := B+C;
END
	START
	    A0 := B0+C0;
	    A1 := B1+C1;
	    IF (B0 != B1) OR (C0 !=C1)
	        THEN ERROR();
	    ENDIF
	    END

Figure 6.33. *Protection of double assignment*

In general this algorithm is pretty simple to implement (Figures 6.32 and 6.33), but for some languages like C, function settings management and/or procedures can lead to more changes, as shown in the example in Figure 6.34.

F(A :INTEGER) :B :INTEGER
 	
START
 	
    B := A+1
 	
END
	F(A0,A1 :INTEGER, B0,B1 :INTEGER)
	
	START
	
	    B0 := A0;
	
	    B1 := A1;
	
	    IF (A0 != A1)
	
	        THEN ERROR();
	
	    ENDIF
	
	END

VARIABLE
 	
    X,Y : INTEGER ;
 	
START
 	
    X := 1 ;
 	
    Y := F(X) ;
 	
END
	VARIABLE
	
	    X0,X1,Y0,Y1 : INTEGER ;
	
	START
	
	    X0 := 1 ;
	
	    X1 := 1 ;
	
	    F(X0,X1,Y0,Y1) ;
	
	END

Figure 6.34. *Protection of a function*

The advantage of this generalization is that it can be implemented through an application that takes as input a software application and provides as output a software application with data duplication.

6.2.6.3. *Review*

The duplication of data is a fairly simple technique to implement but it complicates the code. The implementation of a library or a duplication automation enables to ensure maintainability of the code and manage complexity.

It must be noted that we can replace the duplication of each variable by introducing CRC protection which is another form of informational redundancy.

6.3. Other diversities

In the previous sections, we introduced the concepts of redundancy and diversity. Diversity increases the efficiency in terms of fault detection rate and prevents the occurrence of a common mode. The common failure modes may lead to non-detection of ta failure due to the fact that different parts of the system are affected identically or similarly by a failure.

Diversity can, thus, become an element for demonstrating the achievement of safety targets for a given equipment. In addition to hardware diversity (for heterogeneous redundancy) and code diversity, it is also possible to implement a temporal diversity and memory allocation diversity.

6.3.1. *Temporal diversity*

Temporal diversity involves constructing redundant hardware architecture such that the various calculation units are not running the same code at given instance t.

This diversity requirement can be associated to various types of failures:

– systematic failure in calculation and processing units;

– systematic failure in memory or on its management.

6.3.2. *Memory allocation diversity*

Memory allocation diversity involves constructing hardware architecture so that the elements stored in memory (local variables, global variables, constants, application parameters, binaries, exchange parameters between functions, etc.) are never allocated to the same space.

This need for diversity may be associated with different types of failures:

– while using a common operating system such as DOS and DOS extender (to manage a larger memory space), it may be necessary to diversify the memory allocation to avoid common methods for managing extended memory.

6.4. Conclusion

The maintainability of a software application is the most important attribute after safety. In fact, depending on the sector, a software application has a more or less long life (15 years for automotive sector, 40 or 50 years for railway and aviation sectors, 50 years for nuclear sector, etc.); therefore, the ability to maintain a software application with respect to safety is essential.

It is clear from this discussion that the only activity to establishing safety of a software application and ensuring its maintainability is quality management. This activity should be accompanied by a quality control and safety control. A dependable software application is a simple application. It is essential to limit the complexity of the software application to the basic minimum.

Therefore, the standards (DO178 [ARI 92, RTA 11], IEC 61508 [IEC 08b], CENELEC EN 50128 [CEN 01, CEN 11], ISO 26262 ([ISO 11]), IEC 60880 [IEC 06], etc.) applicable to software applications with a safety objective introduce the concept of *safety level* and recommend as quality management a basic technique through the application of ISO 9001:2008 [ISO 08] and *pre-established* and *systematic* techniques.

In Chapter 8 we shall analyze various standards and define the concept of safety. Moreover, quality management will be presented in Chapter 9.

6.5. Glossary

ALU: Arithmetic Logic Unit

CENELEC[6]:   *Comité Européen de Normalisation Electrotechnique* (European Committee for Electrotechnical Standardization)

CRC: Cyclic Redundancy Check

E/E/PES: Electric/Electronic/Programmable Electronic systems

EEPROM: Electrically Erasable Programmable Read-Only Memory

EMC: Electromagnetic Compatibility

EPROM: Erasable Programmable Read-Only Memory

FPU: Floating Point Unit

IEC[7]:   International Electrotechnical Commission

ISO[8]:   International Organization for Standardization

OS: Operating System

PLC: Programmable Logic Controller

---

6 http://www.cenelec.eu/Cenelec/Homepage.htm.
7 http://www.iec.ch.
8 http://www.iso.org/iso/home.htm.

PROM: Programmable Read-Only Memory

QA: Quality Assurance

RAM: Random Access Memory

RAMS: Reliability, Availability, Maintainability and Safety

RAMSS: Reliability, Availability, Maintainability, Safety and Security

ROM: Read-Only Memory

SA: Safety Assurance

SIL: Safety Integrity Level

VRAM: Video RAM

7

Assessment and Certification

7.1. Introduction

We are currently in a transition phase where software applications are increasing in number (office automation, telephony, automotive, leisure, life, etc.) and becoming larger (moving millions of lines of code). It is important to note that developing a software application is not an epic[1] act but has become a layman's act (see modeling tools, website production tools, etc.).

Given the diversity of use of software applications, it is important to measure the impact of their faults on human life, financial aspects, degradation of installations and goods of a company as well as their environmental impact.

As it is, we must be able to demonstrate the safety of software applications. This safety demonstration may be made necessary by defining a frame of reference (standard, regulatory environment, state of the art, etc.) and introducing an obligation of compliance with this referential.

The concept of certifiable application [BOU 07, IET 14, OZE 09a] is related to the ability to demonstrate compliance with the standard. The objective of this chapter is to introduce the concept of certifiable software applications and the various applicable standards (in aeronautics, railways, automobile and general).

Certification is an activity that is based on the ability to demonstrate the safety of an application, the ability to assess the safety of an application and the objective of certification itself, determined by the conformity of a product to a referential.

---

1 There was a time when developing a software application (satellite, aeronautics, video games, etc.) was considered an epic act, however, today, it is possible to develop a fairly complex application without producing any code manually.

In this chapter, we will introduce the certification process (with a link to standards such as NF 45011, ISO/IEC 17065 and ISO/IEC 17020) and its impacts on safety demonstration. We will also introduce the concept of cross-acceptance; this concept defines a framework for the acceptance of certificates of another domain.

7.2. Product

As shown in Figure 7.1, a product is not only the description of a set of interfaces but also a set of assumptions, constraints and restrictions.

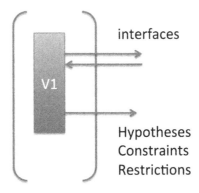

Figure 7.1. *A product*

DEFINITION 7.1 (Product).– *A product is an element that autonomously renders services. It is characterized by a set of interfaces, hypothesis of use and the services it can provide.*

From Definition 7.1, we can conclude that a software application is not a product but a system, subsystem, equipment or generic platform.

7.3. Assessment

Assessment [BOU 06, BOU 07, BOU 09b, OZE 09a, OZE 09b] of a product (or system or software) is to analyze all product elements to evaluate the conformity of the product with respect to a referential (typically a standard, a part of a standard or a set of standards), according to a given method. An independent assessment is thus carried out by an Independent Safety Assessor (ISA) who, ideally, is not part of the company that makes the product.

DEFINITION 7.2 (Product Assessment).– *Product assessment involves analyzing the compliance of a product against a repository. The compliance analysis follows a predefined process.*

From Definition 7.2, it must be noted that the assessment of a product uses two components as inputs: a repository and all the elements produced during product development.

Figure 7.2 shows the overlap between the development of the software application and assessment. It also shows product assessment as an assessment report.

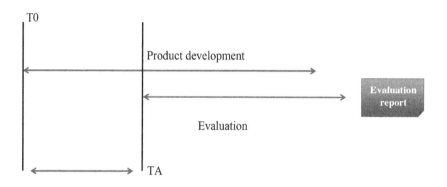

Figure 7.2. *Development and assessment*

As shown in Figure 7.2, between the start of a project (T0) and the start of an independent assessment (TA), there is a lag time. If T0 = TA, the independent assessor will have very little activities to perform at the beginning of the contract. If TA is significantly higher than T0 (or, at worst, the project is finished), the work of the independent assessor may generate work overload, or even a complete re-development cycle.

Finally, the start date of assessment (TA) must be selected for the assessor to have enough elements and to allow the project to take into account the requirements of evolution.

Figure 7.3 represents the assessment process and the four major phases:

– drafting the assessment plan that describes the organization, input referential, methodology and scope of evaluation;

– audit phase of analyzing the methodological plans, preparing an audit plan and performing the audit;

– assessment phase of all the elements produced by the software implementation process (descending phase, ascending phase, safety analysis, etc.);

– the last phase involves drafting the assessment report.

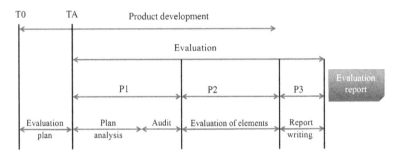

Figure 7.3. *Three phases of assessment*

The assessment work (see Figure 7.4) involves analyzing all the elements and producing a questions and remarks form (QRF). The QRFs serve as a medium of exchange with the customers; they help formalize the questions and remarks and customer responses. The customer responses can lead to proposals for change.

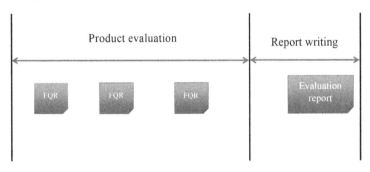

Figure 7.4. *Assessment*

The result of an assessment should state whether or not the product is compliant with each of the requirements of a referential:

– if a product complies with the requirements, the assessment result states that the product is "consistent with the requirement";

– if a product does not comply with the requirement, the assessment states a "deviation";

– if a product complies with each of the requirements of a standard, the assessment states the compliance of the product with the standard;

– if one or more requirements are not satisfied, the product cannot be declared to comply with the standard.

There may be several types of deviations (sensitive points, notes, non-compliances), classified according to "the risk" when a requirement is not met.

This classification of "risk" is very subjective, and it is customary that the standards make clear the "mandatory", "optional" or "recommended" requirements.

This allows the assessor to classify the deviations in a conclusive manner:

– a deviation from a "mandatory requirement" calls into question the compliance of the product with the standard;

– a deviation from a "recommended requirement" does not, in itself, question the overall product compliance to the standard.

Assessment of a product, component or software results in an assessment report. Certification [BOU 07, IET 14, OZE 09a] is to formalize the assessment results in a certificate of compliance.

The assessment of a product, component or software is carried out by an entity that must be independent of the developing entity; it must be noted that in some countries, it is acceptable that the assessment team be part of the same company (e.g. in Germany).

7.4. Certification

7.4.1. *Product certification*

Certification is an administrative act which reflects the confidence gained by the competent authority on the system's ability to perform its safety functions.

In the rail sector, certification is the operating license [BOU 07, BOU 08, BOU 09b, OZE 09a, OZE 9b].

The certification relies on the "proof" of safety produced to the supervisory authority by the personnel in-charge as defined in the organizational document.

DEFINITION 7.3 (Certification).– *Certification involves obtaining a certificate which is a commitment that the product meets a normative referential. Certification is based on the results of an assessment and on production of a certificate.*

A certificate (see Figure 7.5) is used to define scope of use and responsibility. An organization is accredited by an organization to issue certificates.

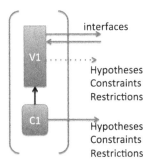

Figure 7.5. *Certificate*

DEFINITION 7.4 (Certificate).– *A certificate is a formal document issued by a certification body. A certificate identifies a product and the repository to which it conforms.*

Several organizations may issue such a certificate through accreditation (Definition 7.5) with respect to the standard EN 45011[2] [AFN 98] or ISO/IEC 17020[3] [ISO 12b]. The standards EN 45011 and ISO/IEC 17065 define the general requirements for organizations processing product certification.

DEFINITION 7.5 (Accreditation).– *Accreditation is the formal process that establishes the competence of a certifying body to conduct assessments for a given sector.*

---

2 The standard EN 45011 outlines the general requirements for organizations issuing product certification. It is replaced by the standard ISO/CEI 17065 [ISO 12a].
3 The standard ISO/CEI 17020 [ISO 12] defines the general criteria for the functioning of various types of organizations that run inspections.

Definition 7.5 introduces the concept of a certifying body (see definition 7.6).

DEFINITION 7.6 (Certifying body).– *A certifying body is an organization that has been accredited for a sector and can provide compliance certificates. This organization is recognized by the authorities of the concerned sector.*

The cost of certification is induced by "strict" compliance with standards (lists of activities to be carried out, list element to be produced and management of all elements); the cost of assessment involves repeated processes of certification activity (implementation of major or minor corrections to rectify the identified non-compliances).

Note that modification of a certified product may require updating of the certificate (major changes) or obtaining a retention letter of the certificate (major changes).

It should be noted that in the absence of a certificate, a company may be required to demonstrate that the product can be introduced into the system it controls. In this case, product qualification is sought (see Definition 7.7).

DEFINITION 7.7 (Product qualification).– *Verification of the suitability of a product and its conformance of use in relation to a specific system through a test activity.*

Qualification of a product can also be performed by the end user to verify that the introduction of the product in its sector had no side effects (environmental problems, accounting problems, procedural problems, etc.).

7.4.2. Assessment and software certification

7.4.2.1. Certification versus certifiable

Product certification is possible because it involves the whole system (hardware, mechanics, software, process). For a considerable time, the certifying organizations are requested to provide certificates for a part of a product, and in many cases for a software application.

DEFINITION 7.8 (Certifiable application).– *A certifiable software application is a software application that has been constructed to be certified in a given context.*

This request is pointless as software alone is not a product; it cannot be executed on its own and its implementation is dependent on the equipment in which it is housed. Nevertheless, several organizations offer Independent Safety Assessment (ISA) certification for software applications. It enables the generation of, in addition to an assessment report, a certificate indicating that the software has been successfully assessed. Therefore, it is not a product certificate.

7.4.2.2. *Assessment of a software application*

7.4.2.2.1. Introduction

The concept of independent assessment exists in several sectors as a way to increase confidence in a product. It is based on the fact that a third party who did not participate in the implementation of the software can analyze the product and its development process.

In a software sector, independent assessment of a software application involves assessment of the development process of software applications (quality-control, organization, competence, project planning, processes, methods, etc.) and assessment of the software application (analysis of the entire documentation).

7.4.2.2.2. Example: the railway sector

Section 6.4 of the standard CENELEC 50128: 2011 [CEN 11] identifies the need to assess the software with SSIL (Software Safety Integrity Level) between 1 and 4. For SSIL0 software, it is simply enough to demonstrate that the standard ISO 9001: 2008 [ISO 08] is implemented; complete assessment is not necessary.

Note that in Appendix B of the standard CENELEC 50128: 2011, Table B.8 identifies the skills of an assessor. Table B.8 (see Table 7.1) shows the need for recognition by an authority, thus imposing restrictions upon evaluators.

As for other activities, evaluation must be formalized using an assessment plan and the results formalized in an evaluation report.

The assessor must, after analyzing the entire product, identify any non-compliance with the requirements of the standard CENELEC 50128: 2011 and assess their impact on software safety; everything must be documented in an assessment report.

If a software is assessed, the assessor must accept that assessment after verifying that the results are applicable. This verification must be carried out through *cross-acceptance* as described in the next section.

Role: **assessor**
Skills:
– must be competent in the sector or technologies in which the evaluation is performed
– must have qualification/license issued by a recognized regulatory authority
– must have/strive continually to acquire sufficient levels of experience in safety principles and application of these principles within the scope
– must be competent to verify that an appropriate method or combination of methods have been applied in a given context
– must be competent to understand the relevant processes of safety management, human resources management, technical and quality management to meet the requirements of EN 50128
– must be skilled in evaluation of approaches/methodologies
– must have ability to think analytically and good observation skills
– must be able to combine various types and sources of evidence and synthesize an overall view on relevance to requirements or constraints and limitations on the application
– must have an understanding and representation of the overall program, including understanding the application environment
– must be able to judge the suitability of all development processes (such as quality management, configuration management, validation and verification process)
– must understand the requirements of EN 50128.

Table 7.1. *Table B.8 of the standard CENELEC 50128:2011*

7.4.3. *Cross-acceptance*

Generally, the activity of designing a rail system, based on certified and assessed products, must be verified for the compatibility of interfaces and compatibility of constraints, hypotheses and restrictions of use. If the assessment/certification referential is not the one used for the railway sector, it must be verified if the standards are compatible.

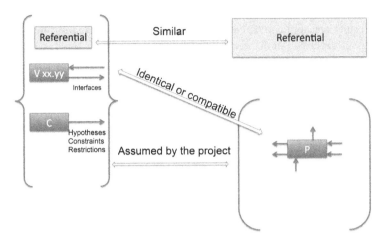

Figure 7.6. *Cross-acceptance*

Cross-acceptance is a phase of verifying that the normative context, hypotheses and exported constraints of an assessment and/or certification report are consistent with the intended use by the project.

The application guide Part 1 of the standard CENELEC 50129 [CEN 07] describes the principles of *cross-acceptance*.

7.4.4. *Change management*

Change management can only be achieved if the software is maintainable and testable. These two properties are identified as essential by all standards but are rather difficult to implement.

One of the difficulties of assessment is the management of changes. As shown in Figure 7.7, a product can be assessed for various versions and it is possible that between two assessments there have been several versions.

Figure 7.7 shows that in general, a certification requires a set of changes leading to version Vx'. The establishment of certification with delta can take into consideration several changes (see V2 + V3).

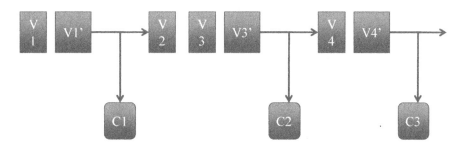

Figure 7.7. *Certification series*

It must then be possible to work with delta and analyze the sum of changes. The standards do not put any constraint on the method of work.

This incremental process raises a number of questions:

– How to manage marketing of products with several certificates?

– After several certifications by delta, is it necessary to have complete certification (if yes, what is the decision criteria)?

It is easy enough to ask the above questions, but to find an answer, we must put in place specific processes to manage changes and the resulting impacts on products already in service. We must have a set of principles that will prevent and/or manage incompatibilities (software/OS, software/software, software/hardware).

7.4.5. Tests

7.4.5.1. Context

The certification of a product takes as the input a large number of works related to design, verification and validation, to demonstrate its safety and quality.

The concept of a test is an integral part of the verification and validation process.

For example, in the railway sector, there are several types of tests such as:

– equipment type tests;

– equipment series tests;

– qualification tests for environmental constraints (vibration, EMC, noise, etc.; see the standard EN 50155 [AFN 01]);

– fire/smoke tests;

– validation tests of sub-systems;

– validation tests of the complete system, (these tests can be carried out on a specific test site or at the final site);

– qualification tests of tools and test methods.

One of the constraints related to laboratory testing is conformity with EN ISO/IEC 17025 [ISO 05] that defines the general requirements with regard to skills for laboratory testing and calibration.

Note that this standard is applicable to all organizations performing tests and/or calibrations. For example, laboratories of first, second and third parties, as well as laboratories where testing and/or calibration form part of inspection and product certification.

Note that the legal texts defining constraints related to commissioning authorization mention the requirement to comply with the standard EN ISO/IEC 17025.

7.4.5.2. *Accreditation*

A testing laboratory is established through a quality framework that takes into consideration the following:

– quality management (there must be at least one ISO 9001 compatible referential);

– skill management (this point is essential; it must be proven that the persons in charge of the tests are skilled in the activities to be carried out);

– documentation management;

– management of sub-contracting;

– management of faults and corrective actions;

– management of registrations.

Therefore, there must be a quality reference describing the experiments and tests for repeating the tests. Repeatability of tests is an essential point as these must last throughout the life of a system (between 30 and 50 years) to demonstrate that the test results are consistent with those expected.

The laboratory cannot be recognized by the state after accreditation from a competent authority (e.g. COFRAC).

This accreditation (see Definition 7.5) is now required for the railway sector.

7.5. Conclusion

In this chapter we introduced the problems of assessment and certification. Assessment and/or certification is a long and expensive process that must be carried out early on in the development cycle.

We can conclude that irrespective of the sector, there is a referential that offers a scale to qualify the criticality level of a system. This criticality level is used to set the effort involved in implementation.

Furthermore, it must be noted that successful assessments are related to skill management, establishment of an organization with adequate independence, formalization of processes and demonstration of compliance with these processes. These processes must cover quality control, development, verification, validation and safety management.

7.6. Glossary

CENELEC[4]:   *Comité Européen de Normalisation Electrotechnique* (European Committee for Electrotechnical Standardization)

COFRAC: *COmité FRançais d'ACcréditation* (French Accreditation Committee)

COTS: Commercial Off-The-Shelf

EMC: Electromagnetic Compatibility

IEC[5]:   International Electrotechnical Commission

ISA: Independent Safety Assessor

ISO[6]:   International Organization for Standardization

---

4 www.cenelec.eu.
5 http://www.iec.ch.
6 http://www.iso.org/iso/home.htm.

OS:	Operating System
QRF:	Questions and Remarks Form
RAMS:	Reliability, Availability, Maintainability and Safety
SC:	Safety Case
SIL:	Safety Integrity Level
SSIL:	Software SIL

Different Sectors and Various Normative Referentials

8.1. Introduction

In this chapter, we shall discuss a few normative contexts. The purpose of this section is not to present all standards and their relationships, but just to locate a few key points that will be useful later.

While safety requirements have always been taken into account in complex systems (railways, air transportation, nuclear centers, etc.), the contractual obligations on performance have paved the way for industries today such as the railway sector, for example, to take total control of parameters related to reliability, availability and maintainability (RAM). The choice of standards and regulations is the responsibility of the designer and/or developer.

The design of critical systems (air transportation, railways, nuclear power, etc.) is subject to compliance with technical references (standards, business documents, technology, etc.).

[BAU 10, BAU 11, BLA 12] provide an overview of applicable standards by sector (aeronautics, automotive, railways, nuclear, space and PLC-based system) and a comparison of these standards (similarities and differences).

8.2. E/E/PE system

8.2.1. *Introduction*

Electrical/electronic systems have been used for years to perform safety-related functions in most industrial sectors (gas distribution, water, production, control, etc.)

The standard IEC 61508 [IEC 11] is a generic standard that can be applied to all complex systems based on electronic and/or programmable electronic systems called E/E/PE systems (electric/electronic/programmable electronic). This standard is published by the International Electro-technical Commission (IEC), which is the international standards organization responsible for electrical, electronic and related technology sectors.

The first version of the standard IEC 61508 addressed the following two problems:

– providing a general framework for safety control and management;

– proposing an approach to cover not only implementation but also installation, commissioning, operation and decommissioning.

Therefore, it provides a global approach to safety[1], that could be compared to ISO 9001 [ISO 08] for the quality of its systematic aspect.

IEC 61508 is fully consistent with the convergence that we observe between the various industrial sectors (aeronautics, nuclear, railways, automotive, manufacturing, etc.), but the content of IEC 61508 is sufficiently complex and unusual that needs to be molded; an interested reader may also read [ISA 05] or [SMI 07].

The standard IEC 61508 [IEC 08, IEC 11] consists of seven parts:

– IEC 61508-1, general requirements;

– IEC 61508-2, requirements related to safety for electrical/electronic/ programmable electronic systems;

– IEC 61508-3, requirements for software;

– IEC 61508-4, definitions and abbreviations;

– IEC 61508-5, examples of methods to determine safety integrity levels;

– IEC 61508-6, directives for the application of IEC 61508-2 and IEC 61508-3;

– IEC 61508-7, overview of measures and techniques.

In most complex systems, safety is achieved by multiple systems using various technologies (mechanical, hydraulic, pneumatic, electrical, electronic, programmable electronic). The safety strategy must take into account all the elements contributing to

---

1 The standard CEI/IEC 61508 [IEC 11] does not cover the confidentiality and/or integrity aspects related to implementation of precautions to avoid unauthorized persons from damaging and/or affecting the safety of E/E/PE systems. The network aspects must be addressed to avoid any intrusions.

safety. Thus, IEC 61508 [IEC 11] provides an analytical framework for application to safety-related systems based on other technologies, and specifically addresses electronic-based systems.

Because of the wide variety of E/E/PE applications and degrees of diverse complexity, the exact nature of the safety measures to be implemented depends on application-specific factors; so in IEC 61508 [IEC 11], there are no general rules but only recommendations regarding the analytical methods to be implemented.

8.2.2. Certification

IEC 61508 [IEC 08b] does not provide any type of certification, but it is the current practice for PLC type devices to achieve product certification with or without EC marking.

The European Machinery Directive (IEC 62061) requires certification associated with the EC marking for the entire machine. This is a self-certification process from the manufacturer.

8.2.3. Safety levels

IEC 61508 [IEC 11] defines the Safety Integrity Level (SIL) concept. SIL is used to quantify the level of integrity of the safety of a system. Safety Integrity Level 1 (SIL 1) is the lowest level, and Safety Integrity Level 4 (SIL 4) is the highest safety integrity level.

The four SIL levels for a safety function are characterized by the impact of failures:

– SIL 4: catastrophic impact (highest level);

– SIL 3: impact on community;

– SIL 2: major protection for installation and production facilities or risk of injury to employees;

– SIL 1: minor protection for installation and production facilities (lowest level).

IEC 61508 describes the requirements necessary to achieve each level of safety integrity. The higher the safety levels, the more stringent the requirements in order to ensure the lowest possible probability of dangerous failure.

SIL enables the specification of requirements for the integrity of safety functions to be allocated to E/E/PE systems.

8.2.4. *Sub-standards*

8.2.4.1. *Introduction*

For several years, the generic standard [IEC 11, IEC 98] has been divided into various sub-standards that cover various sectors, as shown in Figure 8.1.

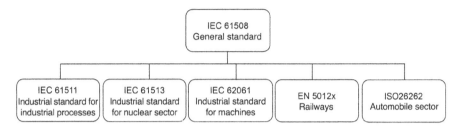

Figure 8.1. *The IEC 61508 standard and its sub-standards*

The standards CENELEC (EN 50126 [CEN 00], 50129 [CEN 03] and 50128 [CEN 01a, CEN 11]) are presented in section 8.3.

Figure 8.1 shows the connection between IEC 61508 and IEC 61513 [IEC 01], but this connection is not correct. In fact, the nuclear standards existed long before the introduction of standard IEC 61508 and the only relationship between the two standards is in the nomenclature.

The version of the standard related to the automobile sector is ISO 26262 [ISO 11] and it is described under section 8.7.

8.2.4.2. *Specific case: Standard 61511*

The "Continuous Process" industry standard named IEC 61511 [IEC 05] provides specifications by limiting the initial scope of application of IEC 61508 [IEC 08b] to the traditional context of continuous processes.

It must be noted that with regard to programming languages, IEC 61511 [IEC 05] is only interested in common programming languages that are specified through the IEC 611131-3 [IEC 03]. This does not in any manner forbid to program an E/E/PE system with ADA or C++ language, but in these cases it is necessary to refer to IEC 61508 [IEC 08b] which provides the framework for using these languages.

8.2.5. Software safety

IEC 61508 [IEC 11] is used for the development of "critical" software in automation and automotive sectors as well as for industrial process control facilities.

The proposed development cycle is derived from the cycle V which involves module testing, software/software and software/hardware integration testing and validation tests.

The standard contains tables (see Table 8.1) that must be used to define the implementation method. As shown in Table 8.1, there are differences between two software techniques with different SILs.

Techniques/measures	SIL 1	SIL 2	SIL 3	SIL 4
Semi-formal methods	R	R	HR	HR
Formal methods	–	R	R	HR
Ascending traceability between the requirements for system safety and requirements for software safety	R	R	HR	HR
Descending traceability between safety requirements and perceived safety requirements	R	R	HR	HR
Computer aided specification tools based on above-mentioned appropriate techniques/measures	R	R	HR	HR

Table 8.1. *IEC 61508-3 – Table A.1*

For high SILs, the standard IEC 61508 requires implementation of systematic and controlled development process. The cost of software is, in general, linked to the value of SIL.

8.3. Railway sector

This section is based on our feedback as an assessor of certifying authority for railway systems (urban and main line). Under [BOU 07], we have analyzed and reported the situation with regard to the implementation of rail standards.

Safety, similar to dependability, is achieved by introducing concepts, methods, and tools, throughout the lifecycle of a system. A safety study requires the analysis of system failures. We must seek to identify and quantify the severity of the potential consequences and, to the furthest possible extent, the expected frequency of such failures. For Europe, the CENELEC referential is used to address this process.

8.3.1. *Introduction*

Railway projects are now governed by texts (decrees, orders, etc.) and a normative referential (CENELEC EN 50126 [CEN 00], 50129 [CEN 03] and 50128 [CEN 01a, CEN 11]) for defining and achieving certain objectives of RAMS (Reliability, Maintainability, Availability and Safety). The three standards cover the aspects related to safety from system to hardware and/or software elements.

The purpose of the CENELEC referential is to:

1) provide a common reference in Europe to promote the expansion of market and interoperability, interchangeability and "cross acceptance" of railway constituents;

2) respond to the specificities of the railway sector.

As shown in Figure 8.2, railway referential CENELEC EN 5012x is a variation of the generic standard IEC 61508 [IEC 08b] that takes into account the specificities of the railway sector and successful experiences (SACEM, TVM, SAET-METEOR, etc.).

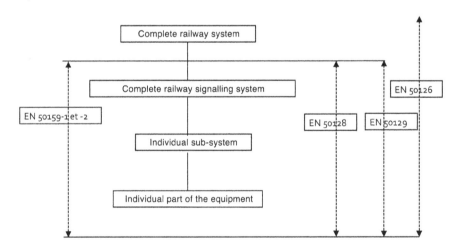

Figure 8.2. *CENELEC referential*

Railway referential CENELEC EN 5012x is applicable to the "urban" type of railway applications (metro, RER, etc.) as well as the conventional railway applications (high speed line, conventional train, freight).

In the railway sector, the normative referential consists of the following standards:

– CENELEC EN 50126 [CEN 00] describes the methods to be implemented to specify and demonstrate reliability, availability, maintainability and safety (RAMS);

– CENELEC EN 50128 [CEN 01a, CEN 11b] describes the actions to demonstrate the safety software. For more information on the 50128 standard and its implementation see [BOU 14c];

– CENELEC EN 50129 [CEN 03] describes the structure of a safety case and the methods to implement for the safety management of hardware.

One of the restrictions on railway referential CENELEC EN 5012x is related to the application scope of the standards CENELEC EN 50128 [CEN 01a, CEN 11b] and CENELEC EN 50129 [CEN 03] that are normally restricted to signaling subsystems (see Figure 8.3). For hardware architectures used in other subsystems, the older standards are still applicable (NF F 00-101, etc.). Work is in progress among the certification organization to extend and generalize these two standards to the railway system as a whole.

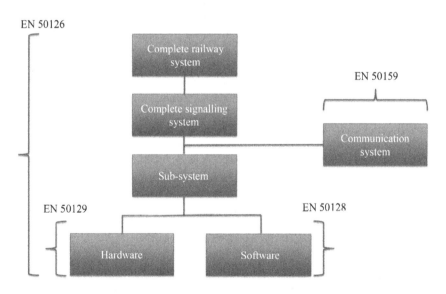

Figure 8.3. *Organization of standards applicable to railway systems*

These standards are complemented by a standard related to the aspects of "transmission". The 2001 version of CENELEC EN 50159 was split into two parts, one part (EN 50159-1 [CEN 01b]) dedicated to closed networks and another part (EN 50159-2 [CEN 01c]) dedicated to open networks. The new version of CENELEC EN 50129 [CEN 11a] replaces the previous version and covers all networks (open and closed). CENELEC EN 50159 covers all the aspects related to security. For more information on the impact of introducing network security on railway systems, refer to [BOU 14b].

CENELEC standards EN 50126 [CEN 00], EN 50129 [CEN 03] and EN 50128 [CEN 01a, CEN 11] describe the requirements in terms of construction and demonstration of RAMS of programmable electronic systems for railway applications. These standards now have a European statute, applying to all Member States of the European Community, and have been endorsed by the International Electro-technical Commission, as application of IEC 61508 [IEC 98] to the railway sector, also conferring them an international status.

CENELEC EN 50129 is more focused on safety management of hardware architectures. In [BOU 10] we presented the principles for safety hardware architectures and in [BOU 09a, BOU 11a] we presented examples of safety critical architecture.

CENELEC EN 50129 introduces the concept of tolerable hazard rate (THR) and the safety concept SIL. SIL values range from 1 to 4. SIL is defined as one of the discrete levels for specifying the safety integrity requirements of the safety functions allocated to safety systems.

Among the risk reduction actions, taken to achieve an acceptable level of risk, CENELEC EN 50129 [CEN 03] describes the allocation of safety objectives for system functions and subsystems. It must be noted that the concept of SIL as defined in CENELEC EN 50129 [CEN 03] is not the same as the concept of SIL defined in IEC 61508 [IEC 08b]. The differences relate to the identification method and impacts. Though, the use made in the standards is identical.

CENELEC standard EN 50128 [CEN 11] is more dedicated to software development aspects for railways. For software, Software SIL (SSIL) defines various criticality levels from 0 (no hazard) to 4 (critical).

Attaining safety objectives for a software application is an expert judgment inferred through a proper assessment (see section 6.4 of the CENELEC EN 50128 [CEN 11].

8.3.2. *Certification*

Railway projects are now governed by regulatory texts (decrees, orders, etc., see [ERA 06, ERA 03]). The regulatory framework of the railway sector has been complemented in recent years by standards (CENELEC EN 50126, EN 50128 and EN 50129, EN 50159, etc.), by European and national regulations and by European bodies such as ERA (European Railway Agency[2]) and national agencies such as the EPSF (*Etablissement Public de Sécurité Ferroviaire*[3] – Public Rail Safety Establishment) and the STRM-TG (*Service Technique des Remontées Mécaniques et des Transports Guidés*[4] – Technical Department of Mechanical Lifts and Guided Transport) for France.

As shown in [BOU 08, BOU 09b], commissioning a rail system (urban, mainline, freight or high speed lines) is subject to approval. Such approvals may be based on certificates of conformance or independent assessment of product(s).

The authorization for commissioning a railway system is done by a state agency in charge of examining the safety case (SC):

– for the urban sector, STRM-TG;

– for the railway sector, EPSF.

In both cases, the safety case contains a description of the system and its implementation, the safety elements of the operator and an opinion on the safety of the system given by an independent party called EOQA (an expert or a qualified expert body). For the urban sector, the mission of the EOQA is defined in the note [STR 06].

For more on the effective implementation of this regulation, refer to [BOU 07]

8.3.3. *Safety versus availability*

The standards describe the processes, methods and tools to achieve and demonstrate the required SIL. This refers to obligation of means, in addition to the obligations of quantitative and/or qualitative results.

---

2 For more information on ERA, see http://www.era.europa.eu.
3 For more information on EPSF, see http://www.securite-ferroviaire.fr.
4 For more information on STRMTG, see http://www.strmtg.equipement.gouv.fr.

For now, we focus on safety as it is the main aspect of dependability which must be analyzed. There is little or no requirement of reliability or availability that comes from the normative framework.

For critical systems (SIL 3 and 4), the safety principles conflict with system availability. For example, in the railway sector, the safety status "stop the train" has a strong impact on overall system availability. However, the obligation for a critical system enables improvement of software reliability. This reliability is induced by managing the complexity and quality of the software.

On the other hand, for non-critical (SSIL 0) and less-critical (SSIL 1 and SSIL 2) software applications, the software delivery process is less constrained (as in the choice of language and tools as well as implemented processes) which indicates a lesser quality of software that results in low reliability. To be more precise, in the context of non-critical or less critical systems, industries can use "commercial off-the-shelf" (COTS) products. However, as quality management has a direct impact on reliability and availability, COTS remains a topical issue.

8.3.4. *Software safety*

The standard CENELEC EN 50128 [CEN 01a] specifies the procedures and technical requirements for the development of programmable electronic systems used in control applications and rail protection. CENELEC EN 50128 is, therefore, normally not applicable to all software applications in the railway sector. In general, the standard EN 50155 [FFN 01] is applicable for all embedded applications on a train.

8.3.4.1. *Standard CENELEC EN 50155*

CENELEC EN 50155 [AFN 07] is applicable to all electronic equipment[5] used in railway vehicles. This standard is not only used for software applications, but section 5.3 describes the detailed rules applicable to all software aspects.

The first requirement is the mandatory application of ISO 9001:2008 [ISO 08]. The second requirement is the implementation of configuration management procedures that cover the developed software applications as well as the tools used for development and maintenance.

The third requirement is the definition of a lifecycle of the development of a software application that must be structured and documented.

---

5 These can be electronic devices used in command, regulation, protection, input, etc.

As shown in Figure 8.4, the development cycle proposed by the standard CENELEC EN 50155 [AFN 01] can be divided into five steps:

– software specification;

– software design;

– software testing;

– hardware/software integration testing;

– software application maintenance.

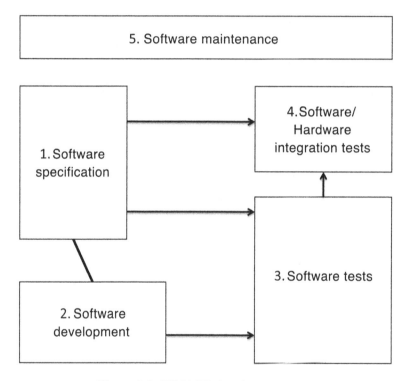

Figure 8.4. *EN 50155 development cycle*

In the specification phase, CENELEC EN 50155 [AFN 07] introduces the concept of the requirement and specification document without providing further details on the concept of requirement.

For the software development phase, section 5.3.2 of the standard CENELEC EN 50155 [AFN 07] indicates that a modular approach (software component broken down into small sizes with size limit, and number of interfaces), an approach (process, documentation list to produce standard plan, standardization, etc.) and a structured method (logical/functional block diagrams, sequence diagrams, data flow diagrams, truth tables/decision) are required and for the code, it is necessary to choose a programming language for *easy* verification (requiring a minimum effort for understanding). The design method and the programming language must facilitate code analysis. The program behavior can then be deduced from code analysis.

For testing, CENELEC EN 50155 [AFN 07] recommends analyzing the limit values, equivalence classes and input partitioning. The selection of test cases can be based on a model and process simulation.

The maintenance phase is a key point; it is necessary to ensure that the modification, addition of functionality or adaptation of software application to another train type does not compromise safety. Maintenance phase management must be completely defined and documented. One of the difficulties of the maintenance phase is to manage the development of multiple versions simultaneously and on-site installations (the trains are of different types and are parked in different places).

CENELEC EN 50155 [AFN 07] recommends that all product components must be saved in a format that allows analysis *a posteriori*. The following is the list of documents to be produced, as specified by the standard:

– software requirement specification with a demonstration of coverage of system requirements;

– description of architecture and design of the software application to meet the requirements expressed in the software requirement specification;

– for each software component, description of the performance characteristics (list of inputs and outputs, etc.), source code, description, and test results must be provided;

– all of the software application data (global variables and global constants) must be described in a "data dictionary";

– description of software application implantation in memory;

– description and references (name, version) of tools used to develop the software application and to produce the executable;

– description of integration tests and associated results.

Under section 8.2, CENELEC EN 50155 [AFN 07] enforces the standards CENELEC EN 50126 [CEN 00], EN 50129 [CEN 03] and EN 50128 [CEN 01a, CEN 11] without clearly stating how and in what areas.

8.3.4.2. *CENELEC EN 50128*

CENELEC EN 50128 [CEN 01a, CEN 11] applies to areas that are related or not[6] to safety and exclusively to software and interaction of the software application with the system as a whole.

This standard specifies the establishment of a V cycle from software specification to software testing. One of the specific points of EN 50128 is the requirement to describe the means of implementation. For this reason, it is called a medium standard.

CENELEC EN 50128 [CEN 01a, CEN 11] clearly introduces the concept of assessment. As shown in [BOU 06b, BOU 07], for software applications, software assessment involves demonstrating that the software application has achieved the safety objectives attributed to it. For more information on CENELEC 50128 and 62279 see [BOU 14C].

Assessment of safety levels of a software application involves:

– setting up audits: how effective is the quality management of the project?

– review of plans (Software Quality Assurance Plan, test plan(s), V & V plan, etc.);

– review of products (documents, source generation chain of the executable, data production processes, scenarios and test results, safety analysis (e.g. SEEA), etc;

– formalization of remarks and potential non-conformities;

– formalization of notices in the form of assessment reports.

8.3.5. *IRIS*

In the railway sector, the International Railway Industry Standard (IRIS[7]) [UNI 09] is redefined to include the conformance with ISO 9001: 2008 as well as CENELEC referential (50126, 50128 and 50129) under a single certification.

Version 2 of IRIS deploys and ensures that a company is able to manage quality as well as the CENELEC standards.

---

6 Standard EN 50128 [CEN 01a, CEN 11] also introduces SSIL0 for software applications without safety requirements.
7 For more information visit www.iris-rail.org.

8.4. Aeronautics

8.4.1. *Introduction*

In civil and military aviation, independent authorities such as the Federal Aviation Administration (FFA) or the European Aviation Safety Agency (EASA), are responsible for the certification of aircraft and their embedded systems for safety.

The aeronautics sector uses a referential (FAR and JAR[8]) that defines the objectives at the system level (10-9/h), and methods and means to be implemented. These standards are segregated at an industrial level by a common "practical" referential which consists of a set of Aerospace Recommended Practice (ARP) including:

– ARP 47.54 [ARP 96b] entitled "Certification Considerations for Highly-Integrated or Complex Aircraft Systems" describing methods for conducting safety analysis for aeronautical systems;

– ARP 47.61 [ARP 96c] entitled "Guidelines and Methods for Conducting the Safety Assessment Process of Civil Airborne Systems and Equipment", describing the certification of complex aeronautical systems.

The methods for safety assessment are detailed and described in document ARP-4761.

From a normative point of view, the aeronautics sector uses the standard DO 178 [RTA 11] for software and the standard DO 254 [DO 00] for electronics.

Figure 8.5 shows the organization and the articulation of the various standards applicable to systems, software etc. in aeronautics.

More specifically, the standard DO-178 provides guidelines to produce code for aeronautical applications. DO-178 is complementary to the ARP 47.54 (see Figure 8.6) which specifies the design processes for control systems and modification of existing systems. The standard DO-178 was updated in 2011 as version C.

---

8 Federal Aviation Regulations, Joint Aviation Requirement.

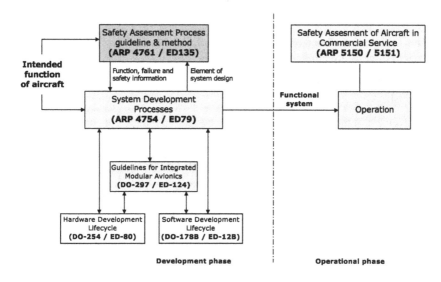

Figure 8.5. *Development cycle for aeronautics*

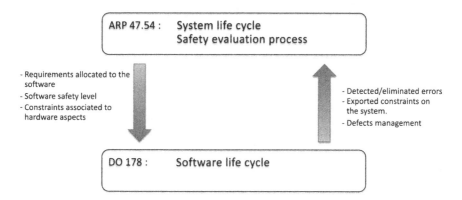

Figure 8.6. *Relation between system and software*

There is no concept of a safety accord in the aeronautics sector that allows for formalization of demonstrating safety.

8.4.2. *Software safety level*

The aeronautics sector uses the concept of Design Assurance Level (DAL) to define a system safety objective.

– Level A: catastrophic problem. Flight safety and landing are compromised. Plane crash;

– Level B: major problem involving serious damages or death of several passengers;

– Level C: serious problems with dysfunction of vital equipment of the flight;

– Level D: problem that may affect flight safety;

– Level E: problem with no effect on flight safety.

The standard DO-178 [RTA 11] proposes an approach that is objective-based: formulate objectives and verify if they have been met, but the specific methods to be used are not provided development (lifecycle is also not specified).

For more information on the implementation of the standard DO-178 version C, see [RIE 13].

8.4.3. *Certification*

Note that aviation agencies (FAA, EASA etc.) do not offer certification for standards EN 45011 and/or EN 17020 and do not provide any specific accreditation.

The concept of certification applies to an aircraft or engine type. Certification authorities treat the software as a component of the system or equipment installed in the aircraft or in the certified engine, which means that the certification authority does not approve the software as an independent product. Currently, the software and hardware are approved for each integration case as system components.

8.5. Space sector

For the aerospace sector, ESA has published the referential Product Assurance and Safety Standards (PSS[9]) which is available for all elements of a system. This referential provides a general safety approach, guidelines to carry out safety studies and objectives to be achieved, etc.

---

9 http://esapub.esrin.esa.it/pss/pss-cat1.htm.

This referential is drafted by the European Space Agency (ESA) and a working group strives continuously to improve the PSS and provide a referential endorsed by industries (ECSS: European Cooperation for Space Standardization). However, this standard is not mandatory, though it serves as a basis for all projects.

The ECSS standards are organized under three main classes corresponding to management and organization (class M), product assurance, quality (class Q) and engineering (class E), to which systems and general aspects (such as the Glossary, S) are added.

Each branch consists of a first level of standards, and if necessary, additional documents (more detailed standards, guides facilitating the implementation of the first-level standards or manuals providing additional, non-normative information).

The standards in the European space sector are developed by the European Cooperation for Space Standardization (ECSS), a cooperative effort of the ESA, national space agencies and European space industries for developing and maintaining common standards.

It must be noted that application of the ECSS standards is not mandatory in the legislative sense, but they are generally proposed and adopted, if necessary with modifications, in each case, within the contractual terms of each project.

8.6. Nuclear sector

Every country operating nuclear power plants must establish a Safety Authority to regulate their use, to protect people and the environment from harmful effects of radiation.

In France, it is the Nuclear Safety Authority (ASN), whose technical support is provided by the Institute for Radiological Protection and Nuclear Safety (IRSN).

Nuclear power plants are not subject to "certification", but have authorizations for creation and operation. These authorizations are issued by Government decrees, further to the proposals drafted by the ASN.

Only the Government decrees are strictly binding. They refer to high-level requirements without going into the technical details. In practice, for computerized safety systems, the documents published by IAEA and IEC TC45 are proposed by the operator as compliance demonstration methods and are acceptable to ASN and IRSN.

The field of nuclear applications specifies that project objectives may relate to undesired events and/or the solicitation of functions. It has a normative referential IEC 61880 [IEC 06] for the nuclear control/order.

8.7. Automobile sector

As shown in Figure 8.1, ISO 26262 [ISO 11] is a variation of the generic standard IEC 61508 [IEC 11] that take into account the specificities of the automotive sector.

8.7.1. *ISO 26262*

The automotive sector does not currently recognize the need for certification. But ISO 26262 [ISO 11] identifies a set of requirements, called "confirmation of measures" to ensure that safety assessment has been correctly performed.

ISO 26262 [ISO 11] provides a safety management process based on the definition of decommissioning management, as shown in Figure 8.7.

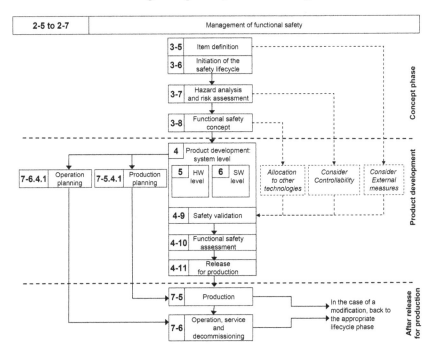

Figure 8.7. *"Safety" lifecycle*

Part 5 of ISO 26262 [ISO 09] is dedicated to the "hardware" safety management of the equipment; see Figure 8.8.

In [LIA 08], there is a demonstration of the impact of implementation of ISO 26262 [ISO 11] on the processes (definition of ASIL, safety management, etc.). Appendix D, Part 5 of the standard ISO 26262 introduces various safety techniques. For example, see [BOU 11] for automobile architectures.

With regard to the application of ISO 26262 [ISO 11], various industries in the automotive sector are beginning to assess the impact of its implementation on the processes currently used as shown in [LIA 08] and [AST 10] .

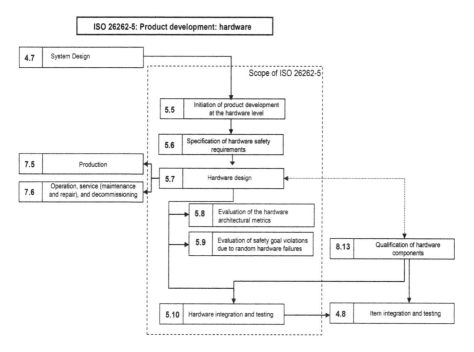

Figure 8.8. *Hardware safety management*

8.7.2. *Safety demonstration*

The people in charge of these confirmation measures must have a minimum level of independence from those in charge of development and decision-making processes related to production. This level of independence increases with the level of requirements listed on the Automotive Safety Integrity Level (ASIL).

It must be noted that contrary to other sectors, the highest level of independence required can be attained within the same organization. These measures are of three types:

– reviews to verify the main products;

– an audit to verify the relevance of the process;

– a safety assessment to evaluate the entire safety case.

8.7.3. *Software safety*

Part 6 of the standard ISO 26262 [ISO 11] is dedicated to the safety management of the "software" part.

8.7.4. *Certification*

The standard ISO 26262 does not require certification, but more and more contracts established refer to the standard and request the demonstration of its compliance. This demonstration is achieved through traceability with ISO 26262, audits and a safety demonstration formalized in a safety case.

8.8. A few constraints

The various standards impose some requirements related to software application, such as:

– implementation of a development process based on quality assurance management;

– management of the complexity of a software application;

– identification of requirements that the software application must comply with;

– implementation of requirement traceability on the entire development process;

– testability of the software;

– maintainability of software application.

8.9. Safety level

This chapter is a brief presentation of the normative standards applicable to various sectors. These various normative standards demonstrate the concept of a "safety level". A safety level can be associated to a system, a subsystem, an equipment, a system function, a software application and/or a software function.

In general, there are two types of safety levels; a safety level related to random failures dependent on the risks[10] and the likelihood of failure[11] and a safety level that is related to systematic failures. The safety level is based on a scale related to the severity of failures.

8.10. Conclusion

We can conclude that irrespective of the sector, there is a referential that offers a scale to qualify the level of criticality of a system. This criticality level is used to define the effort related to implementation. Managing the safety of a critical system goes through the process definition based primarily on test activities that are complemented by verification activities.

8.11. Glossary

ARP: Aerospace Recommended Practice

ASIL: Automotive SIL

CENELEC[12]:   *Comité Européen de Normalisation Electrotechnique* (European Committee for Electrotechnical Standardization)

COFRAC: *Comité FRançais d'ACcréditation* (French Accreditation Committee)

COTS: Commercial Off-The-Shelf

DAL: Design Assurance Level

EC: European Community

ECSS: European Cooperation for Space Standardization

E/E/EP: Electric/Electronic/Programmable Electronic System

EMC: Electromagnetic Compatibility

---

10 It is important to note that risk R is associated with severity G and frequency F.
11 F Tolerable Hazard Rate is in the form 10^{-x}.
12 www.cenelec.eu.

EOQA:	*Expert ou Organisme Qualifié Agrée* (an Expert or a Qualified Expert Body)
EPSF[13]:	*Etablissement Public de Sécurité Ferroviaire* (Public Rail Safety Establishment)
ESA:	European Space Agency
HR:	Highly Recommended
IEC[14]:	International Electrotechnical Commission
ISA :	Independent Safety Assessor
ISO[15]:	International Organization for Standardization
JAR:	Joint Aviation Requirement
M:	Mandatory
MISRA[16]:	Motor Industry Software Reliability Association
NoBo:	Notified Body
NR :	Not Recommended
OQA:	*Organisme Qualifié Agrée* (Qualified Expert Body)
PLC:	Programmable Logic Controller
PSS:	Product assurance and Safety Standards
R:	Recommended
RAM:	Reliability, Availability, Maintainability
RAMS:	Reliability, Availability, Maintainability and Safety
RAMSS:	Reliability, Availability, Maintainability, Safety and Security
SC:	Safety Case
SIL:	Safety Integrity Level
SSIL:	Software SIL
STI:	*Spécifications Techniques d'Interopérabilité* (Interoperability Technical Specifications)

---

13 http://www.securite-ferroviaire.fr.
14 http://www.iec.ch.
15 http://www.iso.org/iso/home.htm.
16 www.misra.org.uk.

STRMTG[17]:   *Service Technique des Remontées Mécaniques et des Transports Guidés* (Technical Department of Mechanical Lifts and Guided Transport)

THR: Tolerable Hazard Rate

UIC: *Union Internationale des Chemins de fer* (International Railway Union)

---

17 http://www.strmtg.equipement.gouv.fr.

9

Quality Management

9.1. Introduction

In Chapter 6, we concluded that the only reasonable safety technique for a software application is to control the quality. In this chapter, we will present the principles of quality control and management for the development of a software application.

Definition 9.1 introduces Quality Assurance (QA) by directing an objective of confidence in obtaining a level of quality required.

DEFINITION 9.1 (Quality assurance) [AFN 87].– *Implementation of an appropriate set of planned and systematic arrangements to give confidence in obtaining the required quality.*

While its role is to *help*, quality is often viewed by the members of a project as:

– either a "word" which is useless, invisible in a project and serves no purpose;

– or as something "bad", which is a waste of time, creates more problems than it addresses and serves as a constraint.

QA is a limitation and control activity that must be understood and accepted. It must provide methods, processes and should enable to manage activities. The establishment of QA thus allows for *pre-established* and *systematic* activities that are understood and controlled.

The general provisions taken by a company for the quality of its products or its services are described in the "Quality Assurance Manual" (QAM) of the company.

Each provision (specification, test, etc.) is defined within a "procedure". The complex provision framework may also contain a guide describing the implementation. Each procedure is associated with a provision that identifies the documents of inputs and outputs. Templates describing the document format are also part of the provision.

Through *pre-established* and *systematic* aspects of the implementation of quality referentials, we can see the emergence of competence and efficiency. In fact, competence is achieved through application and understanding of the processes, whereas efficiency is achieved through improvement proposals, understanding and acceptance of difficulties and feedback implementation.

This chapter is not a general discussion on quality, but it aims to present what should be quality management when implemented a software application.

One of the main difficulties in quality management is the ability to manage improvement. It is not enough to just set up a quality framework, but it must be ensured that the quality framework evolves over time while taking into account any feedback on projects; it is equally important to analyze the difficulties that could be encountered, improve efficiency, etc.

9.2. Continuous improvement

Quality management cannot be limited to the existence of a quality referential, the implementation of projects or the monitoring of this implementation. Quality management must go through a continuous improvement of quality referential.

Therefore, implementation of quality management must be associated with an improvement process such as PDCA (Plan Do Check Act). PDCA is a continuous improvement or problem-solving process, symbolized by the Deming wheel. The PDCA is:

– *P: Plan*: This step is to define the subject or problem, in order to identify sustainable solutions. The completion of this stage involves production of an action plan, including planning and the actors involved.

– *D: Do*: The objective of this step is to implement the actions defined above.

– *C: Check*: Using measures, indicators, or observations, the effectiveness of measures implemented must be verified. If any modifications are needed, we return to step P.

– *A: Act*: Finalization of results and their sustainable implementation involves development or updating of documents such as procedures, processes, good practice guides, or forms. Improvements can be identified and implemented by returning to step P.

Continuous improvement must be based on the results of implementation control on projects. We must analyze the defects identified in the projects, difficulties encountered (delay, impossibility to do, etc.), exemption requests, etc.

9.3. Quality management as well as quality control

As discussed previously, QA not only involves quality management, but also, and above all, quality control. One of the reasons for the failure of projects is related to the fact that there is no quality control in the project.

Quality control must demonstrate that the project meets the set objectives and company's quality management principles. The quality team involved in the project must perform this control.

9.4. Quality management

9.4.1. *Introduction*

It must be noted that more often the term "quality assurance" is used. QA involves implementation of an appropriate set of pre-established and systematic provisions to give confidence in obtaining a required quality.

In this section, we shall briefly introduce the standards related to QA and their characteristics.

The demonstration of the safety level (DAL, SSIL, ASIL, etc.) requires demonstration of quality management at all levels (system design, hardware design and software design).

9.4.2. *ISO 9000*

ISO 9000 is a set of quality management standards that are applicable to several sectors (manufacturing, service, etc.). In order to meet the ISO 9000 standard, the ability of an organization to produce goods and services must be demonstrated. This demonstration goes through a process of certification by an independent body.

The spirit of ISO 9000 standard is "Say what you do, do what you say, and show what you have done".

More specifically, ISO 9000 standard is divided into:

– ISO 9000 is a document outlining guidelines for the selection and use of standards;

– ISO 9001 provides a model for QA in the context of the design, implementation, installation and after-sales services;

– ISO 9002 provides a model for QA in production and installation;

– ISO 9003 is a model for QA in final inspection and testing;

– ISO 9004, along with common guidelines to all companies, completes the three previous standards related to external QA in contractual situations.

ISO 9001 is the most relevant standard for development of software applications, but it must be applied along with the ISO 90003 standard which is an ISO 9001:2008 interpretation guide for developing a software application.

9.4.3. *ISO 9001*

Among the abovementioned ISO standards, ISO 9001 remains the most used because it is dedicated to quality assurance in the context of design and implementation. In this section, we present this standard and its application for developing a software application.

9.4.3.1. *Introduction to ISO 9001:2008*

The international standard ISO 9001:2008 [ISO 08] is a generic standard that specifies the requirements related to Quality Management System (QMS) in an organization. It is used when an organization needs to demonstrate its ability to consistently provide a product that meets customer requirements and applicable statutory and regulatory requirements. It also aims at the continuous improvement of the system and assurance of conformance to these requirements.

All ISO 9001:2008 requirements are applicable to all organizations, regardless of type, size and finished product.

As shown in Figure 9.1, ISO 9001:2008 consists of five main chapters that define five families of activities:

– the quality management system (process approach, general requirements, documentation) – continuous improvement of the QMS;

– management responsibility (responsibility, authority and communication, quality policy, quality objectives, management review);

– resource management (human resources, infrastructure, work environment);

– product development (planning, client processes, purchasing, production, measuring equipment);

– measurement, analysis and improvement (control, nonconforming product, internal audit, corrective action, etc.).

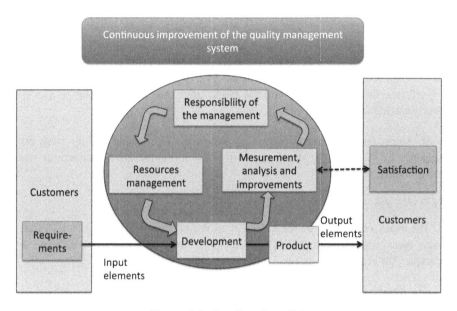

Figure 9.1. *Quality referential*

The standard requirements cover a wide range of aspects applicable to all the activities of an organization, including the quality commitment of the management of supplier, staff competence, process management, etc.

9.4.3.2. *ISO 90003*

The ISO 90003 guide [ISO 04b], while taking into account the 2000 version of ISO 9001, remains a useful application guide for the implementation of ISO 9001:2008 for developing a software application.

It must be noted that certain industry standards also have the same regulatory role, for example, ISO 90003 is not mandatory for the railway sector as CENELEC 50128:2011 and IEC 62279 are used.

9.4.3.3. *ISO 9001 version 2005*

The ISO 9001 standard was recently under revision and the new version was published before the end of 2015 [ISO 15].

The changes include:

– organization of the standard has evolved to introduce compatibility with other standards;

– risk management, even though present in the previous versions, takes more importance in the new version;

– greater emphasis is given to the involvement of management;

– consideration of supply chain;

– change in base language and the terms used in order to be compatible with other standards.

In conclusion, the most important change involves compatibility with other standards to facilitate the demonstration of conformance for organizations using multiple referentials.

9.4.3.4. *Review*

The main interest of this standard is to define business processes in order to make them applicable to all. They constitute knowledge of the company and guarantee the replay[1] and maintainability over time.

The disadvantage of this standard lies in its "administrative" nature and the high cost involved to achieve ISO[2] certification, this being due in particular to the large number of documents (procedures, instructions, etc.) generated by the standard. Ultimately, it is a standard that is widespread and is compatible with other standards.

9.4.4. *Others*

9.4.4.1. *CMMi – Capability Maturity Model for integration*

The purpose of this section is not to describe the CMMi model in detail, but it is interesting to present aspects of the requirements addressed by the model.

---

1 Replay is the ability to replay the same activities ("redo" something). For a replay to be effective, there should not be anything implicit.

2 www.iso.org.

9.4.4.1.1. Introduction

CMMi[3] is a maturity model dedicated to the software industry which includes a set of best practices to be implemented in development projects. This is a model of international reference for evaluation and improvement of the development processes and software maintenance. Deploying CMMi within a company is part of a continuous improvement process and must therefore be adapted to different organizations and project typologies.

CMMi provides a consistent response in terms of the relationship between contracting authority (MOA) and project management (MOE). It allows:

– satisfaction of the end users through explicit and implicit management requirements;

– project management in terms of timelines, budget and quality;

– transparency and clear and shared vision of projects by all the persons involved.

9.4.4.1.2. Maturity levels

CMMi includes practices by maturity level, on a scale from 1 (most basic) to 5 (most developed). Each level of maturity corresponds to process in sectors. The five maturity levels and areas of CMMi process are:

– Level 5 – Optimized:

- organizational deployment and innovation;

- causal and resolution analysis.

– Level 4 – Controlled:

- organizational process performance;

- quantitative management of project.

– Level 3 – Defined:

- requirements development;

- technical solution;

- product integration;

---

3 http://www.sei.cmu.edu/cmmi.

- Verification;

- Validation;

- Focalization on organizational process;

- Definition of organizational process;

- Organizational training;

- Integrated project management;

- Risk management;

- Analysis and decision making.

– Level 2 – Reproducible:

- Requirement management;

- Project planning;

- Follow-up and project control;

- Management of agreements with suppliers;

- Measurement and analysis;

- Configuration management;

- QA of processes and products.

– Level 1 – Initial.

For requirements, CMMi describes best practices for requirement development (Level 3) and requirement management (Level 2). CMMi introduces the concept of customer requirements and product requirements, and presents activities both specific and common to both levels of requirements.

9.4.4.1.3. Review

The CMMi approach allows for controlling the quality of the software, taking into account the needs related to requirements. This approach has many advantages.

As part of consulting activities, it was given to us to see that many companies, which had launched the implementation of CMMi, had reached Level 2 or 3.

Nowadays, organizations are no longer necessarily looking for CMMi certification, but are implementing good practices strongly inspired by this referential.

Similar to ISO 9001, CMMi involves a significant cost for obtaining the certification as well as to maintain it over time.

9.4.4.2. SPICE – Software Process Improvement and Capability Determination

9.4.4.2.1. Introduction

The SPICE [ISO 04a] model provides a reference for evaluation of practices that enable:

– repeatable processes;

– determination of their relevance with respect to the company objectives;

– easy comparison with a referential;

– obtaining products or software services having a pre-defined quality level;

– supporting improved productivity.

The SPICE model provides: a reference model for process and requirement management regarding the use of this model and the evaluations, guidelines for implementation of evaluation, improvement and determination of process capability.

ISO/SPICE management model identifies two dimensions:

– process dimension;

– aptitude dimension.

Aptitude dimension introduces six levels whose characteristics are as follows:

– at Level 0, the process is not carried out or it has only achieved partial objective;

– at Level 1 of a process the objectives have been "achieved";

– at Level 2, the process is "managed". This involves two aspects: the management of processes and management of products obtained from the processes;

– a process at Level 3 is said to be "established" at the organization level. At this level implementation of the process is based on pre-established and documented practices;

– level 4 characterizes a process whose management is based on quantitative approach: the process is measured, and its performances are "predictable";

– at Level 5, the process is "optimized": the organization is capable of improving its processes and adapting them with respect to the objectives of the organization.

The process dimension of a model consists of five process categories consisting each of 4–10 processes:

– the client–supplier (CUS) process category consists of processes implemented by an acquirer to identify their needs, select their supplier and receive the supply. For the supplier, this category includes the activities necessary for supply, commissioning, operation and support of the user;

– engineering (ENG) category includes the development activities of a software application. Consider the software application in its environment from definition phase to the maintenance phase;

– support (SUP) category includes the processes called support functions/media; these can be implemented on an application of another process, such as process documentation, QA and verification or configuration management;

– management (MAN) category contains the process' characteristic of management activities such as project management, quality management and/or risk management;

– The fifth category, organization (ORG), contains processes addressing the global nature of the organization and not at project level.

9.4.4.2.2. Review

The ISO/SPICE framework provides a tool for quality development. This framework can be perfectly integrated with the consideration of other quality management standards, such as ISO 900× standards.

Thus, ISO/SPICE can serve as an analytical tool, either for improvement of the approach, obtaining ISO 9001 certification or for maintenance of an already ISO 9001 certified quality system.

Similar to ISO 9001, SPICE approach involves a significant cost for obtaining the certification as well as for maintaining it over time.

9.4.4.3. *IRIS – International Railway Industry Standard*

In railways, IRIS[4] [UNI 09] includes compliance with ISO 9001:2008 and CENELEC referential (50126, 50128 and 50129) under a single certification.

Version 2 of IRIS deploys and thus ensures that a company manages the quality as well as compliance with the referential CENELEC [CEN 00, CEN 03, CEN 11].

9.4.4.4. *Compatibility of standards*

It must be noted that the 2001 and 2011 versions of CENELEC 50128 (like other standards) only mention ISO 9001: 2008, however, a company could have a QA process compliant with another repository such as CMMi or SPICE.

Obtaining ISO 900× certificate (or another similar referential, SPICE or CMMi can be used but their compatibility with ISO 9001: 200x[5] must be demonstrated) is the first step but the associated quality framework must have procedures that cover various areas and particularly designing of a software application.

9.4.5. **Quality Assurance Manual**

The general provisions (see QMS) engaged by a company for the quality of their products or services are described in the *Quality Assurance Manual* (QAM) of the company.

Each provision (specification, test, etc.) is defined within a "procedure". In the complex provision framework, a guide describing the implementation may be provided. Each procedure, associated with a provision, will identify input and output documents. Types of plans describing the document format are also available.

The quality referential (QMS) of a company involves QAM, a set of procedures, guides and plans that characterize the documents to be produced. This referential must comply with one or more standards. The standards can be generic standards (ISO 9001, SPICE, CMMi, etc.) or industry standards (see Chapter 8).

For critical applications, the quality referential has to take into account the various safety levels (DAL, SIL, SSIL, ASIL or other) and must describe the activities to be performed.

---

4 IRIS stands for International Railway Industry Standard. For more information visit www.iris-rail.org.
5 Currently the standard ISO 9001:2008 is applicable.

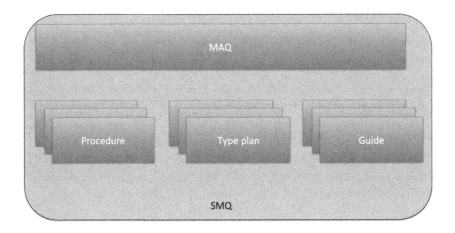

Figure 9.2. *Quality referential*

9.4.6. *Project quality*

9.4.6.1. *Project management plan*

It is necessary to describe the activities that will be carried out to construct the system, subsystem and/or equipment. For a given project, the quality objectives, procedures implemented to develop the product and the conditions of development must be identified.

A *Project Management Plan* (PMP) should describe all activities that are carried out to construct the system, subsystem and/or equipment. This PMP should cover all areas: system design, hardware design and software design. PMP must describe the different teams (system design, hardware design, software design, RAMS, quality, etc.), various activities, resources used, etc.

PMP must describe the overall policy design for development of the element under design (system, subsystem and/or equipment).

9.4.6.2. *Quality Assurance Plan*

Every project must have a *Quality Assurance Plan* (QAP). The Quality Assurance Plan is a document describing the specific steps taken by a company for the quality of the product or service concerned.

The quality management of a software application will require implementation of *Software Quality Assurance* (SQAP).

9.4.6.3. Safety Assurance Plan

The *Safety Assurance Plan* (SAP) must describe the means (human, material, etc.), methods and documents to be produced. SAP must cover all levels: system, subsystem and/or equipment, and the various aspects: hardware, software, etc.

SAP must take into account the fact that off-the-shelf products (COTS) may be used and/or the products may be reused (developed on another project). In that case, the exported requirements must be taken into consideration.

9.5. What is quality of a software application?

The quality applied to a software application can include several areas:

– product quality;

– quality of product in use;

– code quality;

– quality of documentation;

– etc.

For a software application, we must manage the quality of a product but the term quality can be viewed in several ways. There is the quality perceived by the user, which can be expressed through a satisfaction (the software application meets specifications) or dissatisfaction (the presence of numerous faults affects behavior, etc.).

Based on the development process analysis, it is possible to identify the quality of the software application development process using the number of exceptions and number of faults with respect to the final product, etc.

Product quality can be measured through product quality elements (code quality, quality of documentation, efficiency of verification activities).

The quality assurance management for the development of a software application must cover the various points:

– process management: ensure the proper implementation of the software application development process. There must be an indicator to detect that the quality decreases, such as the number of exemptions, number of faults, delays in document production, etc.;

– product management: verify that company plans and procedures are applied;

– component management (code, documents, tools, etc.): ensure that each element is managed in terms of configuration, has a reference, a version and that implementation plans are respected and the company's procedures are complied with;

– management of perceived quality: it is necessary to have technical facts management processes that enable to address complaints or requests from customers for improvement.

9.6. Development of a software application

Note that the term development refers to *creation* of a software application and not to *development* of a software application. Creating a software application (see Figure 5.2) contains development activities but also verification, validation, production, installation and maintenance of the software application.

The activities of verification and validation are important and are more or less developed depending on the level of safety required. Regarding the production activities of the final application and installation, they are crucial and require implementation of specific processes. Withdrawal of a software application is mentioned but it does not cause any concern unlike the removal of a complex system, for example, the withdrawal of a nuclear power plant or the withdrawal of railway installation.

Maintenance of software application is a very sensitive activity; following a change, we must maintain a level of safety while controlling the cost of change and minimizing the impact on the system in service.

Maintenance of a software application is confronted with a difficulty: life of software application. For railway sector, the lifetime is 40 to 50 years, for aeronautics sector, it is 40 years, for nuclear sector, it is 50 years, for automobile sector, it is 15 years. In view of these long lifetimes, we must take steps to ensure the maintenance of service and the software application.

9.7. Software quality

In this section, we shall discuss few fundamental points with regard to software applications.

9.7.1. *Characteristics of a software application*

It is possible to characterize a software application, using the following properties:

– it is visible *but* intangible: a person can implement a software application and identify the behaviors but the application remains a series of bits copied to a memory, any alteration to which gives another application;

– it ages *but* does not wear out: a software application has systematic faults but it does wear out with time; however, it ages in the sense that its performance degrades (version change of the operating system, for example), it does not correspond to the standard, or its behaviors on new architectures are not the same;

– it *does not* deteriorate as a result of tests: crash of a software application does not lead to its loss and does not induce cost as can the implementation of a crash test in the automotive sector, for example;

– it is *still* and *always* has been handmade: man remains the biggest player in the development loop of a software application. The implementation of code generation tools need to be developed and support on complex tools needs to be worked upon; which leads to tool qualification problems that are discussed in Volume 2 [BOU 16a];

– it is (too?) *easily* reproducible: the ease of reproduction of a software application leads to the availability of n versions on m media of the same software application;

– it is (too?) *easily* modifiable: a simple hexadecimal editor can help edit the program in the memory, an EMC[6] field and/or particle can change a memory bit thereby changing the program or associated data etc.;

– It is highly complex: cost (too?) *high*: the size of software applications has grown from a few dozen to a few thousand to currently over a million code lines, and the question is how to manage this complexity.

This list of characteristics remind us that a software application is not a simple object but a complex one that must be managed from its development to its installation and maintained well through its lifecycle. This management involves establishment of a set of rules that must be taken into account to control activities carried out throughout the verification activity.

---

6 Electromagnetic Compatibility.

9.7.2. *Quality objective*

9.7.2.1. *Example of indicator*

ISO 9001:2008 [ISO 08] recommends the setting up of indicators to monitor the quality of the software product and the implemented processes.

The 2001 version of the CENELEC 50128 standard [CEN 01], in section 15.4.5 – item 7, states that the metric definition (quantitative measures) needs to be applied to the processes and products. It introduces an explicit link to ISO/IEC 9126 [ISO 91, ISO 04c].

ISO/IEC 9126 defines and describes a series of quality characteristics of a software product (internal and external characteristics, characteristics of use). These characteristics can be used to specify the functional and non-functional requirements of customers and users.

The characteristics identified by ISO/IEC 9126 are:

– functional capacity: does the software respond to the specified functional requirements?

– reliability: does the software maintain its service level under specified conditions and for a definite period of time?

– usability: does the software require effort to use?

– efficiency: does the software require a cost-effective and proportionate sizing of hosting platform for other requirements?

– maintainability: does the software require effort for its evolution with respect to new requirements?

– portability: can the software be transferred from one platform or environment to another?

CENELEC 50128:2011 [CEN 11] and IEC 62279:2014 [IEC 14] transfer the request for compliance with the ISO / IEC 9127 at the development level of software requirements specification (section 7.2.4.1 of CENELEC 50128). The standard CENELEC 50128:2011 [CEN 11] introduces the need to manage the complexity in line 8 of Table A.12. This complexity management refers to HR for all levels of SSIL.

For the state-of-the-art aspect, the ISO 25000 standard [ISO 14] must be preferably considered for the requirements and evaluation of software quality. The latter is also referred to as SQuaRE (Software Quality Requirements and Evaluation).

9.7.2.2. Reliability

In section 5.2.1 we discussed the concept of reliability of a software application. The perceived quality of the implementation of a software application (installation, performance, use, update, etc.) is often interpreted as reliability, but as already explained, the software reliability cannot be quantified or calculated.

There are two types of software: software having several users and other software. For software with many users, we may want to discuss reliability but many users does not mean that it refers to the same version of software and that all faults are actually attributed to developers. For other software, fault management is fairly well done, but the number of users or the use does not allow for characterizing an indicator.

9.7.2.3. Usability

A software application must be usable. This means that its use is documented and reproducible for a given period. The concept of given period is important because the life of a software application may be of some minutes (the time to do a complicated calculation), some months (transient application), a few years (current application, your text processing, for example) or several decades (15 years in automotive sector, 40 years in railways, 50 years in nuclear sector, etc.).

The use must take into account the context of use; it is as difficult to update the software of a car as reprogramming of a satellite if it has not been planned from the beginning. Hence, in the space sector, it is possible to develop systems which support dynamic reconfiguration of software applications.

Furthermore, documentation cannot be limited to technical documentation of the development but it must have documentation for installation, daily use and for managing updates. Using the documentation, it should be possible to train people in the use of software applications throughout the operating life of a system.

9.7.2.4. Efficiency

A software application is executed on a platform and its efficiency is related to the resources required to run it. There exists a relationship between the level of services and the required resources.

9.7.2.5. *Maintainability*

In section 5.2.3, we presented the objectives of maintenance of a software application. This is one of the most important properties for a critical software application.

Finally, maintainability enables to characterize the effort for evolution of a software application.

Maintainability introduces constraints on:

– design: it is necessary to implement abstraction, modularity, readability and complexity management, taking into account best practices;

– execution: this involves taking into account performance constraints to ensure the possibility of being able to change the application (available memory size, processor load, cycle time, size of the data handled, number of processed messages, etc.);

– documentation: it must be complete and correct, legible, stored in a format to allow analysis and manipulation;

– diagnosis: ability for diagnostics such as logging, access to important variables, etc.

9.7.2.6. *Portability*

Portability is an important issue for software applications and can be summarized by the question: can the software application be transferred from one platform or runtime environment to another?

For critical software applications, that point is more difficult because it is necessary to revalidate the entire software application on a new platform, or redo the evaluation/certification.

This subject is associated with the concept of interoperability and encapsulation that characterizes the modular architecture (see section 2.3.3). AUTomotive Open System Architecture (AUTOSAR) and Integrated Modular Avionics (IMA) in the field of aeronautics) are environments that allow decorrelation of software application execution support.

9.7.2.7. *Reusability*

Reusability of a software application is often seen as an important property, but it is poorly understood. Reusability of software is often seen as the ability to use a *piece of code* for different projects. To do this, the code must be restricted to the minimum necessary for the current project and documented.

In most cases, implementation of a *piece of code* that can be reused involves developing a code with a superset of possibilities. The development team defines all the uses of this *piece of code*, but it is not possible to list out all uses for a given project.

While developing a software application, we must implement a decomposition module/component through an interface (API). The entire code must be simple and documented.

9.7.2.8. No defects

Sometimes a software application is considered to be "without fault". This property characterizes a software application that has followed a strict process involving several layers of verifications.

9.8. Measurement of complexity of a software application

Before we introduce effective quality management, we must introduce the concept of complexity of a software application. Complexity is a property that will impact testability of an application, code readability, ability to maintain the code, effort involved in verification and validation and ultimately the evaluation effort and/or certification of the software application.

Complexity can be expressed in terms of object sizes characterizing the software application such as the size of object name (variable, function, etc.), size of code lines, size of a function/procedure/service, number of instructions, execution path, size of conditions, etc.

Complexity is a method of characterizing the effort to understand, verify and maintain. The size and complexity of elements characterizing a software application must be balanced.

The measurement of complexity is based on the metric definition (measurements performed on documentation, code, testing, etc.) and objectives to be followed. In Volume 2, we introduce the various metrics used and their uses.

9.9. Development cycle

9.9.1. Introduction

As stated earlier, the development of a software application is divided into several steps (specification, design, coding, testing, etc.). This refers to lifecycle. A lifecycle is required to describe the dependencies and sequencing between activities.

Lifecycle must take into account the progressive refinement aspect of development and possible iterations. In this section, we shall discuss the lifecycle used to achieve a certifiable software application.

As shown in Figure 9.3, there are several cycles (1) V cycle, 2) cascade cycle, 3) spiral cycle, etc.) for developing a software application, but the cycle recommended by the several standards (EN 50128 [CEN 01a] DO 178 [ARI 92], IEC 61508 [IEC 11] ISO 26262 [ISO 11]) is cycle V.

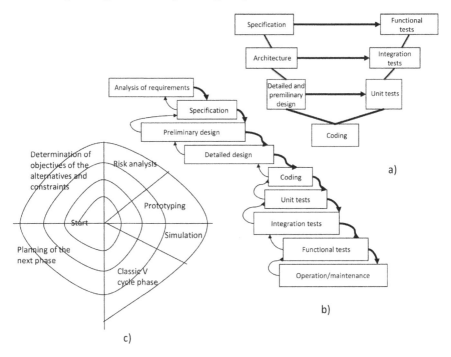

Figure 9.3. *Three possible lifecycles*

9.9.2. *Various lifecycles*

9.9.2.1. *Iterative cycle*

An *iterative* cycle is a development mode in which the activities were carried out in a predetermined order for iteration and this sequence is reproduced identically as many times as necessary.

This development mode implies that the project is divided into a number of iterations. The duration of the iterations is not necessarily identical, "agile" approaches where the duration is fixed.

The initial iterations enable, in general, to remove major risks of a project and take into account the requirements and priorities for future structuring of the project. It is during the initial iterations that the architecture of the software application is defined. This architecture will accommodate the later productions of each iteration.

9.9.2.2. Incremental cycle

An *incremental* cycle is intended to successively create functional elements of the product used directly. The project is divided into a number of deliverables and these elements are called increments. Each increment is an operational product, partially at the beginning of the cycle (with reduced scope) and totally at the end of the cycle (with full scope).

An increment is a functional sub-part consistent with the final product. It is characterized by the following:

– each increment adds new functions;

– each increment is tested as a final product;

– increments are defined *a priori* (this implies a prior classification of requirements).

9.9.2.3. Cascade cycle

The cascade or "waterfall" cycle is undoubtedly the oldest development cycle. In this mode, shown schematically in Figure 9.4, the project activities are linked sequentially with little or no retro-gradation. An activity starts when the previous one is completed. There may also be some more or less parallelization or overlapping activities. Each stage is connected downstream to an upstream stage; the deliverables of one stage are inputs for the other. At the end of the cycle, the deliverable of all activities is the finished product, ready to be commissioned.

Figure 9.4 is limited to a short cycle; the test step can be divided into several steps as shown in Figure 9.3(b).

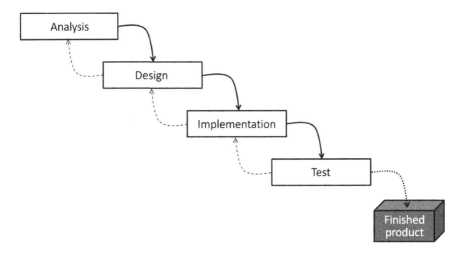

Figure 9.4. *Cascade or "waterfall" cycle*

9.9.2.4. *Spiral cycle*

A spiral development mode (see Figure 9.3(c)) combines the iterative mode and incremental mode. It combines the advantages of both approaches and is very well suited for developing applications or systems where requirements change constantly or when the scope of the product is not well known at the beginning of the project.

9.9.3. *V cycle*

Finally, definition of a development cycle involves management of various aspects such as: implementation of development cycles, management of requirements traceability, change management, configuration management, tool management, etc.

Figure 9.5 shows the V cycle as it is usually presented. The objective of requirements analysis is to verify the adequacy of customer expectations and technological feasibility. The objective of the specification phase is to describe what the software should do (not how it should do it). In general, while defining the architecture, we try to create a hierarchical decomposition of the software application as module/component and identify the interfaces between these elements. A description of each module/component (data, algorithms, etc.) is given as part of the design. Often the design phase is divided into two steps. The first step, called preliminary design, aims to identify the manipulated data and services required, the second step, called detailed design, describes all services using their algorithms. Coding phase then follows design phase.

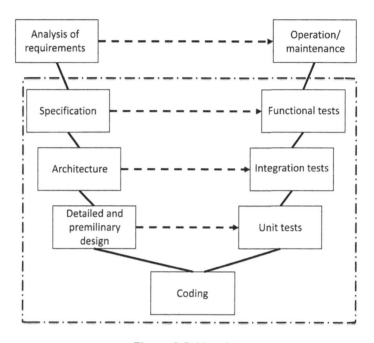

Figure 9.5. *V cycle*

Figure 9.5 shows that there are different phases of testing: unit testing (focused on lower-level components), integration testing (focused on software and/or hardware interfaces) and functional testing which demonstrates whether or not the product conforms to its specification. Operation/maintenance phase is related to the operational life and management of possible developments.

It must be noted that there is a horizontal correspondence (dotted arrow) between the specification, design and testing activities (see Volumes 2 [BOU 16a] and 4 [BOU 17]). V cycle is split into two phases, descending phase and ascending phase.

Activities of the ascending stage should be prepared during the descending phase. Figure 9.6 is closer to the recommended V cycle.

9.9.4. Verification and validation

Development of a software application must take into account the design of the software application as well as the activities that demonstrate that the software application has attained a certain level of quality. Achieving a quality level involves demonstrating that there are no defects introduced during the design phase and that the product meets identified requirements.

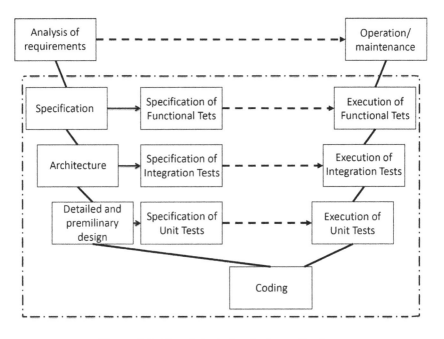

Figure 9.6. *V cycle including test specifications*

As shown in Figure 9.7, verification involves finding faults within the V cycle and validation involves demonstrating that the product corresponds to its requirements, hence its location at the top of the V cycle. Verification and validation activities are introduced and analyzed in detail in Volume 2 [BOU 16a].

9.10. Vocabulary and mode of expression

During all the phases involved in the implementation of a software application, it is necessary that the persons involved in interpreting the documents do it in the same manner.

For this, it is necessary to define a unique vocabulary for the project by creating a glossary (GL) and include modes of expression and description that are understandable to all persons involved in the development of the software application. If it is not possible for historical reasons, to define a unique vocabulary; various meanings of the terms used must be cited with their references.

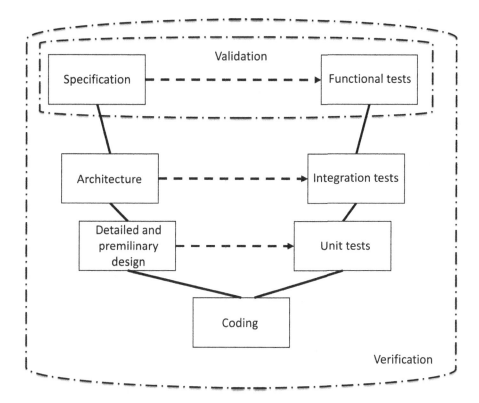

Figure 9.7. *V&V in the V cycle*

Hence, we must identify a glossary in the project documents and in industry processes, and train the personnel by creating a common framework of expressions and drafting documents.

Verification procedures should help to remove ambiguities and incorrect formulations. For this, the associated controls must identify rules to verify understanding of the texts.

9.11. Organization

9.11.1. *Introduction*

One of the major topics in the quality management of a project involves human resource management. Human resource management covers the establishment of an organization (see Figure 9.8) and skills management.

The establishment of an organization should define hierarchical lines for a project, define the connection between the services/departments of the company and ensure independence whenever necessary.

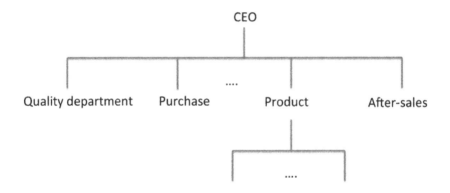

Figure 9.8. *Basic organization of a company*

9.11.2. *Organization type*

For example, the standard CENELEC 50128:2011 provides three types of organizations depending on the safety level. Figure 9.9 represents a complete organization for SSIL3/4 software.

In the gray area, we see two roles (QUA and PM) that are not part of CENELEC 50128:2011 but are introduced by the application of ISO 9001:2008 and safety management request (see CENELEC 50126 [CEN 00] for example).

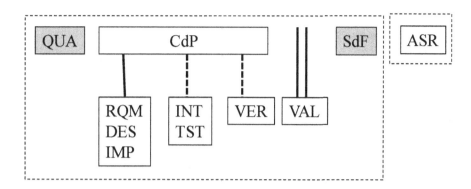

Figure 9.9. *Architecture type for SSIL3/4 as defined in CENELEC 50128*

Figures 9.9 and 9.10 identify reporting lines and independence. The dotted boxes represent two independent organizations.

Development of a software of high-level safety (SSIL3-SSIL4, DAL A, ASIL D, etc.) requires at least eight people on the project who must assume eleven roles:

– QUA: the Quality Engineer is responsible for verifying the proper implementation of quality procedures and company rules on the project as well as the correct implementation of plans (SQAP, PVV, SCMP, etc.);

– PM: the Project Manager is responsible for managing and organizing implementation of activities;

– RQM: the Requirements Manager is responsible for specifying the requirements (see Table 5.2);

– DES: the Designer is responsible for building the architecture and developing software design;

– IMP: the Implementer is responsible for activities from designing to code execution;

– INT: Integrator is responsible for integration of software components that have been already tested, this integration extends until the completion of the software;

– TST: the Tester is in charge of performing tests on a component or the entire software;

– VER: the Verifier is responsible for carrying out checks; these checks may concern a document, a file, process, etc.

– VAL: the Validator is responsible for confirming that on the basis of various activities whether or not the software is validated;

– SM: the Safety Manager is in charge of carrying out safety studies related to the software aspects (SEEA, RCC, followed safety requirements, etc.);

– ASR: the Assessor is an independent evaluator of the production team and must certify SSIL of the software.

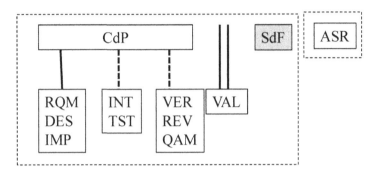

Figure 9.10. *Architecture type for SSIL3 / 4 as defined in IEC 62279*

This hierarchy highlights the fact that a single person cannot develop a software application correctly and that a skill set is required for each phase.

It must be noted that in IEC 62279:2014 [IEC 14], quality has been addressed through the introduction of QAM (Quality Assurance Manager) that was added to from VER's aspect. IEC 62279:2014, thus, uses the same approach, but there are new roles (see Figure 5.7) as the CGM (Configuration Manager) and REV (reviewer); Appendix B of the standard contains the following additional roles:

– QAM: the person in charge of Software Quality Assurance Planning (SQAP) and verification of the correct implementation of plans;

– CGM: the person in charge of configuration management and to produce associated documents (SCMP, SVF[7]);

– REV: the person in charge of document review at the output of each phase.

9.11.3. *Skills management*

The various industry standards recommend skills management. For example, clause 5 of CENELEC 50128: 2011 emphasizes skills management, especially for the formalization of this management.

---

7 SVF is Software Version File, classically known as "release-note".

Ideally, SQAP must contain elements demonstrating the skills of people according to the roles they assume, but this management can be formalized at the company level.

These management skills and/or justifications cannot rely solely on the management of Curriculum Vitae (CV). The suitability of persons must be demonstrated adequately for the attributed roles.

One of the challenges in skills management is the management of the skills of people external to the company (in-house, outsourcing, expert, etc.). The Labour Code and Trade legislation introduced a ban to skills management of external personnel but the ISO 9001: 2008 does not permit external skills management.

In railway projects, we must establish a management process (definition of position, skills identification, identification of expected training, etc.) to demonstrate that external people are competent and can fulfill the roles assigned to them.

When outsourcing (fixed-price projects), it is necessary to demonstrate that the contractor has skills management and allocation management for projects, and the customer must perform at least one audit to check the suitability of skills management processes. In general, the audit of the subcontractor is performed simultaneously with the audit to demonstrate compliance with ISO 9001: 2008.

Appendix B of CENELEC 50128: 2011 and IEC 62279: 2014 identifies the roles and responsibilities and skills for each role (see Table 9.1). Note that for each role the standard (at least the relevant part of the standard) and the regulatory framework must be known.

This example of role definition is applicable/adaptable to any sector.

For the management of external people involved in a project, it is important to ask for a proof of training in CENELEC 50128: 2011 standard (the application may be extended to the entire CENELEC standards) and in the legislative context.

Based on the definition of roles (Table 9.1) it is possible to define job descriptions (Figure 9.10) to be instantiated for each individual project. They are used to define skill levels to be compared with the actual skills.

Role: Requirements manager (RQM)
Responsibilities: – must be responsible for specifying the relevant software requirements – must be the owner of software requirements specification – must establish and maintain traceability to and from the system requirements – must ensure that the requirements related to specifications and to software are taken into account in managing modifications and configurations including the status, version and authorization status – must ensure consistency and completeness in software requirement specification (with reference to requirements of the user and final environment of the application) – must develop and maintain software requirement documents
Main skills: – must be competent in requirements engineering – must have experience in application field – must have experience of safety criteria in application field – must understand the comprehensive roles of the system and the application environment – must understand the analytical techniques and their results – must understand applicable regulations – must understand the requirements of the standard CENELEC 50128

Table 9.1. *Extract of Appendix B of standard*
CENELEC 50128:2011

Figure 9.11 introduces an example of a resource process that is organized around an allocation phase. The input of the allocation phase has the job descriptions for each role, defining the skills and their expected levels, and the list of people (internal and external to the company) who must be involved in the project. Outputs of the allocation phase are the justifications that show that people allocated to each role are competent. For this, we must be able to link a person to a role and must have proof that indicates whether the expected skills are acquired or additional training is needed.

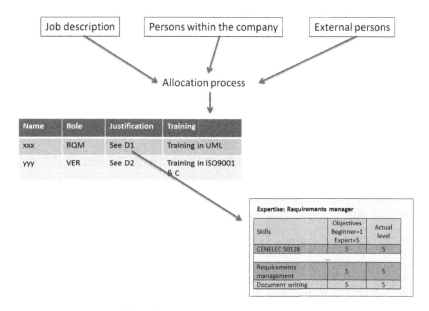

Figure 9.11. *Example of allocation*

9.12. Configuration management

The software is part of the equipment that must be managed in terms of configuration; hence, we must have a *Configuration Management Plan* (CMP). The CMP must cover all aspects of the equipment: pneumatic, mechanical, electrical, electronic, hardware, software, maintenance tools, etc. The CMP describes the naming rules, versioning rules, means of configuration management, organization, responsibilities, etc., and the content of version sheet.

With regard to configuration management of software, we must be able to know, at any given time, the list of items produced in the framework of development of software applications and associated versions.

It must be indicated that the sources and the executable generation process are just a few elements in software development and that all documents produced (drawings, specifications, design documents, test records, verification documents, end phase report, etc.), different scenarios and test results[8] (CT, S/S and S/H IT, GT), results of verification equipped phases (summary files, metric summary file, code analysis report, etc.) and the tools used in the whole process must be taken into account.

---

8 The strategies for components tests (CT), integration tests (IT) and group tests (GT) are introduced in Chapter 7.

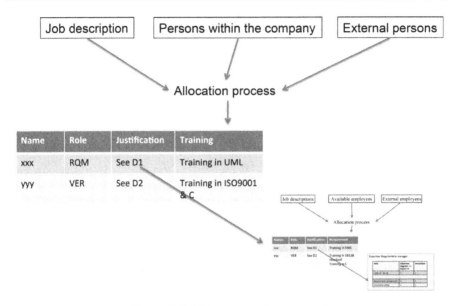

Figure 9.12. *Management process of resources and skills*

Role: Configuration Manager (CGM)
Responsibilities:
– must be the owner of the configuration management system
– must establish that all requirements related to software are clearly identified and are updated in terms of version in an independent manner within the configuration management system
– must prepare delivery sheets mentioning the incompatible versions of the software components
Main skills:
– must be competent in software configuration management
– must understand the requirements of IEC 62279

Table 9.2. *Extract from Table B.10 of standard IEC 62279:2014*

Software configuration management involves the establishment of a Software Configuration Management Plan (SCMP). SCMP defines the general approach (what, when and how) and the arborescence(s) to archive all the elements (source, documents, files, tools, etc.) and people in charge of managing and controlling configuration management. The proposed process is to define the content of the software version file (SVF). The standard IEC 62279: 2014 introduces a specific role for this activity and job description (Table B.10).

The configuration management plan should identify a control activity; it is not acceptable to discover at the end of the project that the elements are lost or the configuration is inconsistent. This verification activity can be done through configuration audits. The quality team may carry out such audits.

Configuration management and definition of the versions are presented in Volume 2 [BOU 16a] of this series.

9.13. Safety assurance management

Consistent with Chapters 4 and 5, the safety team must identify the functional requirements related to safety and the safety integrity requirements, and must follow all requirements throughout the cycle.

Safety team must ensure that all safety-related requirements are assumed by the software application during its development as well as during commissioning on withdrawal. The safety team must therefore ensure that each safety-related requirement is properly addressed during the development of the software application; the team must also analyze all the software residual faults to check the impact on the system and analyze each modification performed during the maintenance phase in order to demonstrate that the changes have no impact on safety.

Figure 9.12 shows an example of a situation for verification of requirements. The requirements of the higher level are divided into the following levels associated with testing. The safety team must ensure that the safety requirements are properly processed, which is indicated by the gray box.

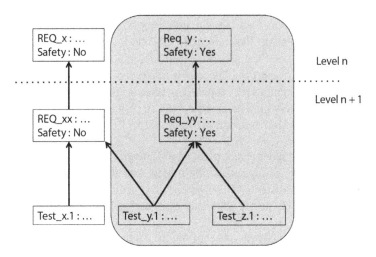

Figure 9.13. *Example of requirements traceability*

The activities of the safety team with regard to a software include the following:

– identification of safety requirements for the software, through summary of safety documents *Preliminary Risk Analysis* (PRA), *System Hazard Analysis* (SHA), *Interface Hazard Analysis* (IHA), *Subsystems Hazard Analysis* (SSHA) and *Hazard-Log* (HL);

– participation as a verifier of the whole document reviews to demonstrate that the safety requirements are met by the software;

– analysis of the coverage of safety requirements by the tests (unit, component, integration, all tests);

– event analysis sheets describing the residual faults;

– identifying exported constraints on software use;

– *a priori* analysis of change requests on software application;

– specific analyses related to the demonstration of software safety as the software effects and error analysis (SEEA – see [AFN 90] and [GAR 94], and/or the critical code review CCR);

– management of the independent evaluation; it is necessary to have proper interaction with the independent assessor (ISA) and manage the impact of comments and questions about the project.

As stated in Chapter 5, it is important that the safety activities related to a software application be formalized, and a SSAP be produced.

9.14. Software Quality Assurance Plan

In order to develop a software application, a Software Quality Assurance Plan (SQAP) must be established. The SQAP defines the organization and methods to be implemented to design and develop a software application, specifying the role of each person involved in the process.

SQAP must also describe management changes and non-conformances that may arise during the implementation or operation of the software. Appendix A (section 9.18) provides the content type of a SQAP.

For a given project, you must identify the software implementation process (e.g. V cycle in Figure 9.7), quality objectives, procedures implemented to develop the product and conditions of development. The V cycle is the implementation cycle that is recommended by various standards for development of software with a safety impact.

For this, each project must develop a Project Quality Plan (PQP). The PQP is a document describing the specific steps taken by a company to ensure the quality of products or services in question at the project level. Generally, all company procedures do not apply to the project and special features are taken into account (innovation, business outsourcing, etc.)

Quality management of a software application requires the establishment of a process for developing a software application as well as defining means for implementation. The means include human resources, material resources, the means in terms of methods and processes and tools.

The SQAP has several objectives (see Appendix A) that include:

– defining project organization, for example organization as identified in Figure 9.10;

– demonstrating the relevance between the persons allocated and the roles;

– defining the software development cycle which must take into account the aspects of development, verification, validation and evaluation;

– for each phase of the cycle, identifying the applicable procedures, guides, input and output elements and activities to be carried out (see Figure 9.13);

– demonstrating conformance with the standards (DO 178, CENELEC 50128, ISO 26262, etc.).

With regard to project organization, as a general rule, SQAP introduces the lifecycle and defines completely the design phases and calls for (see Figure 9.8) a Software Configuration Management Plan (SCMP), a Software Verification Plan (SVEP) and Software Validation Plan (SVAP).

Input documents

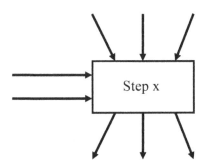

Step x

Output documents

Figure 9.14. *Description of a step*

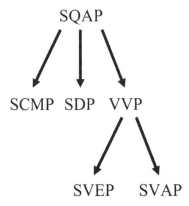

SQAP

SCMP SDP VVP

SVEP   SVAP

Figure 9.15. *Hierarchy of plans*

In some cases, the software verification plan and software validation plan are grouped under the Verification and Validation Plan (VVP) which covers verification of each phase of the lifecycle, unit testing, integration testing (software/software and software/hardware) and validation tests of targets.

The plans related to software implementation (SQAP, VVP and/or SVEP, SVAP) must be checked and the Quality Verification Report (QVR) must contain the results of this verification. This verification must be able to prove conformance with QAM of the company and with the objectives of SSIL standard.

It is necessary to control the quality of a project; for this, we must establish a set of metrics to evaluate the project and to identify difficulties. The possible metrics include: number of faults, number of versions, number of processed and/or tested requirements, etc. These metrics are essential and identify critical situations such as peak load, weak quality control, lack of skill, etc.

9.15. Defect management

The main result of implementing the quality management process is to highlight faults/failures. Formalization of activities associated with a quality control must identify failures (software failure, human failures, failures in the implementation process, etc.) and associated faults (errors). In general, anomalies are generated by verification and tests activites.

It is thus necessary to establish fault management. Defect management is based on a process of identifying faults (software bug, faults in data, faults in documentation, failure in implementation processes, etc.) and analysis process and correction of defect (see Figure 9.15).

A defect is characterized by at least three attributes:

– a unique identifier;

– activity that enables to identify the anomaly;

– description of the fault.

The feedback on the implementation of critical application shows that the testing activities represent 50–75% of cost of implementation and that presence of defects can increase the deadlines by two or three times.

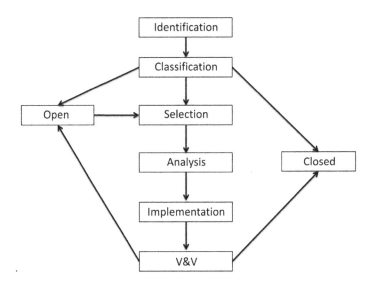

Figure 9.16. *Defect management cycle*

The increase in time is induced by the discovery of defects, identifying, analyzing their effects (impact on safety and/or reliability of the software application), selecting the faults to be corrected, analysis of faults, implementing corrections and verification of corrections (usually verification of proper implementation of the changes requires a series of tests but it will be necessary to check that no further changes are to be implemented).

Defect analysis is performed through impact analysis (definition 9.2) and regression analysis (definition 9.3). In some cases non-regression is said to be total, and for this, it is necessary to re-run all the tests in one or all phases. The objective of non-regression analysis is to minimize the cost of a new version.

DEFINITION 9.2 (Impact analysis).– *The impact assessment of an anomaly is to identify the changes to be made in the descending phase (impact on documents, impact on code, impact on description and implementation of tests) of the development.*

DEFINITION 9.3 (Non-regression analysis).– *Non-regression analysis is to determine a set of tests to demonstrate that the modification carried out has no effect on the rest of the software application[9].*

---

9 It must be noted that a non-regression analysis can be carried out on software application or on a more important element such as an equipment, subsystem and/or a system.

In addition, it must be noted that the cost of the correction of a defect is directly related to the phase in which it was identified. In fact, the detection of a defect in functional test phase costs 10 to 100 times more than a defect identified in unit test phase. This cost is related to the means that have been implemented until the discovery of the defect and the difficulty of performing the functional tests (using a target equipment, need to take into account of real-time observational difficulty, technicality of the people involved, etc.).

Our feedback (as an evaluator/certifier of the railway system) leads us to conclude that the phases of unit tests and integration tests are generally not as effective as the industries consider them to be, and that:

– unit tests are most often useless (in general, unit tests are defined by code);

– software/software integration can be summarized as a big-bang integration (integration of the entire code instead of a module by module integration), and at worst the entire code is compiled in one go and integration comes down to a verification of interfaces by the compiler;

– software/hardware integration is supported by functional tests on target. If the entire software runs correctly on the target machine, the integration is said to be correct.

Cost and time management has two requirements:

– reducing the number of defects introduced in the software application during descending phase of the V cycle;

– early identification of the defects introduced in software application.

In Volume 2 [BOU 16a], there is a more detailed presentation of defect management (defect record, analysis cycle, organization, etc.).

9.16. Maintenance of a software application

To conclude this chapter, it must be noted that the maintenance of a software application is a real challenge. It not only involves the ability to modify a code but to ensure the continuity of services provided by a software application for a longer duration and on various types of equipment.

This point must be taken into consideration in the design of software applications (it must be possible to upgrade software) while completely documenting the software application and the processes of developing it. One of the actions to be implemented is related to the regeneration of the same executable to verify if it is possible to replace a complete runtime environment and if it produces the same executable. This is discussed in more detail in Volume 2 [BOU 16a].

9.17. Conclusion

In conclusion, quality is not just a "word" (and certainly not "bad") but a process. This process must be applied at each stage of the development of a software application and must facilitate management of a product and its components (hardware, software, etc.).

Quality is thus linked to two important words: "pre-established" and "systematic". This requires that the processes, procedures and guides be predefined and used consistently. Software quality management is achieved through process management.

Figure 9.16 shows that quality is the intersection of three requirements; there must be a pre-established and systematically used quality framework (procedures, standard plan, guide, checklist, etc.) and a set of competent persons, organized and independent with adequate tools. Qualification tools will be discussed in detail in Volume 2.

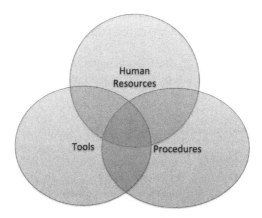

Figure 9.17. *Three quality requirements for a software application*

9.18. Appendix A – Structure of an SQAP

SQAP for a railway project must contain the elements that are described below in this section. SQAP is divided into several documents as shown in Figure 9.12.

The topics include:

– Section 1: identification of standards and mandatory regulations. The objective of this section is to identify the set of standards and regulations to be observed while developing software. It is necessary to clearly identify the titles, references, and versions of these documents;

– Section 2: organization of the project (software part), demonstration of independence and skills justification (it may rely on a processes local to the project and HR management of the company);

– Section 3: presentation of the scope of the software to be developed;

– Section 4: presentation of quality control and management (metrics, control points, audit, etc.);

– Section 5: presentation of development cycle of software (V cycle, etc.) and each phase. For each phase, a subsection must describe the input elements, output elements, activities to be performed, human resources, technical resources (tools, test environments, laboratories, etc.) and acceptance criteria and management of the end stage;

– Section 6: presentation of configuration management (tool, procedure, identification of versions, identifying items to be managed, etc.). The procedure for creation of the software version sheet must be explained;

– Section 7: presentation of the fault management process, requests for amendments and corrections;

– Section 8: presentation of the tool management process (identification, configuration management, etc.) and, more specifically, management of tool qualification;

– Section 9: list of documents to be produced during software development;

– Section 10: demonstration of compliance with the standards identified in Section 1.

9.19. Glossary

ASIL:	Automotive SIL
AUTOSAR[10]:	AUTomotive Open System ARchitecture
CCR:	Critical Code Review
CENELEC[11]:	*Comité Européen de Normalisation Electrotechnique* (European Committee for Electrotechnical Standardization)
CMM:	Capability Maturity Model
CMMi[12]:	Capability Maturity Model for integration
CT:	Component Test
DAL:	Design Assurance Level
EMC:	Electromagnetic Compatibility
EU:	European Community
GT:	Group test
HL:	Hazard-Log
HR:	Human Resources
IEC[13]:	International Electrotechnical Commission
IHA:	Interface Hazard Analysis
IMA:	Integrated Modular Avionics
ISA:	Independent Safety Assessor
ISO[14]:	International Organization for Standardization
IT:	Integration test
MOA:	*Maîtrise d'ouvrage* (Contracting Authority) ‑
MOE:	*Maîtrise d'œuvre* (Project Management)
PDCA:	Plan Do Check Act
PQP:	Project Quality Plan

---

10 http://www.autosar.org.
11 www.cenelec.eu.
12 http://www.sei.cmu.edu/cmmi.
13 http://www.iec.ch.
14 http://www.iso.org/iso/home.htm.

PRA:	Preliminary Risk Analysis
QA:	Quality Assurance
QAM:	Quality Assurance Manual
QAP:	Quality Assurance Plan
QMS:	Quality Management System
SEEA:	Software Errors and Effects Analysis
SHA:	System Hazard Analysis
SIL:	Safety Integrity Level
SPICE:	Software Process Improvement and Capability dEtermination
SQAP:	Software Quality Assurance Plan
SQUARE:	Software QUAlity Requirements and Evaluation
SSIL:	Software SIL
V&V:	Verification and Validation

10

Requirement Management

10.1. Introduction

Requirements engineering is a need that appears in all industry standards (aerospace, automotive, railways, nuclear, electrical equipment, etc.). However, one difficulty is that no industry standards define what a requirement is. Industry standards introduce the concept of traceability (connection between various elements) and the concept of level (in aeronautics we have the concept of LLR and HLR for *Low Level Requirement* and *High Level Requirement*).

This chapter introduces engineering requirements and their implementation. The identified activities can cover the analysis of user requirements and development.

Requirements engineering is the discipline that involves establishing and documenting requirements. The various activities associated with requirements engineering are elicitation, specification, analysis, verification and validation, and management.

In general, a project begins with the requirements acquisition phase which involves constructing a specification of requirements. After requirement specification, the second phase is to achieve the requirements.

In reality, some projects begin with the analysis phase while others do not. Indeed, an institution wanting to develop new equipment must begin with an analysis phase, to build its specifications in the best possible manner.

For other projects, the requirements specification exists, even though it is in the form of functional specifications. It must be noted that for the second family of projects, several companies support the principal or leading industry to achieve the final system, and in this case, the requirements specification is used to manage the consistency of the entire system.

10.2. Requirement acquisition phase

10.2.1. *Introduction*

The first phase (see Figure 10.1), which can be named as the requirements acquisition process, is a four-step process (see Figure 10.2): elicitation of requirements, analysis (negotiation) of requirements, documentation of requirements and verification.

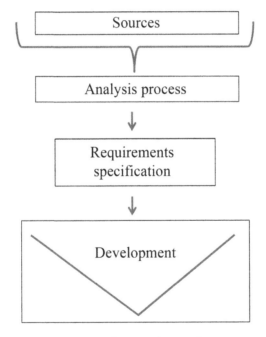

Figure 10.1. *Process in two phases*

The first step, called elicitation, involves identifying the problem (identification of stakeholders, sources, explicit and implicit requirements). The second step is to analyze the problem, to discuss and negotiate. This second step is very important because it is necessary to have the consent/assent of the user(s) on the requirements; the concept of negotiation is very important here to arrive at a consensus. The next step is to develop the requirement specification, which can be textual and/or supplemented by models. The last step involves requirement verification on the basis of the requirement specification; it is necessary to verify that the specification is consistent and complete.

The implementation phase is based on a cycle which must take into account the different life phases of the system.

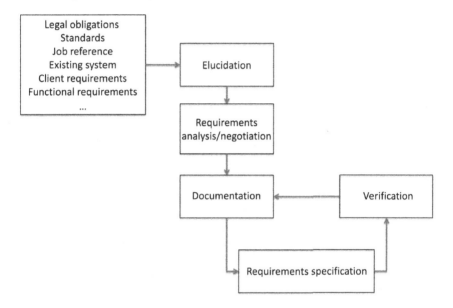

Figure 10.2. *Acquisition process*

In Chapter 2 of Ramachandran [RAM 09] and in Chapter 3 of Ramachandran [RAM 11], we presented examples of requirement management in the automotive and railway sectors.

10.2.2. *Elicitation of requirements*

10.2.2.1. *Introduction*

Table 10.1 is taken from the Standish Group [STA 94]; it highlights that over 30% of the causes of failure in developing systems arise from incomplete requirements, lacking description and unrealistic requirements.

One of the difficulties of requirement management is the definition of the concept of requirement. There are several studies that attempt to identify what a requirement is and how to take it into account. Hull [HUL 05] has one of the most comprehensive syntheses.

Description	%
Incomplete requirement	13.1
Requirement does not represent the user requirement	12.4
Improper resource management	10.6
Unrealistic requirement	9.9
Poor support from managers	9.3
Changes in requirements/specifications	8.7
Improper planning management	8.1
Not a requirement	7.5

Table 10.1. *Distribution of the causes of failure*

We consider definition 10.1, deduced from the studies carried out by the industries through AFIS[1].

DEFINITION 10.1 (Requirement).– *A requirement is a statement which reflects a need and/or constraints (techniques, cost, time, etc.). This statement is written in a language that can be natural, mathematical, etc.*

For clear identification, a requirement is a labeled element (the label allows for unique identification) that characterizes a system component to be developed. For each requirement, it is necessary to know the source which introduces the concept of source attribute. Table 10.2 characterizes a minimum requirement, an identifier, a text and a link on the source.

---

1 AFIS stands for *l'Association Française d'Ingénierie Système* (French Association for Systems Engineering). One of these work groups is specifically dedicated to requirement management. For more information, visit: www.afis.fr.

Attributes	Description
ID	Unique identifier
TEXTE	Requirement text
SOURCE	Element that enables to introduce the requirement

Table 10.2. *Attributes of a requirement*

The elicitation of requirements involves identifying, clarifying and justifying the requirements to be considered. The main difficulty lies in the fact that the requirement sources are numerous (see Figure 10.3): customer specifications, industry referential, existing system, similar system, interface systems, standards and applicable laws, user requirements, etc. The second difficulty lies in the fact that expression of the initial requirement is often incomplete and vague.

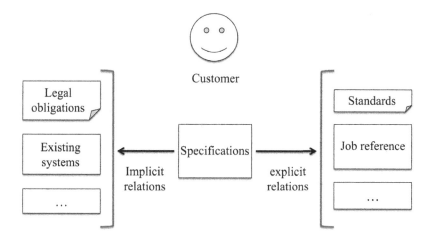

Figure 10.3. *Sources of requirement*

In documented sources, the person in charge of eliciting the requirements (referred to as an analyst) uses all kinds of documents; as the existing product documentation, fault reports written on earlier applications, documents from sectors (standards, laws, etc.) and technology (new technology, etc.) or analysis of previous requests for change.

But immersion with the end user (yet to be clearly identified) will raise expectations and comments on the functional aspects and especially on non-functional aspects. The particularly long response time of an application, problems of accessibility and usability will always be subject to comments that must be recorded for later use.

In the end, it is quite difficult to optimally combine all the means available to the analyst. The elicitation process involves:

– identifying stakeholders;

– identifying all sources of requirements to the extent possible;

– adapt a strategy to analyze the problem being addressed (systematic analysis of documentation, immersion with the customer, immersion with the end user, brainstorming session, etc.).

These three activities will be analyzed later in this chapter. There are different types of requirements, as shown in Figure 10.4.

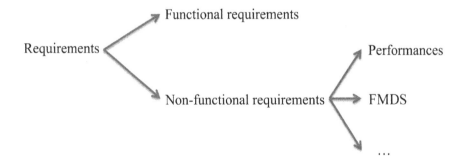

Figure 10.4. *Acquisition process*

The requirements can be classified into two families: functional requirements and non-functional requirements. Functional requirements are related to behavior and are therefore testable, whereas non-functional requirements are characterized by properties such as safety (due to damages to people, property and/or environment), security (compliance with labor rules, intrusion, data manipulation, etc.), availability, reliability, performance, maintainability, etc.

10.2.2.2. Identification of stakeholders

Generally, projects involve updating an existing product, and therefore the project stakeholders are well known; however, innovative projects are often characterized by some freedom. Hence, the stakeholder identification step is often overlooked. This neglect has a consequence on the construction of requirements referential that may result in incomplete coverage of requirements.

For certifiable systems, this can result in a lack of knowledge of applicable laws and standards. Thus, overlooking the stakeholders is often a cause of failure or significant delays of projects as the products delivered do not match the expectations of stakeholders (operators, managers, system managers and/or infrastructure, maintenance, users, authorities, certification body, etc.).

A stakeholder, by definition, is a person or entity that has an interest in the project. One way to obtain a complete overview of stakeholders is to ask the following questions:

1) Who is financing the project? Who is handling the budget?

2) Are there any sponsors for the project? If yes, who?

3) Who are the future users of the system? User, obviously but not exclusively, means the end user. We must consider system operation (operator, administrator, etc.), maintenance and withdrawal. Figure 5.4 shows several users (operators, road drivers, train drivers and maintenance staff).

4) Who are the people designing and testing the system?

5) Who is deploying the system and training the end users?

6) Are there authorities in charge of authorizing the system? There can be national, European and international authorities, each with a legislation and representative body.

7) Are there any existing systems in interface?

8) Are there any certification requirements?

Stakeholder-related requirements can be analyzed by creating a model of the environment in context and identifying the flows between parties. For this, we can create a context diagram, or ("horned beast") a bête à cornes diagram, as defined used in APTE[2] [BRE 00] methodology.

As part of a project to connect the railway equipment to a global network, we can build a bête à cornes diagram, that identifies the new system and the persons involved in interaction. On this basis, it is possible to identify functional constraints (without which the system cannot function) and main functions (expected services). Figure 10.5 formalizes the result of this study.

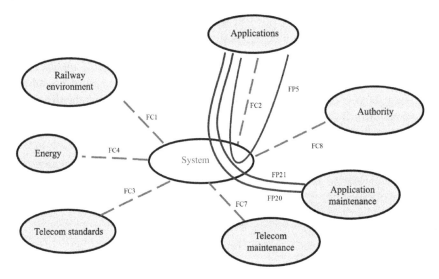

Figure 10.5. *Example of a bête à cornes (horned beast) model*

Figure 10.6 is an example of modeling (class diagram) that identifies users and user interactions. This model uses UML [OMG 11, ROQ 06, ROQ 07] and shows that the system to be developed (DRBCS) is a decentralized system that interacts with several types of actors (operators, train drivers, maintainers, road users).

---

2 The APTE method is a functional analysis and value analysis method. This method is also applicable to products, manufacturing processes, equipment and organizations. For more information visit http://cabinet-apte.fr.

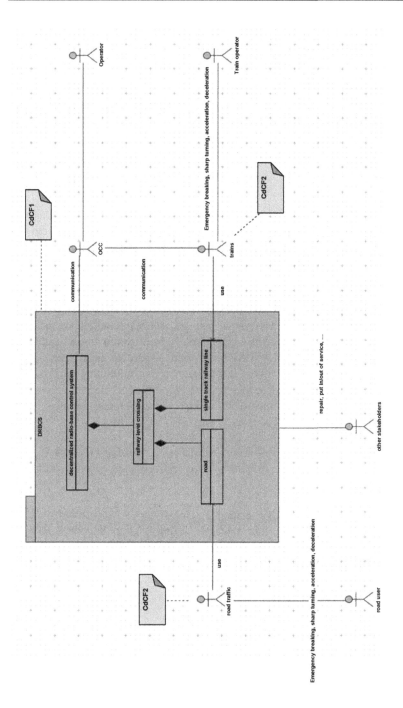

Figure 10.6. *Passage to computerized level and its users*

For each stakeholder, we must identify and clearly state what their interest in the project is. In general, a table with columns (see, for example, Table 10.3) responds to this need to identify stakeholders.

Name	Organization	Roles	Coordinates	Availability	Sector	Level of expertise	Objective/interest in the project

Table 10.3. *Example of stakeholder identification*

10.2.2.3. *Identification of sources*

Generally, a project is a response to a demand (usually in the form of an updated set of functional requirements) which is expressed by a stakeholder, who is the customer. Therefore, functional specifications are the primary source.

The functional specifications may contain requirements specific to the sector (aerospace, automotive, railways, nuclear, service, telecom, etc.) and/or refer to industry documents. If the product is subject to authorization (commissioning authorization, certification, etc.), the functional specification must state the standards (IEC[3], DO, CENELEC[4], ISO[5], etc.) and applicable legal texts (laws, orders, decrees) to be respected, except if they refer to basic information about the sector, but in general, it is preferable that they be properly identified. In addition to the standards and laws, the objectives (safety objective, performance, time, maximum load, certification objectives, etc.) must also be identified.

On a similar principle, if the system is intended as a replacement of an existing system, the documentation of the existing system and feedback become sources to be taken into account.

Note that in railways, the GAME principle (globally at least equivalent) is used while designing a new system; this principle enables us to benefit from past experiences (reuse of justifications, renewal of original principles, etc.) when designing a comparable system.

---

3 www.iec.ch.
4 www.cenelec.eu.
5 www.iso.org/iso/home.htm.

In general, functional specification is incomplete and based on the list of stakeholders; therefore, it is necessary to identify the associated sources. Figure 10.7 shows a summary of what may be the sources of a project.

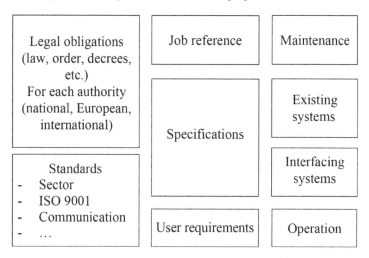

Figure 10.7. *Identification of sources*

10.2.3. *Analysis process and documentation*

10.2.3.1. *Process decomposition*

Based on the identification of stakeholders and knowledge of sources, it is possible to establish an analysis process (see Figure 10.8) which can be broken down into two stages: problem analysis (or requirements analysis) and the production of a product description.

This two-stage process is important, and many projects go directly to the production phase. This introduces a risk of not managing all requirements and, therefore, producing wrong or inadequate systems.

The analysis phase involves identifying requirements, analyzing all sources and selecting the known requirements and then, on the basis of stakeholders, it is possible to establish a requirement allocation step for stakeholders; this phase is followed by an analysis phase that analyzes the interactions between stakeholders and the system in order to identify the additional requirements.

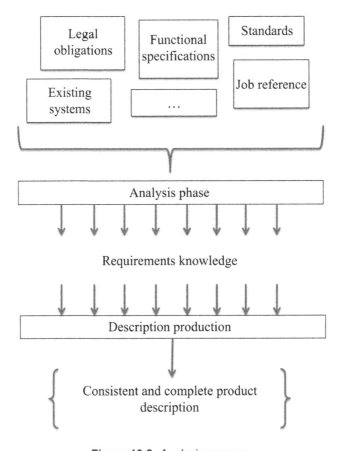

Figure 10.8. *Analysis process*

10.2.3.2. *Requirement analysis phase*

10.2.3.2.1. Objectives

The requirement analysis phase aims to collate all stakeholders' requirements. Note that the analysis phase enables us to identify the limits of the product (see Figure 10.9) and characterize interfaces with other products.

Figure 10.9 shows the environment of a system and/or application that comprises three inputs (E_i), two outputs (S_j) and three interfaces (I_k) with existing means (reused systems, power supply, etc.).

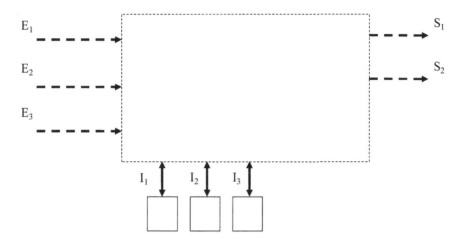

Figure 10.9. *Environment of the software application*

The requirements of stakeholders form the basis of whether or not a system is accepted, negotiation and agreement on the project, system development and management of changes of requirements. The requirements define the result as expected by stakeholders; therefore, it is necessary to obtain requirements to the best possible ability.

The following must be identified within the system:

– interfaces with the environment (see Figure 10.9); these interfaces can be electrical, mechanical, software-related, pneumatic, etc.

– states: stopped, running, degraded state, etc. (see, for example, Figure 10.10). The concept of state introduces partition between proper functioning, fall-back states and hazardous states;

– the concept of correct behavior, degraded behavior and dangerous behavior;

– the concept of functional and non-functional requirement.

With regard to the system states, Figure 10.10 identifies the correct and incorrect states, but we must go further and introduce all the states attainable by the system that characterize specific behaviors (fall-back, maintenance, degradation, etc.) as shown in Figure 10.11.

During the elicitation phase, it is necessary to consider the non-functional requirements and implement analyses related to dependability, to define the safety requirements but also the availability, reliability and maintainability requirements.

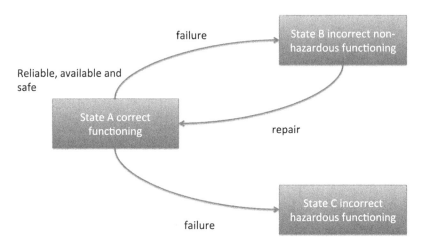

Figure 10.10. *Evolution of status of a system*

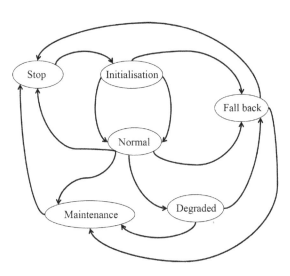

Figure 10.11. *Different states of the system*

Figure 10.12 shows a process taking into account elicitation of non-functional requirements related to RAMS.

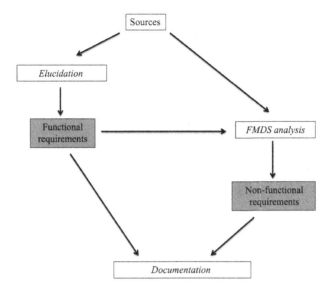

Figure 10.12. *Elicitation process with RAMS analysis*

10.2.3.2.2. Elicitation techniques

The objective of elicitation techniques is to help discover conscious, unconscious and subconscious requirements of the stakeholders. These techniques are selected based on risk factors, human and organizational constraints, business sector and the expected level of detail for requirements. Elicitation techniques can also be selected according to the requirement document to be drafted.

Based on the list of stakeholders and sources, it is necessary to establish a requirement acquisition process. There are various elicitation processes such as [ZOW 05]:

– investigative techniques: surveys, questionnaires, etc.;

– interview techniques;

– creative techniques: *brainstorming, storyboarding*;

– animation techniques: *brown paper*, role-plays, use cases;

– observation techniques: field, learning;

– prototyping and simulation techniques.

In appendix A of Meinadier [MEI 02], the author presents the methodological aspects related to requirements engineering. Requirements engineering is a tool that system engineering offers to implement as shown in the standard EIA-632 [EIA 98].

The best result is achieved when the analyst implements it along with several of these techniques.

As it is not possible to state all these techniques in an exhaustive manner in this book, in the following subsections we shall introduce only two techniques; however, the identified technology is implemented with respect to the project.

10.2.3.2.3. Interview techniques

An interview consists of the following steps:

– Questioning: questions are asked and answers are taken into account.

– Pause: during breaks, most people will find something to say and/or explain, which helps to capture additional requirements.

– Summary and/or reformulation phase: this phase is important because it enables to verify the understanding of the answers.

Interviewing involves a preparation phase, where a set of questions is prepared. This set of questions should identify the requirements of different stakeholders. This set of questions includes:

– Open questions: they require answers other than yes or no;

– Closed questions: they elicit yes or no answers. Closed questions are used to obtain a definitive answer (after reformulation, for example).

Note that during the interview, it is possible to add questions based on the responses and after the reformulation of answers step.

All the identified stakeholders must be interviewed and they must be made aware that their requirements must be considered as a whole (system). It is essential to take stakeholders seriously and not to pass judgment on the expressed requirements. During interviews, it is necessary to process all elements as requirements, document the importance of the requirements for each stakeholder, documenting the results of interviews and formalizing the acceptance of stakeholders of the interview results (notes, documents, etc.).

Conducting interviews requires the skill to stimulate and encourage stakeholders to respond. The person in charge of interviews must have strong abilities to manage a discussion and talk while being able to organize pauses.

10.2.3.2.4. Prototyping and simulation techniques

A model is the initial simplified modeling of a problem. A model helps in modeling certain aspects of the problem to be resolved in a more or less accurate manner. When the model handles the actual elements of the system (such as data files, etc.), it is called prototype.

Models and/or prototypes are a way to confront the vision of various stakeholders and expected behaviors (see Figure 10.13).

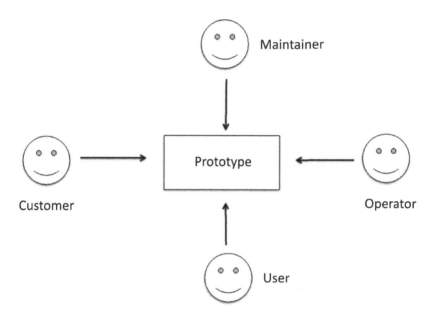

Figure 10.13. *Prototype and expression of requirement*

A prototype can be static, where we try to model the interactions between various elements, including actors, but it can also be dynamic, where simplified behaviors are modeled, and it is possible to run scenarios.

Developing a prototype is a good way to facilitate understanding of requirements, but this involves costs, and often the prototype is considered as the beginning of a solution.

It must be noted that, nowadays, more and more prototypes are used to validate a concept (website, etc.). The challenge with a prototype is not to lose sight that it is a prototype (which can be extremely successful) and that it is not the design of the final product.

10.2.3.3. Production phase of the description

The second step involves identifying requirements. The analysis and transformation processes intend to clarify the requirements text of the stakeholders and identify product requirements. Any conflict (two contradictory requirements or requirements with different objectives), incompleteness, unspoken requirements and others must be highlighted.

This step is an opportunity to remove the descriptive aspects and focus on the essentials. In fact, it is necessary to focus on the requirement and not on pseudo-solutions. At the end of this phase, we obtain a set of requirements that constitutes the description of the requirement.

In the end, we seek to produce a complete and consistent description of the requirements. Requirement specification is described under section 10.3.

10.2.4. Verification and validation of requirements

10.2.4.1. Introduction

In Figure 10.2, we identified the need to verify the requirements after the production phase of the requirements specification document. But we must also mention the concept of validation; in fact, the requirements identified with the customer are the source of customer tests that are usually called acceptance tests.

The development process of a system (subsystem/equipment/application) must take into account the design as well as the activities that show that the system has attained a certain level of quality. Achieving a certain level of quality involves demonstrating that no faults have been introduced during the design phase and that the product matches with the identified requirements.

Under the requirements and verification phase of requirement specification, it is necessary to show through a verification phase that the requirements specification has faults, and through the requirements validation phase that the product matches the customer requirements (see Figure 10.14).

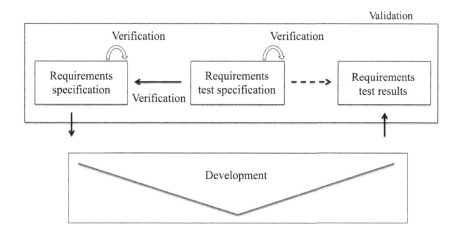

Figure 10.14. *Verification and validation*

10.2.4.2. *Verification*

Verification of requirements can be carried out through various activities such as:

– conducting a more or less formal design review (review, use of control list, etc.);

– creating a model and/or a prototype;

– preparing a list of tests (see Figure 10.15).

It must be noted that we are referring to verifications where the requirements of the stakeholders are properly taken into account; therefore, this verification must be carried out by the customer and supplier.

Requirement validation involves preparing acceptance specification of the system by the customer. This is one of the most important verifications to be performed.

As shown in Figure 10.15, based on requirements we identify test cases (CT_x); the test cases describe a situation to be achieved which is related to an equivalence class. Based on test cases, it is possible to prepare the test scenarios that describe a situation. A test case can, therefore, participate in several scenarios.

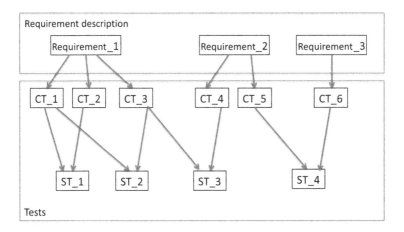

Figure 10.15. *Relationship between tests and requirements*

As the only input element at this level is the requirements specification, the tests are specified in the black box (without knowledge of implementation).

The customer or the entity representing employed by them must normally carry out acceptance tests, but with respect to the contract, maturity of the customer, maturity of the supplier, etc., the customer can decide to create their terms of acceptance tests on the basis of implementation of validation tests conducted by the supplier.

10.2.4.3. *Validation*

The development of acceptance tests requires availability of the system in its real environment. This is an important activity because it involves verifying if the finalized and installed product functions as expected by the customer. This phase is also called the validation phase and in standard CENELEC 50126 it is referred to as the acceptance phase.

10.3. Specification of requirements

10.3.1. *Characterization of requirements*

The requirements specification is a document that contains all the requirements that the product to be developed must meet. Definition 10.1 defines the concept of requirement and Table 10.2 defines the basic attributes that characterize a requirement.

10.3.1.1. *Identification*

A requirement should be uniquely identifiable; hence, in general, an identifier is associated with each requirement. This identifier must be unique. In order not to confuse it with other items that can be numbered (list items, etc.), the identifier is created using a label (e.g. EXI) and a unique number (xxxx). An identifier is therefore of the form: EXI_xxxx.

[EXI_0001]

The software must be updated.

[PROJECT] AAAA

[DOCUMENT] DDD

A requirement is associated with a project and especially to a document, and therefore has an identifier EXI_AAAA_DDDD_xxxx where AAAA represents the project number, DDDD is the document reference number and xxxx is the requirement.

Management of the project reference and document reference can, therefore, be integrated with the identifier or considered as an attribute.

[EXI_AAAA_DDD_0001]

The software must be updated.

To create a unique identifier, it is necessary not to reallocate the requirement numbers in case of deletion of requirement. For the same reason, mechanisms for automatic identification (e.g. the auto-numbering style in Word tool) must be avoided.

For identification of a requirement, it can be difficult to detect the end of a requirement, hence, it is useful to set up identification in the form of tags; see the following example.

[EXI_0002]

Software cycle must run in 100 ms.

[FIN_EXI]

10.3.1.2. *Some important characteristics*

Before defining requirements, we must develop a set of criteria. These criteria must enable to qualify requirements. An analysis of literature (scientific and/or normative) allows identification of the criteria related to a requirement and others relevant to a set of requirements.

For each requirement, the following criteria are often applicable:

– Atomic: the requirement is an identifiable and not a decomposable element; it expresses a simple fact;

– Concise: when it is described in natural language, a requirement should be written as a single sentence that does not exceed a few lines;

– Clear: the meaning of the requirement is easily understood on reading; the structure of the sentence must be simple and not use any literary subtleties;

– Accurate: all the elements used in the requirement are identifiable and fully characterized (no ambiguous questions such as: what is the unit used?);

– Abstract: a requirement is at appropriate level of abstraction; it must not impose a solution (technical or functional), but it should describe the need;

– Unambiguous: reading of the requirement allows understanding of the need with only one possible interpretation; it is necessary not to use phrases or words with several interpretations or complicate the understanding of the requirement;

– Up-to-date: the requirement reflects the current state of the system/its knowledge;

– Complete: all the concepts used in the requirement are defined and no information is missing;

– Verifiable: there are (reasonably) possible means to verify the requirement;

– Consistent: the requirement is consistent (all terms used in the requirement are the same and have the same meaning);

– Coherent: the requirement is not in conflict (requirement does not have any contradictions), consistent with the terminology (with glossary);

– Correct: it corresponds to a real requirement of a stakeholder (external consistency);

– Traceable: it is necessary to trace the source, change, impact, and use of the requirement.

There are other criteria that may also be necessary, for example, a requirement must be achievable, i.e. it must be possible to implement the requirement while respecting the constraints of cost, time and development.

Furthermore, even though there is a scope to add other criteria, the above-mentioned ones provide a good basis for requirement development methodology.

There are two main rules for understanding the requirements:

– use short sentences and paragraphs;

– formulate one and only one requirement per sentence.

10.3.1.3. *Characterization of all requirements*

For all requirements, the main criteria are coherence, completeness and non-redundancy.

All requirements must be:

– Complete: no requirement is missing and each requirement is complete. Completeness of all requirements is a difficult point, as it is linked to a comprehensive identification of the requirement. For example, it is easy to forget to mention the software behavior during undesired events (hardware failure, errors in the data entered by the user, etc.) in a specification. In such situations, it is not the developer's responsibility to invent the program behavior during implementation. It is necessary to ensure that the requirements include the following elements when identifying requirements:

– all manipulated objects;

– all states of manipulated objects;

– all use conditions;

– all use scenarios that have been considered;

– all applicable standards and industry referential, etc.

The best way to assess the completeness of a set of requirements is to create a document template;

– Consistent: there is no ambiguity or inconsistency in the requirements referential; there is no contradiction between the requirements, there is a unique identification of the document. Consistency of requirements involves the proper definition of concepts of all requirements; in other words, each word must be used in the same way for all requirements;

– Non-redundant: there must be no redundancy in all requirements; same information and/or same requirement must not appear more than once.

10.3.1.4. *Process characterization*

In terms of processes, all requirements must be:

– Identifiable: each requirement must be associated to a unique identifier (see the first attribute in Tables 10.2 and 10.4);

– Verifiable: all requirements must be verifiable. Verification can be in the form of review, modeling, specific analysis and/or test (see the fourth attribute of Table 10.4);

– Modifiable: It must be possible to manage changes in requirements throughout the life of the system (production, manufacturing, commissioning, maintenance, withdrawal); for this, configuration management process must be implemented (see the fifth attribute).

Attributes	*Description*
ID	Unique identifier
TEXTE	Requirement text
SOURCE	Element introducing the requirement
VERIFICATION	Associated verification activity
VERSION	Version associated to the requirement

Table 10.4. *List of attributes characterizing a requirement*

Table 10.4 introduces a second identification of attributes describing a requirement. We shall add this description as we progress in the chapter.

10.3.1.5. *Additional attributes*

The list of attributes can be complemented by the following requirement qualifying attributes:

– family (functional, RAM[6], safety, performance, etc.);

– state of the requirement: in process, to be validated, validated, implemented, etc.;

– priority (to be defined with respect to project);

– verifiable (yes/no);

– verification type (review, specific analysis, simulation, etc.);

---

6 Reliability, Availability and Maintainability.

– testable (yes/no);

– test types;

– source (who, when, etc.);

– state (to be processed, analyzed, rejected, etc.);

– document type;

– version;

– effort;

– allocation.

Attributes	Description	Values
ID	Unique identifier	EXI_AAAA_DDDD_xxxx
TEXT	Requirement text	
SOURCE	Element that introduces this requirement	
FAMILY		FONC, FMD, SEC, PERF
VERIFIABLE		YES / NO
VERIFICATION	Associated verification activity	Review Calculation Unit tests Integration tests Group tests
...		
VERSION	Version associated with the requirement	xx.yy

Table 10.5. *List of additional attributes characterizing a requirement*

Attributes must be defined at the beginning of the project and they must be properly defined; see Table 10.6.

Name of the attribute	*Version*
Semantic of the attribute	Version associated to the requirement
List of possible values	x.y
Semantic of values	x is the major indicator y is the minor indicator
Unit	NA

Table 10.6. *Definition of an attribute*

10.3.2. *Characterization of the requirements specification*

It has been indicated that a set of requirements must be non-redundant, consistent and comprehensive, but the requirements specification document must also verify the following additional criteria the document must be:

– structured: it must have a clear structure, easily read by all and allowing for targeted reading;

– modular: the requirements that belong together are combined under a clear structure, and are logically located with respect to each other;

– extensible (taking into account maintenance): it must have a flexible structure to accommodate changes;

– sufficient: there must be no need to refer back the source documents to understand the product;

– traceable: relationships must be established between requirements documents and other engineering documents.

10.3.3. *Expression of requirements*

10.3.3.1. *Natural language*

It is essential to express the requirements in natural language. Natural language is the foremost and easiest way to communicate requirements and achieve mutual understanding. The expression of a requirement in natural language aims to express the requirement as clearly as possible without any design detail.

It should be noted that this approach may seem the opposite of common approaches which aim to highlight the model, but the model can never replace the requirements in natural language. In fact, if a drawing can replace a thousand words, it is not easy to understand and we may require a thousand words to make sure the design is correct and complete.

The difficulty of natural language lies in the ability to express in different ways the same concept, and in the use of literary phrases that complicate a sentence and may introduce ambiguities. It is therefore necessary to establish rules for drafting requirements in natural language.

The first rule is to use and comply with a requirement template that must be defined for the project. This template can be based on the following rules (not exhaustive):

– a requirement to be of "subject + verb + predicate" form;

– consistently use the word "must", conjugated in present;

– use of active form;

– use of uniquely defined terms; this can be done through use of glossary (refer to the following section);

– avoid the use of adverbs that can be ambiguous;

– avoid negations; their use must be limited to safety requirements (the system must not…).

Here are a few examples of textual requirements:

[EXI_1]

A firearm must propel a bullet in a given direction.

[FIN_EXI]

[EXI_2]

A bullet must be expelled from the weapon chamber if the firearm is stopped or fired.

[FIN_EXI]

10.3.3.2. Creating a glossary

A difference in interpretation of the terms used by stakeholders is a common source of conflict and misunderstanding in requirements engineering. Therefore, it is especially important to agree on common terminology.

It is then possible to define all the relevant words in a glossary. We will find the business terms or specific technical terms under abbreviations and acronyms. If necessary and in order to make the link between the stakeholders, the glossary can identify synonyms and homonyms, but the general idea is to define a single vocabulary reference for the project.

The use of a glossary must follow strict rules:

– the glossary must be centralized and versioned; it is a referential;

– responsibilities related to maintenance of the glossary must be defined;

– the glossary must be maintained and accessible throughout the project;

– the use of the glossary is mandatory for stakeholders;

– all stakeholders must approve the glossary.

It is recommended to create a glossary at the earliest point, as all misunderstandings can lead to repetitions and especially to difficulties in understanding that may be discovered at a later stage and have a strong impact on effort and cost.

10.3.3.3. *Formalization*

The expression of requirements in natural language have a difficulty that is the declarative nature of the requirements; it can be quite difficult to translate a requirement in text, or its formulation may be longer than a small drawing or a mathematical formula. Hence, a requirement in textual language must rely on graphical representations and/or mathematical expressions.

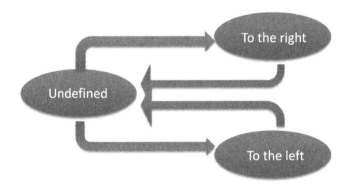

Figure 10.16. *Textual requirement complemented by a drawing*

Therefore, it is not uncommon to see requirements that are a mixture between a textual description and a drawing (see, for example, Figure 10.16).

```
MACHINE
     Example
SETS
            TRAIN
     ;      POSITION
VARIABLES
            Field
NON-VAIRANT
            Field : TRAIN - - >POW(POSITION)
     &      !(t1,t2). ((t1,t2: TRAIN*TRAIN) => (Field(t1) Λ Field(t2) = {}))
INITIALISATION
            Field :(              Field : TRAIN - - >POW(POSITION)
                          & !(t1,t2). ((t1,t2: TRAIN*TRAIN) => (Field(t1) Λ Field(t2) = {}))
                    )
END
```

Figure 10.17. *Model B of anti-collision property*

Formalization may involve development of mathematical equations and/or construction of a formal model. For example, Figure 10.17 shows an example of model B which is a formalization of property P1: there must be no risk of collision. The property can be expressed mathematically as follows:

$$\forall \{t_1, t_2\} \in [T], \text{ alors } D_{t_1} \cap D_{t_2} = \varphi, \text{ si } t_1 \neq t_2$$

10.3.3.4. Formulation using a pattern

The formulation template is an effective tool for the drafting of a requirement. Using a requirement template helps in preventing common mistakes when drafting the requirements in natural language.

A template is an excellent educational tool, especially effective in the learning phase. It is a guide to the syntactic structure of a unit requirement and is well suited to writing functional requirements. An example of a template is shown in Figure 10.18.

Combining glossary and drafting templates, we can reduce the ambiguity introduced by natural language.

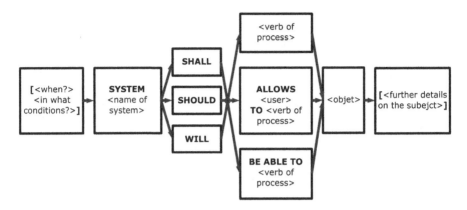

Figure 10.18. *Example of a formulation pattern of a requirement*[7]

10.3.3.5. *Modeling*

In order to ensure the correction and completeness of requirements, it might be advantageous to create one or more models. A model is an abstract description of a system and/or a process. Since this is a simplified representation, there is a reduction of complexity; the model is easy to handle and allows for justification and/or enables a number of verifications. The closer the modeling to the actual system, the closer the results observed on the final system.

Therefore, a model can be a tool for communication between various stakeholders.

A good model must focus on the problem, but it can describe a solution and must, therefore, be able to manage all or part of the final code. Thus, a model can be either executable or not.

In general, it is possible to have models dedicated to each step of the system implementation process; this refers to Model Based Development (MBD). In France, this is referred to as IdM for "*Ingénierie des Modèles*" (Engineering Models).

Modeling must be used in addition to a textual description of requirements; it must be able to express the requirement to be modeled. Implementation of a model without textual requirement refers to a requirement that has not been expressed and leads to the question of how to verify whether the model corresponds to a requirement.

---

7 Source translated from Pohl [POH 10].

A model, in general, consists of two complementary parts:

– static modeling describing the entities constituting the system and states that may be associated with it;

– dynamic modeling describing the status of authorized changes.

In Volume 3, there is an entire chapter dedicated to modeling.

10.3.4. *Validation of requirements*

A requirements specification enables identification of the user requirements based on which the customer can prepare the campaign of acceptance tests for the system.

The system acceptance tests are intended to show that the product meets the system requirements; acceptance tests must cover all user requirements.

10.4. Implementation of requirements

10.4.1. *Processes*

Figure 5.1 (Chapter 5) shows that once the requirements are specified it is possible to proceed to the second phase related to requirements development; must follow a cycle that demonstrates that the final product fulfills the requirements.

It must be noted that the term development refers to creating an application and not just developing an application. The implementation of an application involves development activities but also includes verification, validation, production, installation and maintenance of the application (see Chapter 9).

10.4.2. *Verification*

10.4.2.1. *Objective of verification*

Verification of a phase requires verification of the implementation of quality requirements (application of procedures, conformance of formats, etc.), process application (conformance with plans, with organizations, etc.), correction activities and proper consideration of safety requirements.

For each phase of the development process, there must be a verification phase with three objectives:

– the initial requirement must be considered: traceability between requirements of the higher level and requirements of current level must be established. This traceability must be verified: there must be a link and these links must be justified;

– the requirements must be correct: it must be demonstrated that the requirements are understandable, unambiguous, verifiable, feasible, etc. We must demonstrate that all requirements are complete and consistent (there must be no conflict);

– there are no non-traceable items introduced: the purpose of this verification is to check that all requirements being drafted are traceable to requirement of higher level. Very often, we see design and/or architecture requirements that have no connection to the next level. An analysis of these requirements shows that they are most often not specified and are very rarely design requirements. Further, a design and/or architecture requirement must be properly defined.

DAL	DCP
DAL_EX_1	DCP_EX_11, DCP_EX_12, DCP_EX_13
DAL_EX_2	
DAL_EX_3	DCP_EX_11

Table 10.7. *Example of a traceability table between architecture and design*

Under the first and third point, the traceability study (analysis of each line of traceability matrices) must enable to show that all requirements have been implemented and also that all requirements that are implemented are required.

10.4.2.2. *Document review*

The verification is done through a quick read (walkthrough) or a design review. A design review (see Figure 5.12) is a document verification which must have an objective. This can be formalized as a checklist.

This checklist (see Table 10.8) must define the control points. These are related to the knowledge of the types of faults that can be introduced during the activity which produced the documents to be verified.

Point	Rule	OK/KO state	Comment
R_1	All parent requirements must be traced or justified		
R_2	All document requirements must be traced with at least one parent requirement or justified		
R_3	All identified interfaces participate in at least one requirement		
R_4	All states of the system participate in at least one requirement		
R_5			
R_6	Is each requirement atomic (not necessary to read all requirements to understand one requirement)?		
R_7	Is every requirement verifiable?		
R_8			

Table 10.8. *Example of a list of controls with respect to requirements*

10.4.3. *Traceability*

Figure 10.19 shows how the customer recommendations can be distributed over the system and how the process can continue over the software and hardware elements. For the verification phase of level n_i, it must be possible to demonstrate that the requirements of this level are related to the higher level n_{i+1}. This linking is done by implementing a tracing action.

Implementation of traceability (see definition 10.2) requires definition of at least one link between two objects. For requirements, traceability links must be able to demonstrate that a requirement level n_i is related to a requirement of the previous level n_{i-1}. The reverse link can show that no requirement has been forgotten during the implementation process.

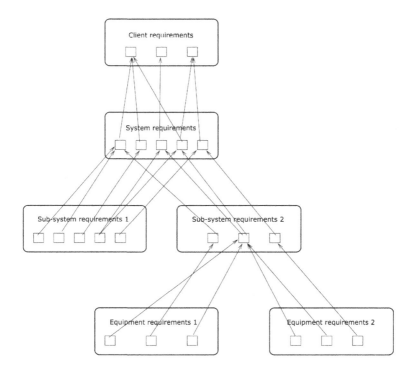

Figure 10.19. *Partial traceability between customer requirements related to equipment*

DEFINITION 10.2. (Traceability).– *Traceability involves creating a link between two objects.*

Traceability must be bidirectional and we must be able to establish:

– vertical traceability: trace a requirement from its highest level to its lowest level to show that irrespective of the level, all requirements are related to a need;

– horizontal traceability: trace a requirement through development and implementation process phases with the objective of demonstrating that a requirement is satisfied.

In requirements engineering, there are three traceability classes:

– upstream requirements traceability;

– downstream requirements traceability;

– inter-requirements traceability.

When traceability must be established for requirements, the following must be evaluated and defined:

– the level of granularity of a traceability link corresponds to the granularity of related elements. Should we trace unit requirements? Requirement sets? Use cases? Complete documents?;

– the semantics of traceability link: "derive", "satisfy", "develop", "verify", "use", "depends on", etc.

There are several ways to set traceability:

– through textual reference;

– through hyperlink reference;

– through internal reference to tool.

As shown in Figure 10.19, there are several requirement-based transformations. Among these, two cases are particularly interesting: adding and deleting a requirement. In either of these cases, it is essential to provide justification for the requirement.

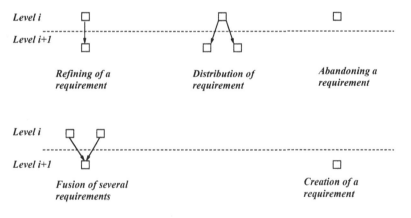

Figure 10.20. *Basic traceability of requirements*

Traceability defines the links between requirements. As shown in Figure 10.21, the basic link allows for connection between two requirements belonging to two consecutive levels.

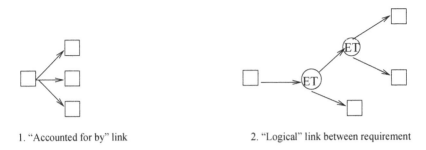

1. "Accounted for by" link   2. "Logical" link between requirement

Figure 10.21. *Link between requirements*

The requirements are associated with system functionalities. A functionality is an expected system behavior. The term functionality is used because at system level, there is no service such as a function but rather a comprehensive expected service (which is the result of a set of actions). Therefore, this process is divided over subsystems, equipment, hardware and software aspects.

Figure 10.22 shows a traceability matrix that allows for linking between requirements and functions but also between requirements and derived requirements.

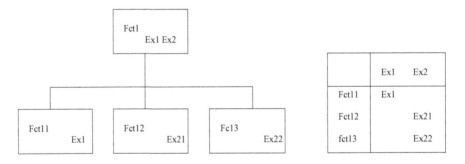

1. Functionality tree   2. Traceability matrix

Figure 10.22. *Requirements traceability matrices*

Item 1 of Figure 10.22 shows the functional relationship and association of requirements on both the levels. The function Fct1 is available in three sub-functions. As shown in item 2, the requirement Ex2 consists of two requirements (EX21 and EX22) that are associated with two sub-functions (Fct12 and Fct13) of function Fct1.

10.4.4. *Change management*

10.4.4.1. *Introduction*

Figure 10.1 shows a process whose requirements development phase can only be launched if all the requirements characterizing the needs are acquired and managed. In the event of a premature launch of the requirements development phase, the changes in requirements may have an impact on cost and time [STA 94, STA 01].

There are two types of projects:

– the requirement acquisition phase is carried out by the contracting authority and is part of a highly controlled process; in this context, the referential which is the output of requirements acquisition phase is quite stable and any change to this referential will result in a change in the contract;

– the acquisition phase is part of the project where the response to tender is prepared before the acquisition phase is finalized. In this case, all the requirements are not known and may change over a certain period. Therefore, it is necessary to have a change management process;

In addition to these two project families, we must also modulate the fact that certain products should be developed taking into consideration the regulatory and normative objectives. These latter are actually additional requirements that must be taken into account, but they have an impact on product management and prevent repeated engagement of requirements development in the finalized acquisition phase.

10.4.4.2. *Nothing is perfect*

As we have seen through the previous sections, definition of requirements is a process that is based on non-formalized elements and tries to identify the requirements that the system must meet. For this, the process must be iterative, and must accept that the requirements are subject to change. This means that the initial requirements can be improved during the application design.

These changes can be induced by difficulty in interpreting at the refinement and/or allocation of requirements on components, by change requests, by a difficulty (see impossibility) in performing tests, etc.

In order to handle this iterative process, a specific attribute defining the state of a requirement may be added. This attribute enables the consideration of, for example, proposed values, values under analysis, and accepted values.

10.4.4.3. *Accept the change*

Nowadays, customers no longer accept rigidity and feel free to ask for functional changes in a project under development. The designers of new products must, therefore, welcome this change in a positive manner.

Development of intelligent products (smart products) must respond to a dynamic market where customer needs are changing very rapidly in a very competitive environment. In this rat race, innovation must be the key to defining and developing new products, and it is better to be the first to bring to market a revolutionary product.

Changes in regulations, which impose increasingly heavy constraints on functionalities and the design of these products, also contribute to change dynamics, but in a moderate manner.

As a product designer, we must act quickly when faced with new requirements or a change in understanding customer requirements in the development process. This acceptance of change is a key strength of agility. We must, therefore, think of a new engineering process to respond to the "natural" development of requirements during the project.

These "agile" processes should be defined in advance at the earliest point and must not be the result of *ad hoc* processes. In this context, the requirements engineering process is a central process, as it ensures the satisfaction of customer requirements and traceability between requirements and the end product. Requirements must be considered as evolutionary artifacts that are always essential for the success of a project.

10.4.4.4. *Impact of change*

The analysis of changes is carried out through impact analysis (Definition 9.2) and non-regression analysis (Definition 9.3). In some cases non-regression is said to be total. For this, it is necessary to re-execute all the tests for one or all phases. The objective of non-regression analysis is to minimize the cost of a new version.

Requirement management is a tool to control developments. Thus, it is possible to define the impact cones associated with a requirement.

As shown in Figure 10.23, based on the modified requirements, it is possible to perform the impact analysis. For this, we extract the cone from the modified requirement and move toward code; this code is used to identify all the requirements of lower levels that are potentially affected by the modification and the associated test case.

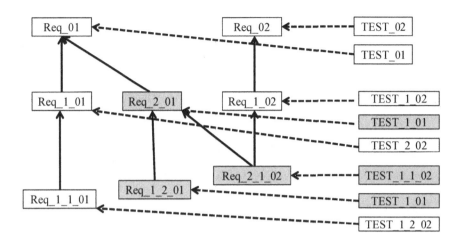

Figure 10.23. *Impact analysis*

The second analysis (see Figure 10.24) involves carrying out non-regression analysis. Non-regression analysis is used to construct a cone that, through modified requirement, goes back to requirements of input specifications. Based on the requirements cone, we can select the non-regression tests to be carried out and show that the change has no impact on the system requirements.

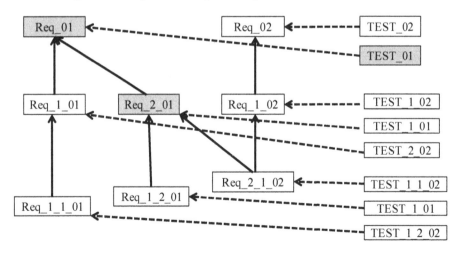

Figure 10.24. *Non-regression analysis*

10.5. Requirement management

10.5.1. *Activities*

Requirements are used to create links between documents (specification files, design files, encoding files) as well as test objectives. The different test categories (unit, software/software integration, software/hardware integration, functional and recipes) can be linked to the requirements on the basis of the "verification type" attribute. Thus, we obtain a requirement management process that enables the creation of a link between the initial needs and the choices made during the implementation and validation phases (see Figure 10.25).

The verification phase involves verifying requirement coverage and consistency of links that have been established. From the perspective of the project, management of requirements coverage can quantify the work that has been carried out and the remaining work.

Managing requirements changes and analysis of impacts on related requirements and products are the key points of requirements engineering. However, the real difficulty of requirements engineering lies in managing developments.

In summary, requirement management involves the implementation of simple mechanisms such as:

– introduction of management of identifiers;

– description of requirements;

– definition of traceability table.

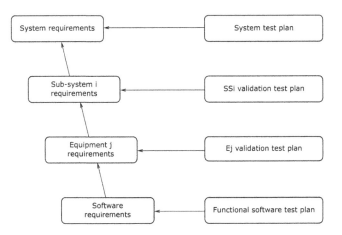

Figure 10.25. *Relationship between activities*

10.5.2. *Two approaches to requirement management*

Requirement management is implemented according to two approaches.

10.5.2.1. *Database-centric approach*

The first approach, called the database-centric approach, involves bringing together all the requirements (and associated elements) within a database and establishing all the links within this database.

Implementation of this approach requires the ability to import all the elements (documents, models, source files, test scenarios, test results, etc.) within this database. It is then possible to produce traceability matrices and justify the links between requirements (impact analysis, management changes, etc.).

Centralization within a database has several disadvantages:

– the size of the database depends on the size of the documents processed;

– in the case of source document development, it is necessary to reimport it into database or in general, it is difficult to automate the reintegration of information related to requirements;

– etc.

10.5.2.2. *Document-centric approach*

The second approach, called the document-centric approach, is used to introduce within documents (documents, models, source files, test scenarios, test results, etc.) information on links between objects. This information comprises of tags, attributes and links.

Implementation of this approach requires the ability to add information and capturing them through requests.

The advantage of this approach is that there is no need to change the process already implemented for project development, and it is limited to reformulating documents.

10.5.3. *Implementation of tools*

The Standish Group [STA 01] mentions that the implementation of a requirement management environment is the best way to have a strong impact on the success of a project. The definition of a minimum of requirements provides a base that can be managed, where the tool is a vector of communication between the teams.

A text[8] editor tool can therefore be used (table, identifiers management, link between documents, etc.) to process one or several documents. For complex systems, the number of documents and the number of steps (see Figure 10.26) involve implementation of a requirement management process based on tooling.

But this tool requires involvement of a requirement management process.

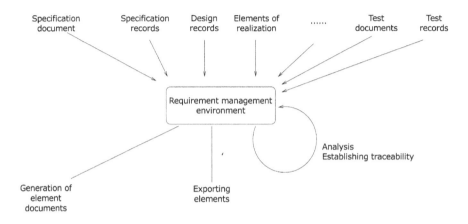

Figure 10.26. *Contours of a requirement management environment*

Choveau and de Chazelles [CHO 01] present the approach called Common Airbus Requirements Engineering (CARE) which is designed to allow the development of the Airbus A380. This approach is based on the definition of a global methodology that originates and is equipped in the standard EIA 632 [EIA 98].

Tools that allow requirements acquisition, establishment of traceability, reporting and documentation generation support requirements engineering. This list contains, for example, DOORS (distributed by IBM), RTM (Integrated Chipware Inc.), Rational Requisite Pro or Reqtify (DASSAULT tool dedicated to traceability aspect). However, one of the challenge of implementing the tools is to integrate the company's business processes.

---

8 As part of the double validation implemented by RATP for SAET-METEOR that equips line 14 of the Paris Metro, Interleaf test processing has enabled to define and manage all requirements (related to system up to three software written with the formal language called Method B).

10.6. Conclusion

Requirements engineering is a process in itself, hence it is essential to create a requirement management plan that describes:

– organization implemented for requirement management for a project during all phases (acquisition phase of a requirement in withdrawal phase);

– concept of requirement: syntax, principle of drafting, list of attributes, etc.;

– implementation methods to manage requirements: tools and processes;

– management principles and document production;

– changes to management processes (change identification, impact analysis, non-regression analysis);

For more information on requirements, refer to Boulanger and Badreau [BOU 14], Hull *et al.* [HUL 05], and Pohl [POH 10].

10.7. Glossary

ASIL:	Automotive SIL
AUTOSAR[9]:	AUTomotive Open System ARchitecture
CARE :	Common Airbus Requirements Engineering
CENELEC[10]:	*Comité Européen de Normalisation Electrotechnique* (European Committee for Electrotechnical Standardization)
CT:	Component Test
DAL:	Design Assurance Level
EMC:	Electromagnetic Compatibility
GAME:	*Globalement Au Moins Equivalent* (Globally At Least Equivalent)
GT:	Group Test
IEC[11]:	International Electrotechnical Commission
ISA:	Independent Safety Assessor

---

9 http://www.autosar.org.
10 www.cenelec.eu.
11 http://www.iec.ch.

ISO[12] :	International Organization for Standardization
IT:	Integration Test
MOA:	*Maîtrise d'ouvrage* (Contracting Authority)
MOE:	*Maîtrise d'œuvre* (Project Management)
PQP:	Project Quality Plan
SIL:	Safety Integrity Level
SSIL:	Software SIL
V&V:	Verification and Validation

---

12 http://www.iso.org/iso/home.htm.

Conclusion

In this first volume we introduced the relationship to be established with the system architecture. It is necessary to ensure that the software application works correctly in an environment that is generally fairly complex. In the context of complex systems such as transportation, energy and production, the dependability of the system depend directly on the software application.

The behavior of the software application will have an impact on the behavior of the system and its reliability. But as we have shown, it is not possible to quantify the software reliability. The main difficulty is related to the concept of residual *bug*. Due to the manual process involved for developing software application and because of its intangible nature, a software application contains bugs. It is possible to reduce the number of residual bugs to zero but this requires establishing processes such as quality assurance, safety assurance and verification to prevent, detect and correct defects.

Hence, the following three concepts were introduced in the first volume:

– What is a software application and what is it made up of?

– What is quality assurance?

– What is safety assurance?

In the next volumes we will define the support processes required to develop a software application and implementation of the software application process that will be divided into two phases: the descending phase of the V cycle, which produces the code for software application, and the ascending phase, which determines whether the application is functioning correctly.

Bibliography

[ABR 96] ABRIAL J.R., *The B Book – Assigning Programs to Meanings*, Cambridge University Press, 1996.

[AFN 87] AFNOR NF F 67-130, "Systèmes de traitement de l'information – Recommandation de plan qualité logiciel", April 1987.

[AFN 90] AFNOR NF F 71-013, "Installations fixes et matériels roulants ferroviaires, Informatique, Sûreté de fonctionnement des logiciels – Méthodes appropriées aux analyses de sécurité des logiciels", December 1990.

[AFN 98] AFNOR EN 45011, "Norme française, Exigences générales relatives aux organismes procédant à la certification de produits", May 1998.

[AFN 01] AFNOR EN 50155, "Norme française, Applications Ferroviaires, Equipements éléctroniques utilisés sur le materiel roulant", December 2001.

[AFN 07] AFNOR EN 50155, "Norme française, Applications ferroviaires, Equipements électroniques utilisés sur le matériel roulant", October 2007.

[ANS 83] ANSI, Langage de programmation Ada, ANSI/MIL-STD-1815A-1983, 1983.

[ARI 92] ARINC, "Software Considerations in Airborne Systems and Equipment Certification", DO 178B and EUROCAE, no. ED12, edition B, 1992.

[ARI 00] ARINC, "Design Assurance Guidance for Airborne Electronic Hardware", DO254 and EUROCAE, no. ED80, 2000.

[ARI 11] ARINC, "Software Considerations in Airborne Systems and Equipment Certification", DO 178C and EUROCAE, no. ED12, Issue C, 2011.

[ARL 06] ARLAT J., CROUZET Y., DESWARTE Y. *et al.*, "Tolérance aux fautes", in *Encyclopédie de l'informatique et des systèmes d'information*, Vuibert, Paris, France, 2006.

[ARP 96a] ARP4754/ED79, Certification Considerations for Highly-Integrated or Complex Systems, SAE, no. ARP4754 and EUROCAE, no. ED79, 1996.

[ARP 96b] ARP, Guidelines and Methods for Conducting the Safety Assessment Process on Civil Airborne Systems, SAE, no. ARP4761, EUROCAE, no. 135, 1996.

[AST 10] ASTRUC J-M., BECKER N., "Toward the application of ISO 26262 for real-life embedded mechatronic systems", ERTS2, Toulouse, France, 19-21 May 2010.

[AUT 14] AUTOSAR, "Main requirements AUTOSAR Release 4.2.1, reference ID 054", 2014

[BAK 97] BAKER S., CORBA Distributed Objects: Using Orbix, ACM Press/Addison-Wesley Publishing Co., New York, USA, 1997.

[BAR 90] BARANOWSKI F., Définition des objectifs de sécurité dans les transports terrestres, Technical Report 133, INRETS-ESTAS, 1990.

[BAU 10] BAUFRETON P., BLANQUART J.P., BOULANGER J.L. et al., Multi-domain comparison of safety standards, ERTS2, Toulouse, France, 19–21 May 2010.

[BAU 11] BAUFRETON P., BLANQUART J.-P., BOULANGER J.-L. et al., "Comparaison de normes de sécurité-innocuité de plusieurs domaines industriels", REE Review, vol. 2, 2011.

[BEL 02] BEL G., BONIOLA F., DURRIEU G. et al., Modèles comportementaux pour l'avionique modulaire intégrée, Unpublished, 2002.

[BIE 98] BIED-CHARRETON D., Sécurité intrinsèque et sécurité probabiliste dans les transports terrestres, Technical Report 31, INRETS-ESTAS, November 1998.

[BLA 08] BLAS A., BOULANGER J-L., "Comment améliorer les methods d'analyse de risques et l'allocation des THR, SIL et autres objectifs de sécurité", LambdaMu 16, Avignon, France, 6–10 October 2008.

[BLA 12] BLANQUART J-P., ASTRUC J-M., BAUFRETON P. et al., "Criticality categories across safety standards in different domains", ERTS 2012, Toulouse, France, 1–3 February 2012.

[BOU 06a] BOULANGER J.-L., Expression et validation des propriétés de sécurité logique et physique pour les systèmes informatiques critiques, Thesis, University of Technology, Compiègne, France, 2006.

[BOU 06b] BOULANGER J-L., SCHÖN W., "Logiciel sûr et fiable: retours d'expérience", Revue Génie Logiciel, vol 79, pp. 37–40, December 2006.

[BOU 07a] BOULANGER J-L., BON P., "BRAIL: d'UML à la méthode B pour modéliser un passage à niveau", RTS Review, vol. 95, pp. 147–172, April–June 2007.

[BOU 07b] BOULANGER J.-L., SCHÖN W., "Reference systems and standards for safety assessment of railway applications", ESREL 2007, pp. 2247–2253, Stavanger, Norway, 25–27 June 2007.

[BOU 08] BOULANGER J.-L., GALLARDO M., "Poste de manoeuvre à enclenchement informatique: démonstration de la sécurité", *Conférence Internationale Francophone d'Automatique (CIFA)*, Bucarest, Roumanie, November 2008.

[BOU 09a] BOULANGER J.-L., "Le domaine ferroviaire, les produits et la certification", Ecole des mines de Nantes, 15 October 2009.

[BOU 09b] BOULANGER J.-L. (ed.), *Sécurisation des architectures informatiques. Exemples concrets*, Hermes-Lavoisier, Paris, 2009.

[BOU 10] BOULANGER J.-L., "Sécurisation des systèmes mécatroniques. Partie 1", *Technique de l'ingénieur*, dossier BM 8070, November 2010.

[BOU 11a] BOULANGER J.-L., *Sécurisation des architectures informatiques industrielles*, Hermes-Lavoisier 2011.

[BOU 11b] BOULANGER J.-L., Sécurisation des systèmes mécatroniques. Partie 2, *Technique de l'ingénieur*, dossier BM 8071, April 2011.

[BOU 11c] BOULANGER J.-L., Maîtrise du SIL et gestion des certificats – Domaine ferroviaire, *Technique de l'ingénieur* No D5560, série Transports et technologies, 2011.

[BOU 13] BOULANGER J.-L., *Safety Management for Software-based Equipment*, ISTE, London and John Wiley and Sons, New York, 2013.

[BOU 14a] BOULANGER J.-L., BADREAU S., *Ingénierie des exigences – Méthodes et bonnes pratiques pour construire et maintenir un référentiel*, Dunod, Paris, 2014.

[BOU 14b] BOULANGER J.-L., ZHAO L., "Sécurité, confidentialité et intégrité dans le domaine ferroviaire", Lambda Mu19, Dijon, France, 21–23 October 2014.

[BOU 14c] BOULANGER J.-L., *Mise en œuvre des normes CENELEC 50128 et IEC 62279*, ISTE Editions, London, July 2014.

[BOU 15] BOULANGER J.-L., *Techniques de sécurisation des applications à base de logiciel*, ISTE Editions, London, 2015.

[BOU 16a] BOULANGER J.-L., *Certifiable Software Applications 2*, ISTE Press, London and Elsevier, Oxford, forthcoming.

[BOU 16b] BOULANGER J.-L., *Certifiable Software Applications 3*, ISTE Press, London and Elsevier, Oxford, forthcoming.

[BOU 17] BOULANGER J.-L., *Certifiable Software Applications 4*, ISTE Press, London and Elsevier, Oxford, forthcoming.

[BRE 00] BRETESCHE B., *La méthode APTE: Analyse de la valeur, analyse fonctionnelle*, Pétrelle, Paris, 2000.

[CAM 14] CAMPBELL R., EVANS R., "Cyber Security: Raising Awareness and Providing Guidance", IT Security in Railway Signalling Workshop, Frankfurt, 14–15 May 2014.

[CEN 00] CENELEC, Applications Ferroviaires. Spécification et démonstration de la fiabilité, de la disponibilité, de la maintenabilité et de la sécurité (FMDS), EN 50126, January 2000.

[CEN 01a] CENELEC, Applications Ferroviaires, Système de signalisation, de télécommunication et de traitement – Logiciel pour système de commande et de protection ferroviaire, EN 50128, July 2001.

[CEN 01b] CENELEC, European standard, Applications aux Chemins de fer: Systèmes de signalisation, de télécommunication et de traitement – Partie 1: communication de sécurité sur des systèmes de transmission fermés, EN 50159-1, March 2001.

[CEN 01c] CENELEC, European standard, Applications aux Chemins de fer: Systèmes de signalisation, de télécommunication et de traitement – Partie 2: communication de sécurité sur des systèmes de transmission ouverts, EN 50159-2, March 2001.

[CEN 03] CENELEC, European standard, Railway applications – Communication, Signalling and processing systems – Safety Related Electronic equipment for signalling, NF EN 50129, February 2003.

[CEN 07] CENELEC, Railway Applications – Communication, Signalling and Processing systems – Application Guide for EN 50129 – Part 1: cross-Acceptance, May 2007.

[CEN 11a] CENELEC, Applications Ferroviaires. Système de signalisation, de telecommunication et de traitement – Logiciel pour système de commande et de protection ferroviaire, EN 50128, July 2011.

[CEN 11b] CENELEC, Applications aux Chemins de fer: systèmes de signalisation, de télécommunication et de traitement. Communication de sécurité sur des systèmes de transmission, EN 50159, August 2011.

[CEN 11c] CENELEC, Applications Ferroviaires. Système de signalisation, de télécommunication et de traitement. Logiciel pour système de commande et de protection ferroviaire, EN 50128, October 2011.

[CHO 01] CHOVEAU E., DE CHAZELLES P., "Application de l'ingénierie système à la définition d'une démarche d'ingénierie des exigences pour l'airbus A380", Génie Logiciel, vol. 59, pp. 13–18, December 2001.

[COU 96] COUNCIL DIRECTIVE, Council Directive 96/48/EC on the interoperability of the trans-European high-speed rail system, Commission of the European Communities, Brussels, 23 July 1996.

[DO 178] DO 178B/ED12, "Software Considerations in Airborne Systems and Equipment Certification", l'ARINC, no. DO 178B and par l'EUROCAE, no. ED12, édition B, 1992.

[EIA 98] EIA, Processes for engineering a system, Technical report, EIA-632, April 1998.

[EUR 06] EUROCONTROL, "Safety Case Development Manual", 13 October 2006.

[EVE 06] EVELEENS R.L.C., "Integrated modular avionics development guidance and certification considerations", Mission Systems Engineering, vol. 4, pp. 4–18, 2006.

[FOU 93] FOURNIER J.-P., *Fiabilité du logiciel*, Hermes, 1993.

[GAR 94] GARIN H., *AMDEC – AMDE – AEEL – L'essentiel de la méthode*, Editions AFNOR, 1994.

[GEF 98] GEFFROY J.-C., MOTET G., *Sûreté de fonctionnement des systèmes informatiques*, InterEditions, Masson-Dunod, Paris, 1998.

[GEF 02] GEFFROY J.-C., MOTET G., *Design of Dependable Computing System*, Kluwer Academic Publishers, Dordrecht, The Netherlands, 2002.

[GEO 90] GEORGES J.P., "Principes et fonctionnement du Systèmed'Aide à la Conduite, à l'Exploitation et à la Maintenance (SACEM), Application à la ligne A du RER", *Revue générale des chemins de fers*, vol. 6, June 1990.

[GOL 06] GOLOUBEVA O., REBAUDENGO M., REORDA M.S. *et al.*, *Software Implemented Hardware Fault Tolerance*, Springer, 2006.

[GUE 08] GUENAB F., BOULANGER J.-L., SCHÖN W., "Safety of railway control systems: a new Preliminary Risk Analysis approach", *XI COMPRAIL 2008*, Toledo, Spain, September 2008.

[GUI 90] GUIHOT G., HENNEBERT C., "SACEM software validation", *Proceedings of 12th IEEE-ACM International Conference on Software Engineering*, March 1990.

[HAD 95] HADJ-MABROUCK H., "La maîtrise des risqué dans le domaine des automatismes des systèmes de transport guidés: le problème de l'évaluation des analyses préliminaires de risques", *Revue Recherche Transports Sécurité*, vol 49, pp. 101–112, December 1995.

[HAD 98] HADJ-MABROUCK H., STUPARU A., BIED-CHARRETON D., "Exemple de typologie d'accidents dans le domaine des transports guidés", *Revue générale des chemins de fers*, 1998.

[HAR 99] HARRIS J., HENDERSON A., "A better mythology for system design", *CHI'99: Proceedings of the SIGCHI Conference on Human Factors in Computing Systems*, pp. 88–95, New York, USA, 1999.

[HEN 94] HENNEBERT C., "Transports ferroviaires: Le SACEM etsesdérivés", in *Informatique tolérante aux fautes*, Masson, Paris, 1994.

[HUL 05] HULL E., JACKSON K., DICK J., *Requirements Engineering*, Springer, Berlin, 2005.

[IEC 91a] IEC, IEC 1069: Mesure et commande dans les processus industriels – appréciation des propriétés d'un système en vue de son évolution, Technical report, 1991.

[IEC 91b] INTERNATIONAL STANDARD IEC 60812, "Analysis Techniques for system reliability – procedure for failure mode and effects analysis (FMEA)", *International Electrotechnical Commission*, Geneva, Switzerland, 1991.

[IEC 98] IEC, CEI/IEC 61508, Sécurité fonctionnelle des systèmes électriques électroniques programmables relatifs à la sécurité, International standard, 1998.

[IEC 01] IEC 61513, "Centrales nucléaires – Instrumentation et contrôle commande des systèmes importants pour la sûreté – Prescriptions générales pour les systèmes", IEC 61513, Edition 1.0, 22 March 2001.

[IEC 03] IEC, IEC 61131-3, Programmable controllers – Part 3: Programming languages 2003.

[IEC 04] ISO/CEI 90003:2004, "Ingénierie du logiciel – Lignes directrices pour l'application de l'ISO 9001:2000 aux logiciels informatiques", ISO, 2004.

[IEC 05] NF EN 61511, European standard, Sécurité fonctionnelle systèmes instrumentés de sécurité pour le secteur des industries de transformation, March 2005.

[IEC 06] IEC 60880, "Centrales nucléaires de puissance – Instrumentation et contrôle-commande importants pour la sûreté – Aspects logiciels des systèmes programmés réalisant des fonctions de catégorie A", CEI 60880, Edition 2.0, May 2006.

[IEC 06a] IEC, IEC 61025 (1990), "Fault Tree Analysis (FTA)", International Electrotechnical Commission, Geneva, Switzerland, 2006.

[IEC 06b] IEC, IEC 60880, Centrales nucléaires de puissance – Instrumentation et contrôle-commande importants pour la sûreté – Aspects logiciels des systèmes programmés réalisant des fonctions de catégorie A, 2006.

[IEC 08a] IEC, IEC 61508, Functional safety of electric/programmable electronic systems related to safety, International standard, 2008.

[IEC 08b] IEC, IEC 61508, Sécurité fonctionnelle des systèmes électriques électroniques programmables relatifs à la sécurité, International standard, 2008.

[IEC 09] IEC 61226, "Centrales nucléaires de puissance – Instrumentation et contrôle-commande importants pour la sûreté – Classement des fonctions d'instrumentation et de contrôle-commande", IEC 61226, Edition 3.0, July 2009.

[IEC 11] IEC, CEI/IEC 61508: Sécurité fonctionnelle des systèmes électriques électroniques programmables relatifs à la sécurité, International standard, 2011.

[IEC 14] IEC 62279, Railway applications – Communication, signalling and processing systems – Safety related communication in transmission systems, IEC, 2014

[IET 14] IET, Assessment of Safety-Related Compliance Claims, The Institutes of Engineering and Technology, September 2014.

[ISA 05] ISA, "Guide d'interprétation et d'application de la norme IEC 61508 et des normes dérivées IEC 61511 (ISA S84.01) ET IEC 62061", April 2005.

[ISO 85] ISO Z61-102, "Traitement de l'information – vocabulaire de la qualité du logiciel" July 1985.

[ISO 91] ISO 9126:1991, Information technology – Software product evaluation – Quality characteristics and guidelines for their use, 1991.

[ISO 99] ISO/IEC, "ISO/IEC Guide 51 Safety aspects — Guidelines for their inclusion in standards", 1999.

[ISO 00] ISO 9000:2000, "Systèmes de management de la qualité – Principes essentiels et vocabulaire", 2000.

[ISO 04a] ISO, ISO/IEC 15504-x Information technology – Process assessment, ISO, several parts published between 2004 and 2011.

[ISO 04b] ISO ISO/IEC 90003:2004, Ingénierie du logiciel – Lignes directrices pour l'application de l'ISO 9001:2000 aux logiciels informatiques, ISO, 2004.

[ISO 04c] ISO 9126:2004, Information technology – Software product evaluation – Quality characteristics and guidelines for their use, 2004.

[ISO 05] EN ISO/IEC 17025, Exigences générales concernant la compétence des laboratories d'étalonnages et d'essais, 2005.

[ISO 08] ISO, ISO 9001: 2008, Quality management systems – Requirements, December 2008.

[ISO 11] ISO, ISO/CD-26262, Road vehicles – Functional safety – ISO, 2011.

[ISO 12a] ISO, ISO/IEC 17020:2012, Conformity assessment, requirements for the operation of various types of bodies performing inspection, 2012.

[ISO 12b] ISO/IEC 8652:2012(E), Ada 2012 Language Reference Manual, December 2012.

[ISO 12c] ISO, ISO/IEC 17065:2012, Évaluation de la conformité – exigences pour les organismes certifiant les produits, les procédés et les services, December 2012.

[ISO 14] ISO 25000, Ingénierie du logiciel – Exigences de qualité du produit logiciel et évaluation (SQuaRE) – Guide de SQuaRE, 2014.

[ISO 15] ISO, ISO 9001:2015, Systèmes de management de la qualité – Exigence, 2015.

[KER 88] KERNIGHAN B.W., RITCHIE D.M., *The C programming language*, 2nd ed., Prentice Hall, New York, 1988.

[KLE 91] KLEIN P., "The safety-bag expert system in the electronic railway interlocking system elektra", *Expert Systems with Applications*, vol. 3, no. 4, pp. 499–506, 1991.

[KOB 14] KOBES P., "Siemens: IT Security from an Industry Automation Perspective: IEC 62443", IT Security in Railway Signalling Workshop, Frankfurt, May 14-15.

[LAP 92] LAPRIE J.C., AVIZIENIS A., KOPETZ H. (eds), *Dependability: Basic Concepts and Terminology, Dependable Computing and Fault-Tolerant System*, vol. 5, Springer, New York, 1992.

[LEV 95] LEVESON N.G., *Safeware: System Safety and Computers*, 1st ed., Addison Wesley Publishing Company, CA, 1995.

[LIA 08] LIAIGRE D., "Impact de ISO 26262 sur l'état de l'art des concepts de sécurité automobiles actuels", *LambdaMu'08*, Avignon, October 2008.

[LIS 95] LIS, *Guide de la sûreté de fonctionnement*, first version, Laboratoire d'ingénerie, Cépaduès, Paris, 1995.

[LIS 96] LIS, *Guide de la sûreté de fonctionnement*, second version, Laboratoire d'ingénerie, Cépaduès, Paris, 1996.

[LOW 03] LOWY J., *Programming .NET Components*, O'Reilly & Associates Inc., CA, 2003.

[MAC 12] MACHROUH J., BLANQUART J.-P., BAUFRETON P. *et al.*, "Cross domain comparison of System Assurance", *ERTS 2012*, Toulouse, France, 1–3 February 2012.

[MAI 93] MAIRE A., "Présentation du système MAGGALY", *Symposium international sur l'innovation technologique dans les transports guidés, (ITIG'93)*, Lille, September 1993.

[MAT 98] MATRA & RATP, Naissance d'un Métro. Sur la nouvelle ligne 14, les rames METEOR entrent en scène, PARIS découvre son premier métro automatique, Numéro 1076-Hors-Série, La vie du Rail & des transports, October 1998.

[MEI 02] MEINADIER J.P., *Le métier d'intégration de systèmes*, Hermès Lavoisier, Paris, 2002.

[MEY 99] MEYER B., "On to components", *IEEE Computer*, vol. 32, no 1, pp. 139–140, 1999.

[MIH 14] MIHALACHE A., BEDOUCHA F., "ISO 26262: application sur le logiciel du Boîtier de Servitude Intelligent (BSI) de PSA", *LambdaMu 19*, Dijon, France, 2015.

[NAU 69] NAUR & RANDELL (eds), *Software Engineering: A Report on a Conference sponsored by NATO Science Committee*, NATO, 1969.

[OMG 11] OMG, Unified Modeling Language™ (OMG UML), Infrastructure, OMG, 2011.

[OZE 09a] OZELLO P., "On Board Assemblies Certification for POS/PBA/PBKA trains", *Rail Transport Workshop on Certification*, 29 October 2009.

[OZE 09b] OZELLO P., "TGV Pis Rolling Stock Certification and safety assessment", *Rail Transport Workshop on Certification*, 29 October 2009.

[POH 10] POHL K., *Requirements Engineering: Fundamentals, Principles, and Techniques*, Springer, Berlin, June 2010.

[ROM 01] ROMAN E., AMBLERS W., MARINESCU F., *Mastering Enterprise Javabeans*, John Wiley & Sons, New York, 2001.

[RAM 09] RAMACHANDRAN M., ATEM D.E., CARVALHO R., *Handbook of Software Engineering Research and Productivity Technologies: Implications of Globalisation*, Information Science Reference, August 2009.

[RAM 11] RAMACHANDRAN M., *Knowledge Engineering for Software Development Life Cycles: Support Technologies and Applications*, IGI Publishers, April 2011.

[RIE 13] RIERSON L., *Developing safety-critical software*, CRC Press, 2013.

[ROQ 06] ROQUES P., *UML 2 par la pratique – Etudes de cas et exercices corrigés*, Eyrolles, Paris, 2006.

[ROQ 07] ROQUES P., *UML 2 – Modéliser une application Web*, Eyrolles, Paris, 2007.

[RTA 11] RTA DO 178:C, Software consideration in airbone systems and equipement certification, Version C, December 2011.

[SAM 78] SAMMET J.E., "The early history of Cobol", *ACM SIGPLAN Notices*, vol. 13, no. 8, pp. 121–161, 1978.

[SMI 07] SMITH D.J., SIMPSON K.G.L., *Functional Safety, a straightforward guide to applying IEC 61508 and related standards*, 2nd ed., Elsevier, 2007.

[SOM 07] SOMMERVILLE I., *Software Engineering*, Addison-Wesley, 2007.

[SPI 01] SPITZER C.R., *The Avionics Handbook*, CRC Press, 2001.

[STA 94] THE STANDISH GROUP, The Chaos Report, Technical report, 1994.

[STA 01] THE STANDISH GROUP, Extreme Chaos, Technical report, 2001.

[STR 06] STRMTG, Mission de l'expert ou organisme qualifié agrée (EOQA) pour l'évaluation de la sécurité des projets, version 1, 27 March 2006.

[SZY 98] SZYPERSKI C., *Component Software: Beyond Object-Oriented Programming*, Addison-Wesley/ACM Press, 1998.

[THI 86] THIREAU P., "Méthodologie d'Analyse des Effets des Erreurs Logiciel (AEEL) appliquée à l'étude d'un logiciel de haute sécurité", *5th International Conference on Reliability and Maintainability*, Biarritz, France, 1986.

[UNI 09] IRIS, International Railway Industry Standard, Revision 02, Unife, 2009.

[VIL 88] VILLEMEUR A., *Sûreté de Fonctionnement des systèmes industriels*, Eyrolles, 1988.

Index

Printed in the United States
By Bookmasters